Reverberating Word

Reverberating Word

Powerful Worship

Michael Denham

WIPF & STOCK · Eugene, Oregon

REVERBERATING WORD
Powerful Worship

Wipf & Stock
An Imprint of Wipf and Stock Publishers
199 W. 8th Ave., Suite 3
Eugene, OR 97401

www.wipfandstock.com

PAPERBACK ISBN: 978-1-5326-3731-5
HARDCOVER ISBN: 978-1-5326-3733-9
EBOOK ISBN: 978-1-5326-3732-2

Manufactured in the U.S.A.

To my wife, Laurie Hein Denham, in whose eyes I found warmth of welcome, depth of kindness, and wealth of blessing

To my children, Daniel, Katharine, Stephen, and Sarah, and my granddaughter, Reagan, commending them to Christ Jesus, in whom are found all the treasures of wisdom and knowledge

To the memory of my late parents, Pat and Jeanne Denham, who adopted me, loved me, prayed for me, and set me on a firm foundation

To my family at The National Presbyterian Church, who have labored and loved alongside me so long and so well

To Earl Frank Palmer, who graciously and winsomely helped me trust the trustworthiness of our Lord

And to Michael Craig Barnes, my brother in faith and life, whose ministry of word and work helped forge my own

Contents

Introduction

Worship can be powerfully transforming. It can do so much more than merely sustain our interest. It can help change us from the inside out for God's glory and our good. It's more than something we attend, it's something we do together. We're less concerned with being entertained and more interested in being edified, a wonderful biblical term that means to be "built up" or "strengthened."

Is it possible to think of worship less as a style and more as a discipline? How can we experience the compelling nature and activity of God apart from heavy filters of personality and taste?

How do we distinguish between felt needs and genuine spiritual needs? How might the one wrongly impact worship, and how can the other rightly shape it? Is there a difference between tradition and heritage? How might our own worship context influence whether we think of these potentially loaded terms in a positive or negative light?

If Christian worship indeed conveys something objective, how might we as worship leaders distinguish between being the merely innovative and the truly creative? Is there a way to creatively convey a received message without obscuring it?

The idea of God's *reverberating* word shapes this notion of creative communication. The metaphor of reverberation is drawn from the sounds of music. Sound and tone are both produced by something vibrating: a violin or piano string, the membrane of a kettle drum, or a column of air moving through an oboe, a trumpet, or a human larynx. If an instrument is energized through plucking, bowing, striking, or blowing, vibrating waves emanate and travel through the air to the ear, where the ear drum receives them sympathetically. This initiates a complex set of signals and responses that we ultimately interpret as intelligible, appreciable, and hopefully beautiful. The communicative force of music confirms the power of this vibrating and reverberating process. We adopt it here as a colorful and apt metaphor for the preaching-hearing-meditating-reflecting-responding dialogue integral to worship.

It's absurd to think that we can become expert worshipers. A rich worship life, however, is a commendable desire that insight and skill can fan. Pastors, worship leaders, musicians, and parishioners alike can ask orienting questions like the following to help catalyze our thinking:

- What is our ground of authority?
- What are revelation, proclamation, and response?
- What roles do preaching and teaching play?
- What is liturgy? Is there both liturgical and non-liturgical worship?
- Are there worship leaders and followers?
- Are worshipers spectators? Participants? An audience? A team?
- What about different age groups of worshipers?
- Who speaks in worship? Who hears?
- Does worship have identifiable, regular, or essential components?
- What is the role of music in worship? Of other art forms?
- What is exposition?
- What is expositional preaching? Is it the only kind?
- Can worship be expositional?
- What is reverberation in the context of worship?
- Are styles of worship influential? Neutral? Normative? Determinative?
- Does expositional worship leave room for cultural or demographic differences?
- Is there a right way to worship? A wrong way?
- What is the goal of worship?
- How does worship affect an individual? A congregation? A community?

Every church has a unique personality drawn from the mix of perspectives within and among the congregation. Some churches think of themselves as worship driven. Others may self-identify as discipleship, fellowship, or service driven. A healthy church is actively involved in all these sorts of things that Christians have been doing since Pentecost (Acts 2:42–47), but no congregation is, or arguably should be, exactly like another, given its own sense of identity, calling, and ministry niche. No matter how we answer all these kinds of questions, asking them can help point us to our task at hand: the wonderful opportunity to love and enjoy God forever through all facets of Christian worship, discipleship, witness, and service.

1

A Different Vantage

Biblical worship is not speculative. It reflects a specific message that is historical and knowable, and which invites our consideration and response.

THE GOD OF HEAVEN and earth doesn't need our worship. God lives in eternity, in the beauty of holiness and the perfect love, communion, mystery, and completeness of the Trinity.[1] Yet the old hymn "Come Christians, Join to Sing" reminds us that praise is God's gracious choice.[2] This is both liberating and empowering. We're freed from slavishly trying to curry the favor of a remote or petulant deity. We're commissioned by God's clear invitation and call. George MacDonald, the Scottish writer who so influenced C. S. Lewis, asserted that God is impossible to satisfy, but easy to please.[3] This is a great blessing because,whenever we come before the Lord, relative to God's righteousness, even our best efforts are feeble.

Old Testament believers couldn't worship without bringing a sacrifice. That was the ticket to worshiping in either the tabernacle or temple. God's holiness simply demanded it. There were all sorts of other sacrifices and offerings available to or required of the Hebrews once they were inside, but a blood sacrifice to cover sin was required to get in the door.

1. For a concise treatment of theology proper, including issues of divine actuality, simplicity, complexity, and tri-unity, see Geisler, *Systematic Theology in One Volume*, 407–612; George, "Nature of God," 157–204; Thielicke, *Evangelical Faith*, vol. 2, 2–258; Boice, *Foundations of the Christian Faith*, 108–46.

2. Bateman, "Come, Christians, Join to Sing"; McKim, *Presbyterian Hymnal*, 150.

3. Paraphrase of C. S. Lewis quoting MacDonald. See Lewis, *Mere Christianity*, 108.

Believers today actually face the same threshold. Our New Testament faith has not changed this. God's holiness still simply demands it. But according to the book of Hebrews, we no longer need to bring bulls or goats to church to get in the front door. The perfect and eternal sacrifice of Jesus Christ, the Lamb of God, cleanses us from all sin and bridges our separation from God that sin brings.

God's gracious choice then, presumes God's cleansing and redeeming. These actions on our behalf are actually what allow us to approach and remain in the divine presence. There, by God's grace, we can learn to feel increasingly at home.

Despite this, none of us will ever be expert worshipers. We all are flawed. We all are "Plan B" people. Over and over again, we need a new start, a reason to keep going, answers that make sense. We need forgiveness, comfort, sustenance, purpose, hope. We want worship to breathe new life back into our souls, so we come with empty hands, seeking to be filled from the inexhaustible supply that is God's alone.

Yet we all could know more about worship. This includes me and every congregation I've been privileged to serve during the past thirty-five years, the last twenty at the National Presbyterian Church in Washington, DC.[4] There's a palpable sense of history and heritage in our nation's capital. People come from across the country and around the world, wide-eyed at its grandeur, or to join the ranks of government to "make a difference." We see how election cycles bring waxing or waning prestige, how influence is a siren call, how information is common currency. Christian churches of all sorts—and other religious houses of worship—dot the landscape. In ways that are increasingly common to all our communities, Washington is remarkably pluralistic.

I was strongly attracted to the idea of doing ministry there, and the opportunity to see the gospel and God's glory come to bear in the lives of leaders whose governing can impact all of us. Worship that speaks into the crucible where God's eternal word mixes with our everyday challenges and needs can powerfully comfort or confront anyone anywhere.

We find a wide spectrum of opinion among Christians about worship. Debate continues today about its basis, content, and style, and the relative

---

4. NPC became the "National" church of the PC(USA) over seventy years ago, though its congregation dates from 1795. As a Reformed body of believers its heritage springs from the Reformation and perspectives of John Calvin. Displayed in the church are a stone excised from the walls of the Cathedral of St. Peter in Geneva, Switzerland, Calvin's last home, and a letter of fellowship from that Swiss congregation.

value of the various approaches people take to it. All kinds of churches cherish (or harbor) disparate traditions, assumptions, and convictions about worship. Not one of us is impervious to cultural, demographic, and spiritual shifts,[5] nor are we immune to resisting change, or insisting on doing things our own way. Theological, aesthetic, and generational impulses are leading many of us to question what has come before, to ask what lies ahead, and to wonder about what to do in the meantime.

In asking these questions myself, I tend to draw a distinction between "tradition" and "heritage." It seems to me that tradition leans toward custom, convention, and established practice. It follows habit, and is inclined toward codifying and a hardening of categories. It can be rigid and stultifying: "We've always done things this way!" "We've never done it that way before!"

I see heritage, on the other hand, as leaning toward origin, legacy, and inheritance. It follows source, heirship, and a sense of being entrusted. It's energized by awareness of the great and historical "cloud of witnesses" who've preceded us and, according to Hebrews 12:1-2, who "surround" us. It can be grounding and centering. Tradition and heritage convey some synonymous values, and are rooted in the same soil, but I typically think of the former as root binding, and the latter as root feeding. Each is rooted in the past, but heritage is nourished, not bound, by it. These distinctions may be artificial to a degree, but for our purposes I believe they're instructive and helpful. Mixing metaphors, my guess is that every ministry leader at one point or another has wanted to say, "The only thing really set in concrete is flexibility!"

Whatever we think of tradition and heritage, it's important that together we guard against a natural and expected sweep of opinion becoming dissonant, caustic, or divisive. All of us have become far too familiar with the expression "worship wars."[6] Too often in these skirmishes our battle cry is, "Ready! Fire! Aim!" When we zero in on each other we truly are off-target. Mark Labberton prophetically cautions us that we can be "so caught up in worship we lose our neighbor."[7]

---

5. Lugo, *"Nones" on the Rise*, 33–34; Smith and Snell, *Souls in Transition*, 103–12; Stark, *What Americans Really Believe*, 101–14; Webber, *Younger Evangelicals*, 13–20; Wolfe, *Transformation of American Religion*, 215–44; Wuthnow, *Struggle for America's Soul*, 19–38.

6. Long, *Beyond the Worship Wars*, 1–14.

7. Labberton, *Dangerous Act of Worship*, 21.

Is it possible for us together to clarify and better objectify what worship actually is and does? Despite our different contexts, can we better ground our worship life to enrich and empower it for everyone? The idea of God's *reverberating* word points to what I have come to call expositional worship—worship that heightens proclamation of holy Scripture as the pathway to that richness and power.

Worship from a Different Vantage

The notion of expositional worship derives from the process of expository preaching, an approach or style sometimes pejoratively identified with sermons tiresomely fixed to verse-by-verse explanation of a biblical passage. This is an overly narrow characterization.[8] Noted preacher Earl Palmer characterizes expository or expositional preaching more positively as a process of letting the Bible "make its own point."[9] A commitment to God's *reverberating* word presumes great value in careful but creative biblical exposition. Preachers, worship leaders, and congregations alike can discover together how proclamation that highly values the biblical witness can center and empower worship.

Good expositional preaching always focuses on the point that holy Scripture is making. Authentic Christian preaching, says the late Anglican preacher and world Christian leader John Stott, is both biblical and contemporary. We want it to open up the text, but also to "meaningfully relate to the world in which we live."[10] Neither biblical preaching nor biblical worship is speculative. Each reflects a message that's historical and knowable, and which invites our consideration and response. Expositional preaching and expositional worship are both chiefly concerned with perceiving and conveying the message of the biblical text itself—its

---

8. For a more detailed treatment of expository preaching as a broad discipline that shares concerns with biblical theology, see Stott, *Preacher's Portrait*, 33–59, and *Between Two Worlds*, 211–54; Robinson, *Biblical Preaching*, 57–70, and "What is Expository Preaching?," 55–60; Chapell, *Christ-Centered Preaching*, 59–81; Kirkland, "Expository Preaching Revitalized," 9–14; Stitzinger, "History of Expository Preaching," 5–32; Thomas, "Expository Preaching," 35–52; Adam, "Relationship of Biblical Theology," 104–8; Hamilton, "Biblical Theology and Preaching," 193–220; Fanning III, "God's Word and God's People," 848–50; and Hagner, "Biblical Theology and Preaching," 137–41.

9. Palmer, "Making of a Sermon," 20–23; and "Case for Expositional Preaching," 8–13. For recent assessment of Palmer see Old, *Reading and Preaching*, 87–169.

10. Stott, *Living Church*, 98.

principal point or big idea—whether focused on a phrase, a paragraph, a book, or the Bible as a whole.

My own training in both music and ministry has been with an eye toward becoming more proficient in the vocabulary of each. Like any other language, music is able to convey and communicate meaning. I believe this. I have experienced its power to evoke insight and express meaning at levels which are simultaneously intellectual, emotional, aesthetic, and even spiritual.

Eminent nineteenth-century British composer and churchman Sir John Stainer served for a time as organist at Magdalen College Oxford, then at that university's Church of St. Mary the Virgin, and eventually at St. Paul's Cathedral in London. He called music that branch of art which most capably fulfills such lofty aims, "as it hovers round the cradle, is the handmaid of worship, the pleasure of the home, and hymns its farewell over our grave."[11] His Victorian-era sentiments may sound a bit arcane to our modern ears, but I think his point is still well taken. Yet if I ask someone why they choose to worship at our church, "Because the music is so beautiful," isn't exactly the answer I'm hoping for. If they worship at a less traditional, more contemporary, or intentionally emergent church, "Because the music isn't old fashioned and stodgy," is likewise not the answer I really want.

Heated debate today often centers on worship music. It can indeed arouse devoted loyalties. Quite apart from any *a priori* value judgment about musical styles or tastes, I would suggest that across the spectrum blurry perspectives can persist which too highly exalt music in one form or another. Musicians might be gratified that worship music touches and moves people, and God has created us to respond in multifaceted ways, but to equate music with worship *per se* is to freight it with a responsibility, and charge it with a task, that is beyond it.[12]

The key point of a recent Gallup Poll emphasizes that a majority of those surveyed identified strong preaching as their principal interest in worship. This actually may surprise some of us, because it cuts cross-grain with what we've been hearing from various sources who are ostensibly well attuned to the vibrations of our popular culture. In an age driven by image and sound, in which medium has become message, at least according to the

11. Dibble, *John Stainer*, 1.

12. For corroborative comment, see Block, *For the Glory of God*, xi, 236–45.

Gallup organization, worshipers remain vitally interested in biblically clear and meaningful preaching.[13]

Even so, how many times might we have seen worship guides that list "Worship of God" and "Word of God" as two distinct halves of a whole, with "Worship" meaning "when we do lots of singing," and "Word" meaning "when we hear the sermon?" I suggest this is a misleading distinction. The better hope is that whatever happens in worship will help us grow in grace and knowledge of the Lord, through glimpses of God gained jointly through proclamation of God's word and its reverberation through music and other regular worship components.

Let's be quick to acknowledge that these encounters—what we might see of God in worship—are only glimpses. We learn from Isaiah 55:8 that God's thoughts are not our thoughts, and God's ways are not our ways. But glimpse upon glimpse upon glimpse can begin to focus and clarify for us an emerging picture. Think of Isaiah's declaration:

> Thus says the high and lofty one, who inhabits eternity, whose name is holy: I dwell in the high and holy place, and also with those who are contrite and humble in spirit, to revive the spirit of the humble, and to revive the heart of the contrite. (57:15 NRSV)

Jeremiah reiterated this fundamental assertion to the Hebrews as they were bewildered and languishing in Babylonian captivity. He reminded them that God wants to be found. God may at times seem silent, God may at times be silent, but God isn't hiding:

> For I know the plans I have for you, plans for welfare, not for evil, to give you a future and a hope . . . You will seek me and find me, when you seek me with all your heart. I will be found by you, declares the Lord . . . (Jer 29:11–13 ESV)

This most wonderful truth is that God wants to be found—by grace through faith—in worship and every activity of Christian discipleship.

What then do we expect or hope for together in Christian worship? Do we aim too low? Do we hedge our bets? Do we short-change ourselves? In one of his inimitably prophetic, sermon-like songs, singer and pianist Ken Medema writes,

> Week by week the Lord's Day comes;
> We go to church with expectations small.

---

13. Saad, "Sermon Content is What Appeals," lines 6–9.

We crave routine, we fall asleep,
And Jesus comes to stand the broken tall."[14]

Is trying to meet a variety of perceived needs among worshipers the best approach? Is a market-driven, church-growth goal the best target?[15] Is there a way to get beneath the turbulent surface of personal tastes and filters in search of something more stable?

Settling for entertainment—whether by a worship band or a Bach choir—can lure us away from a deeper desire to be edified, to be built up and strengthened in our faith. This better goal in no way mitigates our commitment to excellence, aesthetic relevance, and even beauty, but being overly concerned about whether or not we like something may end up masking what the Lord might otherwise actually be saying to us. It's always by the illuminating power of the Holy Spirit through holy Scripture that we can thoughtfully consider its claims, as we place ourselves before God's divine right to judge, God's divine decision to love, and God's divine power to transform.

This isn't to say that we're slavishly and exclusively tied in worship to the proclaimed biblical text(s) at hand. We might also be interested in integrating other themes fed by a biblical theology aware of Scripture's overarching story or meta-narrative, and in patterns of teaching, praying, communing, sharing, and caring that have been ours since the day of Pentecost. Following St. Peter's powerful preaching, thousands of Christian converts gave themselves to hearing the apostles' teaching, to regular fellowship with other believers, to the Lord's Supper as well as communal meals, to the giving and sharing of resources, and to prayers. This pattern shouldn't categorically be dismissed as limited to the early, heady days of the Jerusalem church's explosive growth.[16]

We also might want to emphasize universal purposes of Christian ministry, including promoting justice and social righteousness, and exhibiting in our daily lives and community the "at-handedness" of the kingdom of heaven.[17] Yet the expressive values of worship that are being tethered week in and week out to texts being preached are well worth exploring.

14. From the song "Eye to Eye," which appeared on Ken Medema's album *Stories* (GlorySounds/Shawnee), which was recorded in July 1982.

15. Webster, *Selling Jesus*, 86.

16. Acts 2:42–47.

17. Sometimes called "The Great Ends of the Church," and including the Proclamation of the Gospel for the Salvation of Humankind; the Shelter, Nurture, and Fellowship

What happens before or after God's word has been proclaimed in worship has potential to underline or undermine it. The notion of God's *reverberating* word commends preaching that consistently exposits biblical revelation as part of worship that is oriented around the very aspect of that revelation being proclaimed each time.[18] This may seem self-evident to some, but it's striking how little is being said or done about it.

In my view, there's too little intentional, integrated, coordinated training along paths that pastors and musicians typically take. Pastors are trained to study, understand, and communicate the Bible, to administer the sacraments, to appreciate the historical sweep of Christian theology, to sensitively counsel people in need, and to coordinate the logistical and ministry needs of congregations. Musicians learn about the language, theory, and history of music, and how to sing or play instruments as a soloist or in various kinds of ensembles, in order to express a composer's intention and their own perspectives on that intention in engaging and meaningful ways. Both are long and rigorous educational pathways that may or may not interface in any deeply formative way.

When my theology professors discovered I was a musician, too often some asked, "What are you doing here?" When my university colleagues heard that I had completed seminary before pursuing doctoral studies in music, some of them asked the same thing. This gave me some pause, but didn't deter me. I believed that these two evidently parallel tracks would eventually cross somewhere just over the horizon. For me, that was at National Presbyterian, but I was bolstered along the way by words of Henry Wadsworth Longfellow that my mother had sent me in a timely note years earlier. Apart from favorite Scriptures themselves, these poetic lines have long served me as a personal credo:

> God sent his singers upon earth
> > With songs of gladness and of mirth
> That they might touch the hearts of men
> > And bring them back to heaven again.[19]

---

of the Children of God; the Maintenance of Divine Worship; the Preservation of the Truth; the Promotion of Social Righteousness; and the Exhibition of the Kingdom of Heaven to the World. While not inherently Presbyterian or Reformed, these ends or purposes have been adopted and long embraced among these traditions. See Small, *Proclaiming*, 147–51.

18. Carson, *Worship by the Book*, 11–63; Barnes, *Pastor as Minor Poet*, 73–86.

19. Longfellow, *Complete Poetical Works*, 191.

To me, there's something in this opening stanza of Longfellow's that captures and conveys a calling and deep desire to communicate intellectually, emotionally, and spiritually. Yet pastors sometimes feel ill-equipped to lead their flock week in and week out in arresting, powerful worship. Musicians sometimes are ill-equipped to consistently contextualize and integrate their own musical language, skills, and contribution in worship. Those in each discipline too often seem to talk past each other, or live in parallel universes, when there actually is unbounded opportunity for mutual inspiration and coordination in service of integrated biblical communication.

For biblical preaching, the Bible is the ultimate authority, lest preachers declare an invented rather than a received message. Those who dare to speak for God do so best with a healthy dose of humility mixed with the tacit audacity of proclaiming God's whole counsel. Sensitivity and caution are called for, but the call to preach remains a clarion one, lest congregations are set adrift of biblical revelation to consider and receive. Allen Ross writes,

> Acts of worship are a form of proclamation only if they are understood . . . Whenever proclamation has been lost in worship, worship loses its way and becomes empty ritual. Both the drama of the ritual and the interpretation by the proclamation are necessary for the full worship of God. The Word gives the ritual meaning, and the ritual gives visible form to the Word.[20]

If Scripture is preached accurately (and we would hope, artfully), its own authority becomes central to worship because its exposition offers glimpses of God's person, character, and activity. It's these glimpses that confront or comfort worshipers, leading us to bow low before the Lord even as God bends to us in grace, mercy, and love.[21]

Worship that is expositional seeks through music and the plethora of other worship components to heighten the expression of what's being proclaimed. It's less concerned with whether worshipers are being engaged or entertained, and more with people being vitally connected to what they themselves are hearing, weighing, receiving, and saying in worship. We're not suggesting people gather for worship to have a bad time, to feel wary of enjoying it, or not to hope for or expect from it something meaningful or encouraging. Worship, however, isn't meant primarily to meet our needs,

20. Ross, *Recalling the Hope of Glory*, 142, 146.

21. Ibid., 50. In the Old Testament, worship was sometimes characterized as "bowing oneself low to the ground."

but to center our attention on the One who can and does meet them. It's an important matter of perspective and distinction.

At the root of it all is doxology, our words of glory offered to God, and lives that bring glory to the holy and righteous, but merciful, gracious, and steadfastly loving God that God is. Isaiah 6 and Revelation 4 offer striking glimpses of God in glory, and how that revelation penetrates the depth and illuminates the breadth of human need. The well-known *trisagion* (or "thrice holy"), "Holy, Holy, Holy," acknowledges our plight apart from God as much as it acknowledges God's separateness, God's complete and unique moral majesty. Holiness is what makes God God. It shows us in relative but exquisite relief who we are and what we need.[22] That need isn't partial; it's total.

Whatever else could be said of Christian worship, what we must repeat again and again is the prophet Jeremiah's fundamental assertion that God wants to be found. God says, "I love you." As in any other close relationship the only satisfying response is, "I love you too." In Christian worship this tremendous and tender encounter is available as nowhere else.

Is this what our worship is doing or is designed to do week in and week out? If not, how might it? If so to some degree, how might it be done better? The desire is for proclaimed Scripture to become the touchstone in a process of crafting worship to best convey its message, meaning, richness, claim, or call.

This sort of tethering to the text liberates us in service of that expression, unleashing insight and creativity on every front. Do we recognize the potential for such heightened expression through meditating, reflecting, or commenting on the proclaimed text as it reverberates through what is said, sung, or enacted by the congregation as a whole or its representatives?

Many identify Sunday morning gatherings as their primary weekly involvement in church. While we may characterize preaching as central, or music as a key draw, we're sometimes less clear about how preaching, music, and other elements of worship might interpenetrate and enhance each other. How do we construct a whole that is greater than the sum of its parts?

Toward this, we need to recover or even discover Scripture as the source of authority and coherence in worship. Apart from it worship can to

22. Burge, "Are Evangelicals Missing God?," 21–27; later revised as "Missing God at Church," 147–55.

its detriment be shaped by more subjective criteria, and the otherwise normative variety of worship can become less rooted and grounded in biblical revelation. If, however, worship remains secured to the text and its richness, and seeks to convey through synergism of its various components the message or point of that text, then its normative variety will help heighten the expression of that text, thereby qualifying it as expositional worship.[23]

23. The concept of exposition also has currency in the language of music, referring to how composers introduce motifs and themes they plan to develop in larger musical forms such as a sonata. Sonata form, or sonata process as it is sometimes referred to, generally proceeds by introducing musical material, developing it, and then restating it in some reiterated or recalculated way. Hence sonatas unfold along the lines of the "exposition, development, and recapitulation" of musical ideas and themes. See Rosen, *Sonata Form*, 1, 229, 262, 284, and *Classical Style*, 30, 43. The process is not unlike biblical exposition and proclamation.

2

A Biblical Lens

Holy Scripture offers us glimpses of God's person, character, and work. These glimpses in worship move us to bow before the Lord, even as God bends to us in grace, mercy, and love.

GOD'S SELF-REVELATION IN ACT or word has regularly prompted acknowledgment of the divine prerogative to be feared, obeyed, praised, thanked, or blessed: in a word, to be worshiped. This cause and effect pattern is embedded in the witness of both the Old Testament (OT) and the New Testament (NT), from creation to the new creation. It's wonderfully crystallized in St. Paul's "therefore" at the beginning of Romans 12 (ESV): "I appeal to you therefore, brothers, by the mercies of God,[1] to present your bodies

---

1. "By the mercies of God," or perhaps "in view of God's merciful acts and activities," a phrase gathering or summing up not only Paul's argument in the preceding flow of the letter, but the whole of God's merciful dealings with humankind, including the background of Old Testament worship and its recapitulation for believers living under the new covenant. Cranfield writes, "The Christian's obedience is his response to what God has done for him and for all men in Jesus Christ. Its basic motive is gratitude for God's goodness in Christ. This means that all truly Christian moral endeavor is theocentric, having its origin not in a humanistic desire for the enhancement of the self by the attainment of a moral superiority, not in the legalist's illusory hope of putting God under an obligation to himself, but simply in the gracious action of God. . .Paul is thinking of the divine mercy as that which directs all God's purposes and actions in relation to His creation. . ." (Cranfield, *Romans*, 292–93). "It is because we are already recipients of the mercies of God that we must and can live the true life. We work *from*, not *for*, salvation" (Griffith-Thomas, *St. Paul's Epistle to the Romans*, 324).

as a living sacrifice, holy and acceptable to God, which is your spiritual worship."[2] Leading to this appeal, Paul has written the bulk of his greatest letter to say just who the living God is, and what this true, living, and only God has done for us. The apostle urges us to remember what's been revealed about God as the basis for our response. Biblical worship, then, isn't speculative. It reflects a specific message that is historical and knowable, and invites our consideration and response.[3]

Remembering is a key concept in Scripture.[4] Remembering who God is and what God has done for us reminds us that biblical religion is always characterized as relationship with God. It's not a distant one, but tender and intimate. Recalling this revelatory evidence is *the* motivating factor for worship. It's a spiritual response to be sure but, in view of the divine initiative undertaken, one of a most reasonable kind. The Bible affirms that the one true and living God indeed has self-revealed in history and Scripture. Proclaiming God's acts and words serves as a signpost pointing toward true and spiritual worship, correcting false senses of direction, and calling us to follow a right path.

The power of such proclamation is so valued in my own Reformed circles that a pattern of Reformed worship is often simply delineated as "Preparing to Hear God's Word," "Hearing God's Word," and "Responding to God's Word." This connotes a high view of Scripture, and a high value placed on its ability not just to *inform* but to *transform*. It's a view that God's living word through the agency of God's written word actually invigorates and creates new life (Heb 4:12). A Reformed pattern is a faithful expression of what constitutes Christian worship. Pointing to Calvin's faith in the persuasiveness of the word of God proclaimed, McGrath writes,

2. "Spiritual worship" (*logike latreia*): the carrying out of religious duties by human beings; activity positively characterized as earnest (Acts 26:7), acceptably reverent and awe filled (Heb 12:28), and with a clear conscience (2 Tim 1:3) (Bauer, *Greek-English Lexicon,* 467). The idea is service, religious service, or worship that pertains to speech, reason, or rational mind and soul, a response that in this context is portrayed as incumbent (Ibid., 476).

3. In Acts 17:22–31, St. Paul's interaction with the Athenians about their very careful decision to worship even what was unclear to them ("to an unknown god") echoes Jesus' own admonition to the Samaritan woman in John 4:22. Both assert the revealed, comprehensible, and received qualities of biblical worship.

4. For "remember" in the Old Testament see Allen, "*Zākhar,*" 1100–6; and Eising, "*Zākhar,*" 64–81. For understanding this important term and its cognates in the context of Israel's worship as "a faith word which appropriates the promised gifts of God," see Clancey, "Old Testament Roots of Remembrance," 36.

Fragmentary and broken though human words may be, they nevertheless possess a capacity to function as the medium through which God is able to disclose himself and bring about a transformational encounter of the risen Christ and the believer. . .[5] Calvin does not, and does not believe it is possible to, reduce God or Christian experience to words. Christianity is not a verbal religion, but is experiential; it centers upon a transformative encounter of the believer with the risen Christ. From the standpoint of Christian theology, however, that experience is posterior to the words which generate, evoke and inform it. Christianity is Christ-centered, not book-centered; if it appears to be book-centered, it is because it is through the words of scripture that the believer encounters and feeds upon Jesus Christ. Scripture is a means, not an end; a channel, rather than what is channeled.[6]

Nothing is more powerful than Scripture itself to demonstrate that worship occurs in response to divine initiative in revelatory event or revealed word.[7] Carefully considering its claims is a key step along the way to being persuaded of its truth and transformed by its power. Even a few selected passages sufficiently illustrate that in both the OT and NT, worship closely follows what God says and does.

Creation

From a biblical perspective no act of God is more fundamental than creation. Even before humans were created, even before human response became possible, creation events elicited applause in the heavenly court. This celestial acknowledgment in Job 38:7 is in the context of a *theophany*.[8] In chapters 38–42, God is doing most of the talking. Job has raised some questions about his plight. God's rebuking answer conveys no small amount of irony:

Where were you when I laid the earth's foundations?

5. Calvin's principle of accommodation is explicated in Battles, "God Was Accommodating Himself," 19–38.

6. McGrath, *Life of John Calvin*, 129, 132. For Calvin and preaching, see Leith, "Calvin's Doctrine of the Proclamation," 206–29.

7. Ross, "Worship with Proclamation," 121–51.

8. "Theophany" derives from a combination of the Greek words for "God" (*Theos*) (Bauer, *Greek-English Lexicon*, 356) and "appearance" (*phainen*) (Ibid., 851); in context it refers to the temporary, possibly visible or audible manifestation of a deity. Emphasis is not on actual appearance, but on what God does or says. See Ellison, "Theophany," 719.

Tell me, if you understand.

Who marked off its dimensions? Surely you know!

Who stretched a measuring line across it?

On what were its footings set, or who laid its cornerstone—

while the morning stars sang together, and all the angels

shouted for joy? (Job 38:4–7 NIV)[9]

"Nowhere," of course, would be the appropriate reply. Only the angelic beings had been present, and all they could do was express amazement with a ringing shout of joy.[10] We also see the very essence of such gape-mouthed wonder in praise ascribed to God in Psalm 29:9 (NIV): "The voice of the Lord twists the oaks and strips the forests bare. And in his temple all cry, 'Glory!'"

Exodus and Sinai

Spontaneous praise is also on the lips of God's people following the most dramatic and central moment in the Hebrews' experience and memory: their deliverance at the Red Sea by the hand of God from the Egyptian Pharaoh and slavery (Exod 14–15). Moses and his sister Miriam led Israel in an expostulation of relief and joy: "I will sing to the Lord, for he has triumphed gloriously; the horse and his rider he has thrown into the sea" (15:1 ESV).[11] This unbridled call and response chorus then prompts a fundamental theological question later in Exodus 15:11 (ESV): "Who is like you, O Lord, among the gods? Who is like you, majestic in holiness, awesome in glorious deeds, doing wonders?" The people would all too quickly forget the rescue they had just witnessed. Their memory and interpretation of events would all too fickly fade, but here Moses sharpens the point that there's no other

9. In context, worship language is: recognizing and noting something significant or magnificent by raising a shout (*rûṣ*) (cf. Zech 9:9; Matt 21:5), and exulting joyfully by crying aloud (*rānan* [Brown et al., *Hebrew and English Lexicon*, 929, 943]) (cf. Isa 12:5–6; Ps 98:4). Propriety of heaven and earth jointly praising God is a regular theme of psalmists (e.g., Pss 148; 103:21–22; 145:21; 65:13). This is unbounded worship due to the Creator of all things.

10. Smick, "Job," 1035. For a recent related hymn, see Bayly, "When the Morning Stars Together," McKim, *Presbyterian Hymnal*, 486.

11. See Exodus 8:1 (NIV) for evidence that the Hebrews were saved from bondage to be saved for worship. Cf. Genesis 2:15 for examples of Adam as priest, and the Garden of Eden as a sacred space. From the beginning, the divine project has been to establish or restore true worship throughout creation.

rescuer to be found, much less any more able one, in whom to place faith. There's no other God. Moses adds that the very nature of this rescuing and redeeming God is to be faithful to his word in covenantal loyalty to those called to be his own: "You have led in your steadfast love the people you have redeemed" (Exod 15:13 ESV).[12] A principle and pattern are emerging: God acts, then God's people worship. Responding to divine revelation and provision, biblical worship stands in contrast to prevalent ancient near eastern (ANE) patterns and practices of sacrifice and worship, where sympathetic magic and fertility rites were used with a view to appeasing, cajoling, or manipulating gods for the benefit of seasonal or human fruitfulness. Ancient Sumer, from where God called Abram, and to a degree representative of ANE perspectives and practices, is referred to as "a complex religious state where people worshipped many gods that embodied the earth's forces governing life and fertility. . . responsible for the universe and its cycles and laws."[13] In the Bible, quite the opposite occurs: the Lord God acts and the people respond. Rather than people acting out in some manner to invite or instigate a response from the gods, it is the Lord God himself who acts and then the people respond.

Nowhere is such initiative, provision, and revelation more evident in the Pentateuch than in Exodus 19, as the Hebrews are encamped at the foot of Mt. Sinai:

> The Lord called to him [Moses] out of the mountain, saying, "Thus you shall say to the house of Jacob, and tell the people of Israel: You yourselves have seen what I did to the Egyptians, and how I bore you on eagles' wings and brought you to myself. Now therefore, if you will indeed obey my voice and keep my covenant, you shall be my treasured possession among all peoples, for all the earth is mine; and you shall be to me a kingdom of priests and a holy nation." (19:3–6 ESV)

For Israel this was the fulcrum of history, a moment that defined the exodus, and the event that shaped them for a future in the promised land and the world. Their eventual weakness, hardheartedness, disobedience, and idolatry would tragically soon be demonstrated in the golden calf incident and its aftermath, foreshadowing much of their future (Exod 32); but when Moses brings together the leaders of the people to tell them what God

---

12. For a developed treatment of loyal or steadfast love, see Sakenfeld, *Meaning of Hesed*, 233–40.

13. Ross, *Recalling the Hope of Glory*, 125.

had just commanded and promised, their spontaneous words of obedience are appropriate and full of faith: "All the people answered together and said, 'All that the Lord has spoken we will do'" (Exod 19:8 ESV).

Obedience is inherently worshipful. Such is the case with Abraham's compliance and God's covenantal promise to bless the patriarch because he had obeyed God's voice (Gen 22:19).

A construct of human obedience and divine blessing is also evident in Jacob blessing his son Judah, prefiguring the rules of David and Jesus Christ: "The scepter shall not depart from Judah, nor the ruler's staff from between his feet, until tribute comes to him; and to him shall be the obedience of all the peoples" (Gen 49:10 ESV).

It's also key in Israel's adherence to requirements of the sacrificial system of the tabernacle and temple:

> But the holy things that are due from you . . . you shall take and go to the place that the Lord will choose . . . Be careful to obey all these words that I command you, that it may go well with you and with your children after you forever, when you do what is good and right in the sight of the Lord your God. (Deut 12:26–28 ESV)

It's also operative in the Lord's rejection of Saul as Israel's king, highlighting the tragic contrast of obedience with rote, heartless, or presumptuous sacrifice. "Has the Lord as great delight in burnt offerings and sacrifices as in obeying the voice of the Lord? Behold, obedience is better than sacrifice . . ." (1 Sam 15:22 ESV).

A call to obedience also permeates the message of the prophets. It sounds like, and actually is, an echo of covenant language in Exodus 19:4–6:

> Thus says the Lord of Hosts, the God of Israel . . . For in the day
> I brought them out of the land of Egypt, I did not speak to your
> fathers or command them concerning burnt offerings and sacrifices.
> But this command I gave them: Obey my voice, and I will be your
> God, and you shall be my people. (Jer 7:21–23 ESV)

The Hebrews' identity, opportunity, responsibility, security, and destiny are all tied at Sinai to their obedience to the revealed character and command of God (Exod 19:5), but not before God first reminds them of what already had been done for them in their deliverance from Egypt.[14]

14. This is confirmed in Psalm 90:1–2, the so-called "Song of Moses," which characterizes God's dealings with Israel and the nature of the God they are called and commanded to worship. As in Exodus 19:5–6, Psalm 90 emphasizes the eternality and

Obligations potentially bringing them even more blessing are instituted only after prior blessings of rescue and redemption. All creation belongs to the Lord, but given his specific choice of Israel, and his recent actions on their behalf, the covenant stipulations being offered are both reasonable and a reason to rejoice.[15] It's *before* the command to obey that the reminder comes of what already has been done on their behalf. A pattern thus continues: God acts, then God's people react and respond in trust, obedience, and worship.

The Monarchy

We're less interested in tracking true worship through the checkered history of Israel's and Judah's kings, as we are in simply in noting it in the life of David. His rule largely defined the Israelite monarchy, which was at best an expression of his personality and character. Despite his flaws, David was known as someone "after God's own heart."[16] First Samuel 16 through 2 Samuel 5 portrays David's life as replete with experiences of God's deliverance. These were sometimes recounted in psalms of rejoicing, lament, petition, or confession, each of which are expressions of worship in words of praise, confession, thanksgiving, or trust.[17] Deliverance from his enemies,

---

sovereignty of God, who as Creator, redeemer, and sustainer is alone worthy of trust. This Mosaic prayer "affirms a monotheism that the book of Psalms and the OT as a whole assume. God is the One who in fact lives, speaks, acts, helps, sees, hears, answers, and saves. No other god does any of these things, nor is there any other to do them. This unique, ruling Lord thus merits worship" (House, *Old Testament Theology*, 407). For more on the enduring quality of the Song of Moses, see Revelation 15:3–4.

15. "The invitation to covenant is predicated on the great divine acts of the past which Israel herself has experienced. Above all, the reference is to deliverance from Egypt . . . The covenant responsibility encompasses her whole life, defining her relation to God and to her neighbors, and the quality of her existence" (Childs, *Book of Exodus*, 366–67). "Now, therefore" in Exodus 19:5 is a construction that "usually introduces the conclusion after the prefatory statements. . . The conclusion is a proposal, to wit, that Israel should make a covenant and be chosen as 'a people of special possession' . . . from among all the peoples of the earth" (Cassuto, *Commentary on the Book of Exodus*, 227). St. Paul uses a "therefore" to similarly frame his argument in Romans 12:1.

16. Samuel pronounced divine judgment on Saul: "The Lord has sought out a man after his own heart, and the Lord has commanded him to be prince over his people, because you have not kept what the Lord commanded you" (1 Sam 13:14 ESV; cf. Acts 13:22).

17. David's deliverance from danger or judgment in a variety of historical events became occasion for reflecting on such divine protection or mercy through his poetic gifts

and particularly King Saul, compelled him to write "I love you, O Lord, my strength. The Lord is my rock and my fortress and my deliverer, my God, my rock, in whom I take refuge" (Ps 18:1–2a ESV).[18] The aftermath of his great sin with Bathsheba fostered the insight of Psalm 51:

> Create in me a clean heart, O God, and renew a right spirit within me. Cast me not away from your presence, and take not your Holy Spirit from me. Restore to me the joy of your salvation, and uphold me with a willing spirit. Then I will teach transgressors your ways, and sinners will return to you. (10–13 ESV)

David's penitence here confirms the Lord's earlier assessment of the nature, or at least the intentions, of his heart, but it also measures divine judgment and grace. David knew that the law stipulated no sacrifice to atone for his high-handed sins against Uriah the Hittite and ultimately against the Lord (Num 15:30–31). All he could do was cast himself on the mercy of God. A word of forgiveness eventually would come to him by way of the prophet Nathan as a hammer blow, but a merciful one.[19]

David's appeal to God's mercy has real value for worship. Forgiven, he might humbly recount there its offer in the face of his heinous deeds. Even memory of the worst circumstances could thus become by God's grace occasion for returning to the Lord.[20]

---

and his role as Israel's great psalmist. "History becomes the background for worship, just as surely as worship strengthened David during difficult historical circumstances. Where theology and history intersect in the canon, worship occurs" (House, *Old Testament Theology*, 240); in view of the hope for eventual deliverance, that even a "call of distress" (lament) is appropriate OT worship language, also see Westermann, *Praise and Lament*, 262–67.

18. House indicates that 1 Samuel 16 through 2 Samuel 5 "initiates the canon's emphasis on David as psalmist . . . In the Psalter, Psalm 18:1–30 matches 2 Samuel 22:1–30 nearly word for word. This dual canonical attribution to David not only makes it plausible that David wrote this material but also makes it likely that the psalm acts as a summary of God's great acts on his behalf in both books. Seen this way, Psalm 18 and 2 Samuel 22 interpret 1 Samuel 16—2 Samuel 5 as material that focuses on God's preservation of David in even extreme circumstances" (*Old Testament Theology*, 239–40).

19. "In Israel, if the sin was willful or premeditated, then no simple purification offering could be made. All the penitent could do was plead for mercy and wait for a word of forgiveness from God" (Ross, *Recalling the Hope of Glory*, 199).

20. A simple act of turning back or returning (*šûb*) (Brown et al., *Hebrew and English Lexicon*, 997). Returning to something or someone implies a commensurate turning from, and thus illustrates repentance, here an astonishing and arresting act by a monarch before his people. This riveting turn of events and redemption in David's life is recounted in a remarkable sermon-like song from Ken Medema called, "When You're a King," which appeared on Medema's album *Stories* (GlorySounds/Shawnee), recorded in July 1982.

Prophetic Rebuke and Promise

Considered broadly, the OT prophetic books share perspective and concern:[21] Israel's identity derives from the relationship and covenant God established with the nation and its people, and Israel's destiny depends on its obedience to God and faithfulness to the covenant. The prophets convey a consistent, recurrent message rooted in the law and its commandments, stipulations, and promises: if Israel obeys the Lord their God, they'll be blessed; if they don't obey, they'll be cursed (Deut 11:26).

How this condition unfolds in the life of the nation becomes the balance of the OT message. Prophetic rebuke persistently follows the people's disobedience to God's covenant and their idolatry and points to coming judgment: Assyrian and Babylonian exiles and ultimately a "Day of the Lord" for the Hebrews and even all nations (Joel 1:15; 2:11; Mal 3:2–3; 4:1; Amos 5:18–20; Obad 15).[22] Mercifully, prophetic promise of God's unchanging faithfulness through and beyond this disobedience points to a "new covenant" whereby Israel will be blessed in spite of themselves (Jer 31:31–34).

The implication for worship in this is well illustrated in Malachi, where God's holiness, honor, and covenant loyalty are set in sharp contrast to the people's disobedience and dishonor.[23] God builds a legal case against Judah through Malachi. In an unfolding oracle, the Lord brings several indictments.[24] He has loved Judah but, despite that elective choice, they mock him (1:2). First, they and their priestly leaders have dishonored and disrespected him in bringing diseased and thus defiled animals for sacrifice (1:8). Second, they've broken faith with him and with each other through unsanctioned marriage and divorce (2:11). Third, they've wearied him by doubting his sovereign justice (2:17). Fourth, they've robbed him by failing to bring a whole tithe (3:10). Fifth, they no longer fear God, saying it's futile to serve him (3:14).

---

21. Former prophets (Joshua, Judges, Samuel, and Kings), as well as Isaiah, Jeremiah, Ezekiel, and the Book of the Twelve. House notes that "by distinguishing Joshua to Kings as prophetic literature the Hebrew canon emphasizes the common ground shared by the prophetic books and their more heavily historical predecessors" (House, *Old Testament Theology*, 197).

22. Old, "John Calvin and the Prophetic," 230–46.

23. Gray, "Useless Fires," 35–41.

24. Oracle, or "burden" (*maśśā*; a load, something to bear). The prophetic oracle brought weight of divine judgment (Brown et al., *Hebrew and English Lexicon*, 672). "The great burden of the prophet is covenant violation" (Merrill, *Kingdom of Priests*, 514).

God will judge this disobedience and unfaithfulness in several ways: by thwarting the people's efforts to such an extent that they will eventually see that their privileged position is no reason to boast (1:4–5); by defiling their half-hearted and misguided worship leaders so they themselves will become unfit to worship (2:3); by cutting them off from fellowship in the covenant community (2:12); and by inexorable retribution and purification in a coming day of the Lord (3:1–5; 4:1–6).

Woven through judgment, however, are threads of grace and mercy. Even God's admonition comes as a reminder of covenantal relationship. First, he reminds the Levitical priesthood that they operate under a covenant of life and peace to revere him, to mediate his presence and its implications among the people, and to teach and proclaim true knowledge as messengers of the Lord (2:4–7). Then he singles out and affirms a faithful remnant from among the people, those "who feared the Lord and honored his name," those for whom "a scroll of remembrance was written in his presence" (3:16 NIV). These faithful continue to model true worship:

> "They will be mine," says the Lord Almighty, "in the day when I make up my treasured possession. I will spare them, just as in compassion a man spares his son who serves him. And you will see the distinction between the righteous and the wicked, between those who serve God and those who do not." (3:17–18 NIV)

This remnant is comprised of those who remain faithful to God's covenant. Remembering all he's shown them and done for them in the past is the basis for continued faith. They responded rightly to the prophet as he recalled, reiterated, and recapitulated God's historical acts and words to them. The rebuke was designed to incite repentance which would lead to rejuvenation and rejoicing. Ideally his message would prompt covenantal loyalty, and a life of true obedience and meaningful worship. Ideally, of course, is a long way from reality, but in Malachi's prophecy we see a pattern repeated: the Lord reaches out to us, then we respond.

The Psalter

Focusing on God's acts and words is what clarifies a transforming vision in worship. Worship can do this. Worship should do this. What we come to see in worship can be powerfully transforming when God is both its object and subject. The Psalms convey this in a way that draws together and exhibits theological themes and perspectives of God from the entire OT canon.[25] As Israel's "hymnal,"[26] the Psalter's focus is doxological, but also conveys, through poetry and a variety of literary subgenres, a spectrum of human emotion and expression intimately tied to everyday personal—as well as national—circumstances and concerns.[27]

Worship certainly is in view in Psalm 50. Its author, Asaph, was one of Israel's early worship leaders. He calls the nation to be transformed and reformed by a renewed vision of God. The people had lost sight of the Holy One who had chosen them and consecrated them to be a royal priesthood, a centripetal spiritual draw to the world, and a light to the nations.[28] His legal case against them is not unlike Malachi's against Judah. He raises two serious charges: rote formalism in worship and hypocritical lifestyles. The psalm's opening *theophany* calls all creation to witness the indictments being brought against God's people: elaborate but empty ritual and hypocrisy rather than genuine faith. Religious ceremonies were elaborate. Attention was given to every detail and decoration, and rules were kept meticulously, but rule-keeping and perfunctory ritual don't constitute true worship. Asaph chides the people and the priests for failing to realize that God himself is the one who instituted sacrifice, not because he needed them like other ancient near eastern gods, but because the people desperately needed him. God doesn't depend on our worship to survive. The remedy for this

---

25. "No other Old Testament book has the theological and historical scope that Psalms displays. As a theological document, the book embraces the full range of biblical confessions about the Lord's character, activity and concerns" (House, *Old Testament Theology*, 402).

26. "It is clear from the beginning and ending of the Psalter that some guides have been given for understanding the whole. Psalms 1 and 2 form an introduction which suggests first that one finds here a true Torah piety that will show the way for those who love the Lord and the law, and secondly that these psalms also show the way of God's rule over the larger human communities. The conclusion to the psalms, i.e., Psalm 150, and the title (*t͏ᵉhillîm* = hymns) gives the Psalter to the community as a book of praise to God" (Miller, "Current Issues in Psalms Studies," 132–43).

27. "The Psalms represent the inward and spiritual side of the religion of Israel. They are the manifold expression of the intense devotion of pious souls to God, of the feelings of trust and hope and love which reach a climax in such psalms as xxiii, xlii–xliii, lxiii, lxxxiv. They are the many-toned voice of prayer in the widest sense, as the soul's address to God in confession, petition, intercession, meditation, thanksgiving, praise, both in public and private. They offer the most complete proof, if proof were needed, how utterly false is the notion that the religion of Israel was a formal system of external rites and ceremonies" (Kirkpatrick, *Book of Psalms*, lxxxv).

28. See Isaiah 42:6 and 49:6 for this light embodied in "Servant of the Lord."

profaning of God's worship standards is prescribed to be gratitude, thanksgiving, and genuine faith:

> Offer to God a sacrifice of thanksgiving,
> and perform your vows to the Most High,
> and call upon me in the day of trouble;
> I will deliver you, and you shall glorify me. (Ps 50:14–15 ESV)

The second charge brought against the people and their leaders is hypocritical living. Hypocrisy in this case is a pretense of virtue and piety. Instead they're thieving, morally duplicitous, and slanderous, all contrary to living in covenant with God and each other (Ps 50:16–20). The root of their evils is inadequate acknowledgment of God's character and concerns (21–22 ESV):

> These things you have done and I kept silent;
> you thought I was altogether like you.
> But now I rebuke you and lay the charge before you.
> Mark this, then, you who forget God,
> lest I tear you apart, with none to rescue you. (Ps 50:21–22 ESV)

Asaph might just as well have said, "Don't confuse God's patience with God's approval." Disobedience and disloyalty to God's covenant had led Israel to a subtle but insidious attitude that they were doing God a favor by worshiping him. Amos corroborates that this displeases God:

> I hate, I despise your religious feasts;
> I cannot stand your assemblies.
> Even though you bring me burnt offerings and grain offerings,
> I will not accept them.
> Though you bring choice fellowship offerings,
> I will have no regard for them.
> Away with the noise of your songs!
> I will not listen to the music of your harps.
> But let justice roll on like a river,
> Righteousness like a never-failing stream![29] (Amos 5:21–24 NIV)

---

29. See James 1:12.

God's priorities are perfectly clear. The corrective of Psalm 50 is that God is the one offering favor. Only God's grace and mercy validate our worship.

Restoration and Reform

A period of restoration and reform during Judah's history offers a strong example of true worship that closely follows God's self-revelation in act or word. After wickedness and apostasy in Judah under Manasseh's and Amon's idolatrous rule (2 Kgs 21), righteous reforms occurred under Amon's son, Josiah (2 Kgs 22–23).[30] This followed the discovery and public reading by Ezra of a previously-displaced "Book of the Law."[31] This reading of *Torah* would have emphasized the same kind of centering and reorienting advice Moses gave Israel after their long sojourn in the wilderness just before their entry into the promised land:

> When you have eaten and are satisfied, praise the Lord your God for the good land he has given you. Be careful that you do not forget the Lord your God. . .Otherwise, when you eat and are satisfied, when you build fine houses and settle down, and when your herds grow large, and your silver and gold increase, and all you have is multiplied, then your heart will become proud, and you will forget the Lord your God. (Deut 8:10–12 NIV)

On the strength and impact of this reading of the law, Josiah repented and instituted reforms which the people affirmed:

> All the people answered "Amen, Amen," lifting up their hands. And they bowed their heads and worshiped the Lord with their faces to the ground. . .they read from the book, from the law of God, clearly, and they gave the sense, so that the people understood the reading.[32] (Neh 8:5–8 ESV)

---

30. See Exodus 7:9–10; Nehemiah 8:5–8.

31. Perhaps Deuteronomy itself or some portion of it. See Driver, *Deuteronomy*, 317.

32. ". . .worshiped the Lord with their faces to the ground. . ." The etymology of the word here for "worship" is open to question (Ross, *Recalling the Hope of Glory*, 50), but context clearly conveys a sense of bowing down low to the ground in acknowledgement, as if placing oneself under another's authority.

This led, at least temporarily, to worship renewal based on a clearer understanding of God's character, concerns, and commandments. Revelation and proclamation again elicit sincere worship.

Four random NT examples likewise support the assertion that true worship follows God speaking or acting: in the incarnation, annunciation, and birth of Jesus narrative (Luke 1–2); during Jesus' earthly ministry (John 4); at Pentecost (Acts 2); and in the Apocalypse/consummation (Rev 4).

Incarnation, Annunciation, and Birth of Jesus

When the angel brings word to Mary of God's favor and that the miraculous work within her will result in the conception and birth of Jesus, her amazement prompts a summary comment from Gabriel: "Nothing will be impossible with God" (Luke 1:37 ESV). By her immediate response Mary places herself at God's pleasure and under his authority: "Behold, I am the servant of the Lord; let it be to me according to your word" (Luke 1:38 ESV). Properly acknowledging her creaturely status before the sovereign Creator Lord, she also signals her readiness to respond in obedience and service to what has been said in this astonishing revelation.

When she goes to visit her cousin Elizabeth with this dizzying news, Elizabeth blesses her by the power of the Spirit, concluding, "And blessed is she who believed that there would be a fulfillment of what was spoken to her from the Lord" (Luke 1:45 ESV). Mary's subsequent worshipful response in the so-called "Magnificat" places her squarely under authority of the word of God revealed: "My soul magnifies the Lord, and my spirit rejoices in God my Savior . . ."[33]

Such private reactions and celebrations become public enough after another angel announces to Judean shepherds the birth of the Savior-Messiah in the nearby city of David. Not unlike the heavenly shouts of joy at creation (Job 38:7), a "multitude of the heavenly host" exult in a chorus of doxology that acknowledges both the supreme source of this "good news of great joy" and its immediate and lasting earthly effect: "Glory to God in the highest, and on earth peace, goodwill toward men" (Luke 2:14 NKJV).[34]

33. "Magnificat," Latin from Greek *megalunō*, means to make large or magnify (Bauer, *Greek-English Lexicon,* 497), in context bearing witness to God's person and work. "Rejoices" conveys a sense of full gladness or joy. Mary's reaction is worshipful acknowledgment and celebration.

34. "Good will," perhaps approval, taking delight, or good decision (*eudokeō,*

This singular revelation prompts worship on earth as in heaven, as the shepherds hurry to Bethlehem to indeed "see this thing that has happened," and later return to their workday world "glorifying and praising God for all they had heard and seen, as it had been told them" (Luke 2:16–20 ESV).[35] This is intense worship, immediate response to divine initiative. God breaks in, and we break out in praise.

Jesus' Earthly Ministry

God the Son breaks in in quite another way in John 4, but the results are just as arresting and transforming. His conversation with a Samaritan woman at a water well in Sychar indicates the general manner in which the Son of Man breaks down barriers to "seek and save the lost." (Luke 19:10 ESV)

Jesus and his disciples are walking from Judea north to Galilee, along a possible but improbable path through Samaria. This improbability is evident in the woman's surprise that Jesus would ask her to draw for him a drink of water. He was Jewish and she was a Samaritan. John confirms her reticence in an aside comment that Jews have no dealings with Samaritans. In fact, deeply-seated and longstanding animosities run both ways between the Hebrews and these descendants of those who survived the 722 BC Assyrian conquest of the Northern Kingdom of Israel, and who later intermarried with foreigners sent to repopulate and colonize the region.

Over time, real differences of theology and religious practice have emerged between Samaritans and Jews, but the tensions are even more visceral. Jews condescend to the Samaritans' ethnicity, and consider them half-bred and at least ceremonially unclean. That Jesus asks the woman for water from the well seems to indicate that he plans to drink from whatever bucket or utensil she has, and presumably uses herself. In that he is unconcerned about potential defilement, his request is striking. He not only has chosen to travel to Galilee along what Jews consider to be a questionable route (even though it is the shortest), and to engage in conversation someone whose nationality, gender, and (as we quickly learn) personal morality collectively

---

eudokia); God's sovereign resolve or good decision on our behalf. See Bauer, *Greek-English Lexicon*, 319.

35. Whether or not they understood the full import of what they had just witnessed (How could they?), the intensity of the shepherds' reaction parallels that of the angels' by use of *doxazō* ("glorifying" God [Bauer, *Greek-English Lexicon*, 204]), along with the shepherds' praising (*aineō*) (Bauer, *Greek-English Lexicon*, 23 [Luke 2:14, 20]).

stand as a significant barrier to that engagement, he apparently and remarkably is now asking to share the same cup or ladle of water.

Jesus no doubt is thirsty, but his question probes more deeply than his own need for water, to her need for something far more refreshing. "If you knew the gift of God, and who it is that is saying to you, 'Give me a drink,' you would have asked him, and he would have given you living water." She counters that this is *her* people's well, and wonders incredulously how he is to make good on his assertion. Jesus elaborates that the water from their well only temporarily satisfies, but that the water he's offering will completely and forever satisfy. It will in fact become a source, "a spring of water welling up to eternal life." The woman is intrigued, but is still thinking merely in terms of her physical needs. Jesus bores into the barriers between them by steering away from the metaphorical and theological, taking an unexpected and decidedly personal tack in the conversation. He asks her to bring her husband. It's at this moment that real tension arises in the narrative; tension between Jesus' probing and the woman's apparent embarrassment and dissimulation about her checkered past and morally dubious present. She's been married many times, and is now living unmarried with someone. His goal isn't to expose her, but to lay bare things about her and himself that will lead her to repentance, restoration, and recreation. Palmer writes,

> This one human being is both found and found out by Jesus Christ. There cannot really be good news that means life to the real me without this finding and finding out. Now the Samaritan woman knows that the joyous living water has been offered to the real person behind the mask. The fact that Jesus truly understands who she is has heightened the richness of the gift of life to her. The impact is profound.[36]

The woman evidently is caught off guard at Jesus' awareness but curious about his insight. Her dodge, "Sir, I perceive you are a prophet," paves the way for one of the clearest, most crystalline moments in the New Testament, in which Jesus forthrightly and directly reveals to her both who he is, and what is the nature of true worship. In the context of this passage, this is revelation that leads to belief. "Our fathers worshiped on this mountain," she says, "but you say that in Jerusalem is the place where people ought to

---

36. Palmer, *Book that John Wrote,* 54. These insights signal deep implications for confession of sin in the context of personal and corporate worship. Confession is like no other moment to tell the truth about ourselves, naming silently or with our lips what God already knows is in our hearts.

worship." He counters, "Woman, believe me, the hour is coming when neither on this mountain nor in Jerusalem will you worship the Father. . .the
hour is coming, and is now here, when the true worshipers will worship
him in spirit and in truth."

Jesus moves with speed and precision to recast the woman's question
about where worship occurs, to how it's offered. He transcends both Samaritan and Jewish expectation and proscription by defining God's nature
and person on his terms, and by emphasizing God's relational character
as "Father." This is a surprisingly tender and direct characterization, and
stands over and against her reliance on the traditions of her own people's
"fathers." What will now characterize true worship is access to and intimacy
of relationship with God *the* Father. Jesus further surprises the woman (and
the readers of John's Gospel), by his straight-up assertion that he himself is
the way to that access and intimacy. The woman admits, "I know that Messiah is coming (he who is called Christ). When he comes, he will tell us all
things." Jesus says, "I who speak to you am he."[37]

This is the revelation of God. The content of the revelation is that Jesus
is the one who by his person and work makes it known. John has expressly
said this in the prologue to his book: "No one has ever seen God; the only
God, who is at the Father's side, he has made him known."[38] This revelation,
this relationship between God and humankind based on God's prior initiative, is again *the* motivating factor for worship. We see this impulse here in
the midst of what might well be characterized as cross-cultural ministry
pointing to the universal appeal and efficacy of Jesus' person and work.
Jesus isn't just for Jews, or Samaritans, or Gentiles, but for everyone.

The results of Jesus' revelation and the woman's reaction are quick
and concrete. Her zealous report of Jesus' encounter with her at the well
reaps significant harvest in her home town. He stays there for two days,
at the end of which time her townsfolk exclaim, "It is no longer because
of what you said that we believe, for we have learned for ourselves, and
we know that this is indeed the Savior of the world."[39] This reaction and
affirmation vividly portray both the purpose of John's Gospel,[40] and the

---

37. Morris asserts that what Jesus is presenting or representing is more than either
Jew or Samaritan had comprehended or anticipated of Messiah, or "Christ" (Morris,
"Gospel According to John" 273). Also see Block, *For the Glory of God,* 272–98.

38. John 1:18; Jesus, God the Son, has "exegeted" God the Father for us.

39. John 4:42, ESV.

40. John 20:30.

pattern we're asserting: It's God's revelation that rightly elicits and engenders belief, trust, and worship.

In terms of what worshiping "in spirit and in truth" implies, another conversation between Jesus and his disciples is instructive. In Mark 13, they're walking in the temple grounds in Jerusalem. One of them says, "Look, Teacher, what wonderful stones and what wonderful buildings!" For all Jews the temple was the defining center of their religious, cultural, and social identity. For Galileans, Herod's grand structure must've seemed all the more magnificent. Jesus' countering comment puzzled and probably jarred them, when he said, "Do you see these great buildings? There will not be left here one stone upon another that will not be thrown down."[41] This of course was borne out literally not long afterwards with the Roman destruction of the temple in 70 AD, but the disciples had no way of foreseeing this. It would've seemed impossible to them that something so evidently solid and central to their lives would be so short lived.

In a later private conversation on the Mount of Olives, Peter, James, John, and Andrew ask Jesus, "Tell us, when will these things be, and what will be the sign when all these things are about to be accomplished?" Jesus' ensuing teaching focuses on the close of the age, *the* end of the world, but with a clarion call of hope: the Son of Man will come "in clouds with great power and glory." He will "send out the angels and gather his elect from the four winds, from the ends of the earth to the ends of heaven."[42] If nothing else, this points to Jesus Christ's sovereign authority and principal role in God's eternal plan. If there's any permanence to be found, it's not in the grand tonnage of the temple stones, but in his own messianic person and work as cornerstone.[43] The locus of divine revelation and human response is no longer to be sought on the temple mount (or in the context of John 4 for the Samaritan woman, on Mt. Gerazim), but in Jesus Christ himself.

The implication for worship is that no building, institution, or location defines the gate of heaven. That function is now centered in the incarnate, crucified, risen, ascended, mediating, and advocating Son of God. He now is the eternal face of God. He is seated "at the right hand" of God whose

41. Mark 13:1–2, ESV.

42. Mark 13:26–27, ESV. See Wesley, "Jesus Comes with Clouds Descending," McKim, *Presbyterian Hymnal*, 6.

43. Matt 21:42; Ps 118:22.

essential nature is spirit. To all who love, trust, and follow him, he's sent the Holy Spirit, who will guide them "into all truth."[44]

Pentecost

After the completion of Jesus' earthly ministry, the word of the Lord is revealed powerfully through St. Peter's proclamation at Pentecost (Acts 2:28–37). His preaching recapitulates OT history and theology in such a way that those who hear it are "cut to the heart," and immediately ask, "What shall we do?" (Acts 2:37 ESV). Following Peter's instructions, thousands repent, are baptized, receive the Holy Spirit, and become part of a fledgling entity: Christ's church. At Pentecost, proclaiming God's acts and words elicits belief, faith, repentance, worship, fellowship, and service.

Apocalypse and Consummation

Finally, with the sweep and scope of salvation history in view, three apocalyptic hymns connect in act and word the revelation of God's character and concerns (Rev. 4:1—5:14). These hymns are part of a doxological continuum. They also can be seen as successive verses of an unfolding song of praise, each one focusing on a different facet of God's identity and activity. The first hymn or verse emphasizes God's eternality and uniqueness. What are identified as "four living creatures" around the heavenly throne unceasingly say, "Holy, holy, holy, is the Lord God Almighty, who was and is and is to come."[45] (Rev 4:8 ESV).

The second hymn or verse emphasizes God's role as sole and sovereign Creator. Those identified as "twenty-four elders" cast down their crowns before the throne, and say, "Worthy are you, our Lord and God, to receive

---

44. John 16:12–15; 14:15–16; 14:25–26. Cf. Renwick, *Paul, the Temple*, 41–43; 157; Burns, *Nearness of God*, 168–72.

45 "Holy" (*hagios*) (Bauer, *Greek-English Lexicon*, 9) is a primary worship word derived from the idea of the quality possessed by someone or something that could approach deity, hence consecrated, dedicated, sacred, pure, perfect, worthy of God (cf. Ps 24); applied to the deity itself, it conveys a sense of uniqueness in divine apartness or otherness; the threefold holy only emphasizes the idea (Bauer, *Greek-English Lexicon*, 9). The Hebrew word for "holy" (*kadōsh*) conveys similar notions of "set apart," "uncommon," "unordinary," "distinct," or "unique." "To say that God is holy is to ascribe a uniqueness to him that is almost incomprehensible" (Ross, *Recalling the Hope of Glory*, 43). See Isaiah 40:15–31.

glory and honor and power, for you created all things, and by your will they existed and were created" (Rev 4:11 ESV).

"Crowns" imply position and authority. This is a striking picture of secondary authority acknowledging ultimate authority. One of the chief by-products or benefits of true worship is the proper ordering of reality.

The third hymn or verse emphasizes the Lamb of God's role in salvation: atonement, rescue, restoration, and kingdom rule. Creatures and elders alike fall down[46] and sing,

> "Worthy are you to take the scroll and to open its seals, for you were slain, and by your blood you ransomed people for God from every tribe and language and people and nation, and you have made them a kingdom and priests to our God, and they shall reign on the earth." (Rev 5:9–10 ESV)

This is worship in heaven. It shouldn't surprise us that heavenly worship mirrors the earthly pattern (or more accurately that the earthly resonates with the heavenly).[47] In each, true worship is the response to revelation.

Of this divine revelation, initiative, and intervention St. Peter writes in his first epistle:

> Concerning this salvation, the prophets who spoke of the grace that was to come to you searched intently and with greatest care, trying to find out the time and circumstances to which the Spirit of Christ in them was pointing when he predicted the sufferings of Christ and the glories that would follow. It was revealed to them that they were not serving themselves but you, when they spoke of the things that have now been told you by those who have preached the gospel to you by the Holy Spirit sent from heaven. Even angels long to look into these things. (1 Pet 1:10–12 NIV)

Similar sentiments are devotedly conveyed in words from a nineteenth-century gospel hymn by Johnson Oatman, Jr.:

46. "To fall, fall down" (*piptō*) (Bauer, *Greek-English Lexicon*, 659); in context of throwing oneself down to the ground as a sign of devotion, closely related to "bowing down" (*proskuneō*) (Bauer, *Greek-English Lexicon*, 716); each akin to Old Testament *hishtakhăwăh* (Brown et al., *Hebrew and English Lexicon*, 1010, and Emerton, "Etymology of *Hishtakhăwăh*," 41–55), highlighting a worship posture "clearly understood" (Ross, *Recalling the Hope of Glory*, 52).

47. See Koester, "Distant Triumph Song," 243–62. Palmer's overall perspective on John's Apocalypse also draws on musical and symphonic metaphors in "Revelation," 101–4.

There is singing up in heaven such as we have never known,
>   Where the angels sing the praises of the Lamb upon the throne.
Their sweet harps are ever tuneful, and their voices always clear.
>   O that we might be more like them as we serve the Master here.
"Holy! Holy! Holy!" is what the angels sing;
>   And I expect to help them make the courts of heaven ring.
But when they hear redemption's story, they all will fold their wings,
>   For angels never felt the joy that our salvation brings.[48]

Here near the end of the NT, Peter in a sense has come full circle from the report of angelic exclamation in the OT book of Job. The holy God of glory captures our attention by creation, redemption, and reconciliation that are made known to us by grace through faith in the Savior, who is revealed to us by the Holy Spirit's power through the word and work of God revealed in holy Scripture.

Two functions then help frame a discussion of proclaiming God's word and properly responding to it as God's people: revealing and remembering. From the beginning of the OT to the end of the NT, what God says portrays absolute and ultimate ability and authority. Merely speaking accomplishes God's creative purposes through imaginative, sovereign, but apparently effortless declaration (Gen 1:3–31). God's power is revealed through his spoken word.

Likewise, at the end of the canon what God says reveals his power and person: "I am the Alpha and Omega," says the Lord God, "who is and was and who is to come, the Almighty" (Rev 1:8; cf. 1:17–18; 2:8; 22:13 ESV). God's very word has power to create, comfort, confront, and convey his prerogatives to his creation and his children. The proper response to divine prerogatives and provisions is worship itself: praise not left to speculation, but following closely what is revealed and remembered. Reverberantly proclaiming it in every way possible is integral to worship's power and impact.

Two NT teachings wonderfully come to bear on the nature of this proclamation: the sacrifice of praise, and the priesthood of all believers. First, Hebrews 13:15 exhorts, "Through Jesus, therefore, let us continually offer to God a sacrifice of praise—the fruit of lips that confess his name." The OT background for this exhortation is the "thank offering" (tōdāh).[49]

---

48. Osbeck, *Beyond the Sunset*, 43; Reynolds, *Songs of Glory*, 132.

49. Related to the Hebrew *yād* and *yādāh*, connoting a gesture with the hand; carrying or bringing something in the hand, hence, thanksgiving (Brown et al., *Hebrew and*

Particularly relevant here is how the individual offer of that voluntary OT sacrifice became the basis for corporate praise and a communal meal.[50] Based on the perfect and complete work of Jesus Christ, the book of Hebrews calls for our "sacrifice of praise," characterizing it as heartfelt, verbal testimony.[51]

This arguably has implications today for what may be brought to the Lord as worship. Just as an OT believer could bring a thank offering for any unspecified reason of overflowing gratitude, a NT worshiper may likewise respond to God's blessings. For either to approach God, a blood sacrifice was and is required, but once admitted before the Lord, bringing a thank offering or sacrifice of praise was and is entirely acceptable. The implication is that whatever causes a worshiper's heart to fill with gratitude toward God may appropriately be expressed in worship. In both the OT and the NT, the individual offering becomes the basis for the corporate expression of gathered believers. This essentially precludes performance in worship, but does not preclude desire for or commitment to excellence. Second, St. Peter writes,

> As you come to him, the living Stone—rejected by men but chosen by God and precious to him—you also, like living stones, are being built into a spiritual house to be a holy priesthood, offering spiritual sacrifices acceptable to God through Jesus Christ . . . a people belonging to God, that you might declare the praises of him who called you out of darkness into his wonderful light. (1 Pet 2:4–5, 9 NIV)

The apostle emphasizes the corporate nature of believers' priesthood to one another and, arguably, to the world. It's not a hierarchical, sacerdotal function, but a mediating role that witnesses to God's person, work, and will to others, and brings human needs to God in prayer.

Christian worship is neither entertainment nor something merely to be enjoyed. Rather it's a grateful response to God speaking and acting on our behalf. When this word and work are clearly portrayed in and through

---

English Lexicon, 388, 392). The Hebrews were not to come to worship empty-handed, that is, without a sacrifice.

50. Leviticus 7:11–18. See Ross, *Recalling the Hope of Glory*, 272–75; Bruce, *Epistle to the Hebrews*, 406–7.

51. For such declarative praise as a regular feature of the Psalms, see Psalm 22:22; 50:14, 23; 66:13–16; 107:22; and 116:17.

various facets of worship, the clearer the opportunity becomes for us to know God and to respond knowledgeably.

Expositional worship tied closely to the biblical text proclaimed in the moment, and which seeks to heighten its expression consistently and creatively, conveys the truth of God's word, trusting in its power to transform us and, as God's people, to conform us to the Holy One who ordains our praise. We're thereby edified, built up in Christian faith.

"Dwelling Richly" and Edification

With respect to edification as an enriching and maturing process, apostolic advice in Colossians 3:16 (ESV) (cf. Eph 5:19) should at least be noted.[52] St. Paul writes, "Let the word of Christ dwell in you richly, teaching and admonishing one another in all wisdom, singing psalms and hymns and spiritual songs with thankfulness in your hearts to God." If "the word of Christ" refers essentially to "the Gospel, the 'Word' about or uttered by Christ himself during his life and ministry and through his person, and repeated by each Christian as he proclaims the Gospel by life and witness,"[53] then it's an objective, verifiable body of truth to be personally and communally appropriated and publically proclaimed with a view to teaching, correcting, guiding, and growing in breadth and depth of faith and faithful living. To whatever manner of heightened expression dwelling richly can legitimately be suggested to be referring, that should be the goal of expositional worship. If the "word of Christ" is "at home" within each believer and among a community of believers, it becomes the basis and content of their life together and their corporate expressions.[54]

---

52. For a detailed treatment of Colossians 3:16, particularly with respect to music and worship, see Detweiler, "Church Music and Colossians 3:16," 347–70.

53. Moule, "Epistles to the Colossians and Philemon," 125. Phrase used only here in New Testament; could refer to word *about* Christ (i.e., the gospel) or Christ's own teaching (a message *from* him), but either would be authoritative and regulative (cf. Vaughan, "Colossians," 216).

54. "Dwell in you richly"; from the root word for "house" (*oikos*), the verb (*enoikeō*) can convey both a regular or specialized sense, as simply to dwell in or inhabit, or to have some idea, conviction, or even faith becoming stronger or infixed in oneself, or to convey a sense of particular presence such as the Holy Spirit (Bauer, *Greek-English Lexicon*, 267). The adverb (*plousiōs*) carries a sense of largely, abundantly, or richly (Bauer, *Greek-English Lexicon*, 673).

It's therefore not surprising that the apostle's advice about the value of worship tethered to recall and reiteration of God's acts and words should characterize it as a wise undertaking. The Psalter itself, Israel's great hymnal and worship guide to millennia of worshipers, begins by pointing to the wisdom of "walking not in the counsel of the wicked," nor "standing in the way of sinners," nor "sitting in the seat of scoffers," but "delighting in the law of the Lord," and "on that law meditating day and night" (Ps 1:1–2).

Remembering what God has said and done is what produces true and proper worship. Expositional worship essentially refers to those practices in the congregational gathering which heighten the expression of this revelation and its proclamation with celebration through various biblically sanctioned, time-honored, and freshly articulated patterns, rubrics, and components. This is its essence and ethos.

3

A Theological Perspective

The reverberating word moves by the power of God's Spirit from inspired text, to illumined text, to transforming text, to commissioning text in our worship and every facet of Christian living.

BEFORE THE REFORMATION, MARTIN Luther was a dedicated Augustinian monk, but one laboring under a heavy load of guilt and an excruciating personal sense of the gulf between sinful humanity and a righteous, remote deity. His intense personal struggle to find a gracious God points us down a proper theological path leading to where the study of theology ought to lead: a life of righteousness, service, value, and joy. Luther recognized that it's not merely "the reading of books or speculating," but "living, or rather dying, and being damned that make one a theologian."[1]

When John Calvin returned to teaching in Geneva several years after he'd been summarily dismissed from leadership there, he offered no recrimination or rebuke to that Swiss congregation and civil consistory. He simply picked up where he'd left off in his previous preaching ministry and exposition of the biblical text.[2] This is remarkable testimony about Calvin's faithfulness

---

1. *D. Martin Luthers Werke*, 5.28–29. "It is through undergoing the torment of the cross, death and hell, that a man becomes a 'theologian of the cross.' It is precisely this consideration which underlies Luther's celebrated statement concerning the qualifications of a true theologian . . . *vivendo immo moriendo et damnando fit theologus, non intelligendo, legendo aut speculando*" (McGrath, *Luther's Theology of the Cross*, 152).

2. "Following the practice of many of the Church fathers, but even more extensively, Calvin preached through whole books of the Bible Sunday after Sunday or day after day.

to the importance of God's self-revelation in Scripture, and of his confidence in its power to accomplish what God intends for it to do.

All Theology as Spiritual Theology

As principal Protestant reformers, Calvin and Luther help illustrate a concern that good Christian theology should be no arcane, academic pursuit. It's rooted in real life, and its abiding and nurturing insights should help cultivate spiritual fruit in our lives. All theology in this sense is *spiritual* theology, never an end in itself, but a catalyst toward alloying right thinking with righteous, faithful, joyful living.[3] Developing a spiritual theology may call for dedicated and rigorous study in cultivating the life of the *mind*, but it is the *heart* of the matter that arguably most interests God (1 Sam 16:7). The heart is apparently where the Holy Spirit focuses God's transforming work. Consider St. Paul's contrast:

> For those who live according to the flesh set their minds on things of the flesh, but those who live according to the Spirit set their minds on things of the Spirit. To set the mind on the flesh is death, but to set the mind on the Spirit is life and peace . . . And God, who searches the heart, knows what is the mind of the Spirit . . . A person is not a Jew who is one outwardly, nor is true circumcision something external and physical. Rather, a person is a Jew who is one inwardly, and real circumcision is a matter of the heart—it is spiritual and not literal.[4](Rom 8:5, 27; 2:29 NRSV)

God is at work at the seat of our inner life, the controlling interest within us. "Our lives," writes Eugene Peterson, "are, after all, the stuff that is being formed."[5] This isn't to artificially divide heart, mind, and body. We aren't compartmented, but integrated wholes. By our Lord's own warrant all God's people are called to love him with every facet and faculty of be-

---

Indeed, to such a length did he carry this that as he wrote in a letter soon after his return to Geneva in 1541, on his first Sunday in Saint Pierre [St. Peter's Cathedral] he continued from the place where he had stopped on Easter Day 1538, 'by which I indicated that I had interrupted my office of preaching for a time rather than that I had given it up entirely'" (Parker, *John Calvin,* 91; cf. Dennert, "John Calvin's Movement," 345–65).

3. Two recent books on spiritual theology are helpful: Peterson, *Christ Plays in Ten Thousand Places,* 5–6; and with respect to the Bible's role as the formative text for Christian spirituality, his *Eat This Book,* 59–77.

4. Hebrews 8:10. Cf. Lemke, "Circumcision of the Heart," 299–320.

5. Peterson, *Eat This Book,* 23.

ing (Deut 6:4–5; Matt 22:37). Synergism between intellectual, emotional, volitional, and physical aspects of our lives is what makes the integration organically and spiritually vital. Is it any wonder that the writer of Hebrews speaks of the word of God as "living and active" (Heb 4:12), and able to discern the most intimate and intricate parts of who we are? God wants what we come to know of him to transform who we are. True and spiritual theology should do this.

Such transformation is a fitting concern in considering God's *reverberating* word. It's the biblical text, and understanding and embracing the drama of God's salvation story and the power of God's truth, that foster spiritual formation through preaching, teaching, and all forms of Christian communication in worship and beyond.[6] It's not just any story that we tell, nor is it primarily our story. We may be in on it and we may be part of it, but ultimately the story isn't about us.[7] What we tell again and again is God's story. It alone best identifies and most satisfies us.

In his *Miracles: A Preliminary Study*, C. S. Lewis explores Christ's incarnation in a chapter, "The Grand Miracle," effectively illustrating this identification and satisfaction. He writes,

> Let us suppose we possess parts of a novel or a symphony. Someone now brings us a newly discovered piece of manuscript and says, "This is the missing part of the work. This is the chapter on which the whole plot of the novel really turned. This is the main theme of the symphony." Our business would be to see whether the new passage, if admitted to the central place which the discoverer claimed for it, did actually illuminate all the parts we had already seen and "pull them together." Nor should we be likely to go very far wrong. The new passage, if spurious, however attractive it looked at first glance, would become harder and harder to reconcile with the rest of the work the longer we considered the matter. But if it were genuine, then at every fresh hearing of the music or every fresh reading of the book, we should find it settling down, making itself more at home, and eliciting significance from all sorts of details in the whole work which we had hitherto neglected.[8]

6. Ibid., 17. Also see Webster, "Stay in the Story," 45–88.

7. Warren, *Purpose Driven Life*, 17.

8. Lewis, *Miracles*, 175–76.

Scripture as Authoritative and Forming Text

Might we infer that Lewis's insights about the incarnation of God's living Word help illustrate what could be called the "fleshing out" of God's written word through proclamation and other forms of communication in worship? The Bible's ability to orient, inform, elicit significance, and transform is key. Christian spirituality involves being "formed by the Holy Spirit in accordance with the text of holy Scripture."[9] If we want worship to play an important, even central, part in our Christian spiritual formation, we need to proclaim in every possible way, invite people to consider, and ultimately inculcate Scripture as God's word revealed and illumined by the Spirit of God.

Worship isn't a performance, but it can be seen as a drama in which we are offered and play our best roles. This was, in part, Kierkegaard's observation. Without overly stressing the metaphor, his notion is instructive.[10] We might hope this would challenge us to worship in ways that tell God's story as creatively and winsomely as possible, with all the heightened expressive qualities we can muster and engage. Peterson writes,

> Scripture . . . in the course of revealing God pulls us into the revelation and welcomes us as participants in it . . . It reveals a God-centered, God-ordered, God-blessed world in which we find ourselves at home and whole.[11]

Our goal is to draw others while being drawn ourselves into this greatest of dramas: the gospel, the unfolding drama of redemption.

Commitment to such formation faces something of an uphill climb today. As an authoritative and forming text, says Peterson, Scripture today has taken a back seat to the "sovereign self."[12] Let us illustrate this with an admittedly extreme example. Among the plethora of world views and personal philosophies dotting the modern landscape, even something called "meism" has emerged as an alternative to truth claims we find in the Bible.[13]

9. Peterson, *Eat This Book*, 15.

10. See Kierkegaard, *Purity of Heart*, 180–81, and Vanhoozer, *Faith Speaking Understanding*, 20–24; 75–109.

11. Peterson, *Eat This Book*, 16.

12. Ibid., 16.

13. It is self-orientation defined as "self-importance without any evidence that we (or our world view) actually matter," http://www.urbandictionary.com/define.php?/term=meism, line 1.

Authority rests no longer in that text, nor even in one's opinion about that text, but in the self as it's seen transcending that or any other text. Many would recognize the rank selfishness of meism, but modern popular culture's barrage about the fulfillment and happiness of "Me, Myself, and I" can inure and numb us to the dangerous thinness of placing ourselves at the center of our reality.[14] George MacDonald reminds us: "The one principle of hell is—I am my own."[15]

Over and against this perspective stands the richness of the gospel and God's salvation story, as articulated by our Lord in John 10 using metaphors of shepherding.[16] Jesus calls himself "the good shepherd" who "lays down his life for the sheep." He's no mere hired hand. He cares for the sheep as his own. They know him and his voice because they are known by him. He also calls himself "the sheep gate," the only secure passage and protection for the sheep amidst dangers all around. Whether in the pasture, passing through dark valleys, or safely penned within a makeshift fold with the shepherd serving as the door across its opening, the sheep are safe.

These metaphors aren't mixed. They beautifully amplify each other with respect to Jesus' claims for himself, and the authority he claims for our lives.[17] When we recognize and embrace his authority, we find both identity and security. As "good shepherd" his guidance is fully trustworthy. As "sheep gate" the identity and security he offers supersedes all other potentially life-orienting principles, programs, places, or people, including ourselves. Jesus is claiming that he's the only able and therefore worthy door for our lives. What becomes of a pilot who goes blind, a ballerina with a broken leg, or a business leader after a nervous breakdown or a heart attack? Jesus is claiming that he's the only life door that will never disappoint. His claims to ability and authority parallel those of God's written word already alluded to in Hebrews 4:12. Strikingly, this affirmation in Hebrews is set in an immediate context of comments about "Sabbath-rest," a theologically-rich term hearkening back to both creation and Israel's conquest of Canaan:[18]

---

14. For a powerful alternative vision, see Brooks, *Road to Character*, 105–29.

15. MacDonald, *Unspoken Sermons: Third Series*, 40.

16. John 10:1–16.

17. Palmer, *Book that John Wrote*, 96–100.

18. A *sabbatismos*, or "Sabbath-keeping." The verb *sabbatizō* used in the Septuagint (LXX) with the meaning "keep Sabbath" (Bauer, *Greek-English Lexicon*, 738–39), usually rendering the Hebrew *šābbat* (cf. Exod 16:30; Lev 23:32; 26:35) (Brown et al., *Hebrew and English Lexicon*, 991. "What is this Sabbath rest that awaits them? It is evidently an experience which they do not enjoy in their present mortal life, although it belongs to

> If Joshua had given them rest, God would not have spoken later about another day. There remains, then, a Sabbath-rest for the people of God; for anyone who enters God's rest also rests from his own work, just as God did from his. Let us, therefore, make every effort to enter that rest. (Heb 4:8–11 NIV)

Whatever else this Sabbath-rest is, it also may be likened to the kind of peace, security, identity, and community to which Jesus alludes in John 10. As seen in God's salvation story, apart from the good shepherd and his task as the sheep gate, there is no other real, lasting, and integrating relationship available from which we can derive true meaning and purpose in life. This is what God's salvation story asserts. Scripture asserts truth claims that ultimately and fully meet our human need.

Some may only accept the truth, authority, and love of Christ in the face of competing claims for our loyalty by our providing an account of the gospel that is true, easily grasped, and attractive. We must ask ourselves what we can do in worship to be good tellers of the story.

Worship can help strengthen our biblical literacy; it can also help clarify and correct theological imprecisions. This guiding corrective is all the more important for some today who harbor deeply held convictions about things of which they know little or nothing at all.[19] This mercifully is a condition that the Lord is keen to remedy.[20]

Our Story in the Biblical Story

In his *Living in Tension*, Douglas Webster argues that the Bible "reveals the tension between our fallen condition and God's redemptive provision," that a theology of ministry is "shaped and energized by the whole counsel of God and salvation history," and that innocuous preaching—and I would add worship—is "overcome by letting the tension in the text lead to the passion of the passage."[21] This of course presumes a high enough view of Scripture for it to serve as the *sine qua non* for preaching, worship, and spiritual formation. If staying in the story includes doing what we

---

them as a heritage, and by faith they may live in the good of it here and now" (Bruce, *Epistle to the Hebrews*, 78).

19. Prothero, *Religious Literacy*, 27–48; Balmer, Review of *Religious Literacy*, 66–67; cf. Jones, *End of White Christian America*, 197.

20. See Jeremiah 33:3.

21. Webster, *Living in Tension*, vol. 2, 45.

can to let the Bible make its own point in our lives, this presumes it has a worthwhile point to make. That this is no universal presumption simply adds urgency to our need to be more familiar with, and graciously, wisely faithful to God's saving story. If we believe that Scripture speaks with clarity and authority, we have the opportunity and responsibility to invite others to consider its claims, even in cultural contexts where detractors are increasing and intensifying.[22] At the same time, those who hold the Bible to be true in any really meaningful sense recognize the need for careful, unbiased examination of it.

With biblical preaching and worship we're at once dealing with a finite text but infinite truth. We're also seeking to speak something timeless and universal, though historical, into contextualized everyday realities of different people, sometimes vastly different people. Without delving into theologies and methodologies of preaching,[23] we can suggest that no one *hears* God's saving story the same way, though the story *remains* the same. The word of God is God's word whether or not we recognize, understand, or appropriate it. But we all read and hear Scripture through our own capacities, propensities, limitations, and filters. An important task of preaching and worship then is to build *kerygmatic*, confessional bridges between Scripture and its intended recipients, who seldom share the same background, outlook, or goals.[24] But however God's story is best told in any given context,

22. Zuckerman, *Living the Secular Life,* 55–77. Also, a recent *Washington Post* article quotes a sociology researcher's following assertion: "Western atheism has evolved into a forward-looking movement that has the wind at its back, is behind the success of the best run societies yet seen in human history, and is challenging religion as the better basis for morality." Paul, "Atheism on the Upswing," lines 26–59. Accompanying the article is a photo of a June 2011, Columbus, Ohio billboard highlighting an affable-looking young man smiling and affirming to passersby, "I can be good without God." This offers at least anecdotal testimony of some antithetical views toward religion in America today. More pernicious are the views expressed in Hitchens, *god is not Great,* which includes two chapters, "Revelation," 97–108, and "'New'" 109–22. Cf. Dawkins, *God Delusion,* 269–87, and Ehrman, *God's Problem,* 1–20. Many might not embrace such views, yet may be unaware of their contemporary currency. Over and against a diet limited to these is Ward, *Why There Almost Certainly,* 141.

23. Recent contributions include Goldsworthy, *Preaching the Whole Bible,* 22–30, 63–80; Greidanus, *Modern Preacher and the Ancient Text,* 157–87; Johnson, *Glory of Preaching,* 53–75; Pasquarello III, *Christian Preaching,* 39–62; Quickie, *360-Degree Preaching,* 44–63, and *Preaching as Worship,* 83–138; Robinson, *Biblical Preaching,* 233–34; Sunukjian, *Invitation to Biblical Preaching,* 87–127; and Willimon, *Guide to Preaching and Leading Worship,* 51–62.

24. See Cherry, *Worship Architect,* 221–42; Jones, "We Are *How* We Worship," 346–60; Stringer, *Sociological History of Christian Worship,* 20–21; and Nelson, "At Ease with

it must be allowed to invite us into its story, helping us to see how our own stories run parallel or perpendicular to it. "Everyone has a story," writes Webster, "but only one story redeems our story."[25]

The Bible is clearly a story of creation, of how we and everything around us have come to exist. Our identity and nature are inextricably intertwined in Genesis' affirmation: "In the beginning God created the heavens and the earth" (Gen 1:1 NIV). The Bible is clearly a story of redemption. Our security and worth are grounded in God's gracious initiative: "In him we have redemption through his blood, the forgiveness of sins, in accordance with the riches of God's grace that he lavished on us with all wisdom and understanding" (Eph 1:7 NIV).

The Bible is clearly a story of reconciliation. Our status and our calling as Christians are defined by God's embrace:

> All this is from God, who through Christ reconciled us to himself and gave us the ministry of reconciliation, that is, in Christ God was reconciling the world to himself, not counting their trespasses against them (2 Cor 5:18–19 ESV).

The Bible is clearly a story of re-creation. Our destiny is determined by God's sovereign purpose and will: "And he who was seated on the throne said, 'Behold, I am making all things new. Write this down, for these words are trustworthy and true'" (Rev 21:5 ESV).[26]

The clarity of this story cuts cross-grain with the personal narratives by which many of us try to organize, summarize, and legitimize our lives. This creates what Webster calls a tension between our and the Bible's way of expressing reality.[27] If we continue to insist on self-direction and self-actualization this tension will remain a rub. But if we place ourselves within God's saving story, it will become a positive force for good, for change, and for our lives moving into parallel posture alongside and within God's narrative.

Tension exists, not only between the biblical narrative and our own, but also within them. We need to embrace this tension. If we're willing to look at it, and not past it, we can learn to see that the Bible pulls few

---

Our Own Kind" 45–68.

25. Webster, *Living in Tension*, vol. 2, 52.

26. This recreation of all things includes the *restoration* in Jesus Christ of Adam's roles as king and priest (rule and worship). Cf. Genesis 1–2 and Revelation 21–22.

27. Webster, *Living in Tension*, vol. 2, 52.

punches, and skirts few issues. If we're willing to keep looking at it, we can discover its passion through tensions in the text.[28]

If we return to the story of King David's high-handed sin against Bathsheba and her husband Uriah in 2 Samuel 11–12, we see that it's filled with striking, even shocking details. Glossing over them and their theological and emotional tension obscures that narrative's focus on the heinous depth of sin into which even God's anointed leader can sink. It cheapens the breadth of God's grace extended in the face of a sin for which no sacrifice or offering was prescribed or even available in the law. It mocks the honesty and sincerity of David's heart-felt repentance. It weakens our grasp of how this passage portrays God's provision in the face of total human need. It fails to properly connect the impact of this story with David's meditation on it in Psalm 51. There we learn that, even after great sin, a true sacrifice acceptable to God is "a broken spirit, a broken and contrite heart." Letting the tension in this passage linger can ultimately bring us where David as psalmist beseeched God to bring him and his fellow worshipers: "Restore to me the joy of your salvation, and uphold me with a willing spirit. Then I will teach transgressors your ways, and sinners will return to you."[29]

We also take note of Jesus and Zacchaeus in Luke 19. The palpable tension in this passage demands to be noticed. On his way through Jericho, our Lord is being followed by crowds. The text tells us Zacchaeus is among them. He is short. He is the chief tax collector in the community, and thus he is rich. These details invoke great subtext tension. Zacchaeus would be easily passed over by others, had he not systematically become wealthy at their expense. He is a hated collaborator with Roman government oppression. After Zacchaeus has climbed a sycamore tree to catch a glimpse of Jesus, our Lord stops right beneath it, and calls to him by name, "Zacchaeus!"

Palmer suggests that we can well imagine an electric pause in this passage, a moment filled with tension.[30] The crowd thinks this new and admired itinerant preacher is going to call down and call out this despised tax collector, this traitor who had been making their lives so miserable. But Jesus said, "Hurry and come down, for I must stay at your house today." Sometimes, Palmer adds, the Bible says the people murmured. Sometimes it says the scribes and Pharisees murmured. Here, Luke's Gospel says,

---

28. Ibid., vol. 2, 53.

29. Cf. Psalm 51:13–17 (ESV) for restoration of worship.

30. Palmer, "Love of Jesus Christ," audio recording.

"Everyone murmured, 'He has gone in to be the guest of a sinner.'"[31] In this tense and energized moment, Jesus places himself between admittedly sinful Zacchaeus and the judgment of the crowd. He places himself between their hatred and Zacchaeus' need. This is not "merely an example of love," Palmer asserts, "but the very thing itself.[32]

Not staying in the story, as Webster demonstrates, not plumbing the "texts and subtexts" of Scripture, as Barnes argues,[33] impoverishes not only our insight into God's saving story, but our own spiritual formation by it through the Holy Spirit's illuminating power. Through preaching that does stay in the story of Scripture's unfolding narrative, and through worship that seeks to tell the same story as faithfully and creatively as possible, we stand a far higher chance of seeing and hitting God's intended target for us: transformation, spiritual formation, and discipleship.

The Bible is filled with songs, poems, letters, lists, history, theology, prophecy, tragedy, wisdom, humor, and gripping apocalyptic literature. Written by many authors over the course of many years, it is yet strikingly unified in its core affirmations and its overarching message.[34] Understanding it asks for careful reading and open, honest consideration. Honestly considering it calls for trust in its power to engage and change us. Changing us leads to our being recreated incrementally to be more like its central character, though these changes typically come in fits and starts. MacDonald writes,

> God regards men not as they are merely, but as they shall be; not as they shall be merely, but as they are growing, or capable of growing, toward that image after which He made them that they might grow into it. Therefore a thousand stages, each in itself almost valueless, are of inestimable worth as the necessary and connected gradations of an infinite process. A condition which of declension would indicate a devil, may of growth indicate a saint.[35]

31. Luke 19:7.

32. Cf. Palmer, *Love Has Its Reasons*, 82–85.

33. Barnes, *Pastor as Minor Poet*, 73–86.

34. House, *Old Testament Theology*, 7–9; Thielman, *Theology of the New Testament*, 19–42.

35. MacDonald, *Unspoken Sermons*, Series One, 14; also quoted in Lewis, *George MacDonald*, 3.

Christlikeness derives from being transformed more and more through exposure to and deepening intimacy with Jesus Christ, as seen in Scripture. Webster writes,

> The Word must be read in the light of the Incarnation. Otherwise, we will miss something important. The paradigm for all Christian communication is the Incarnate One: Truth in Person, absolute truth, independent of all contingencies, spoken into the personal, earthly contingencies of daily life.[36]

Such a paradigm tethers our reading of Scripture, the content and contour of our worship, and our way of witness in the world around us, whether that world is open to us or hostile. Such tethering to the text, to staying in its story, helps us become and remain, as Webster characterizes it, "resilient saints."[37]

Resilient and Reverberant

In his biography of Dietrich Bonhoeffer, Eric Metaxas paints an intricate and intimate portrait of the great twentieth-century Christian leader, who near the end of World War II went to the gallows at the hand of Hitler's Nazi regime. Bonhoeffer was a brilliant theologian who recognized that Christian faith doesn't rest merely in the realm of ideas, but is rooted in the physical and concrete world around us. He paid the ultimate price under the implications of this truth, following Jesus to the end. "At the heart of Bonhoeffer's theology was the mystery of the Incarnation," writes Metaxas, who then quotes the German pastor: "No priest, no theologian stood at the cradle in Bethlehem. And yet, all Christian theology has its origin in the wonder of all wonders that God became man."[38]

This radical and personal center of Christian faith, this "enormous exception," as Chesterton characterized it, is what gives meaning to our faith and to the telling of God's salvation story. In response to H. G. Wells's *Outline of History*, Chesterton concludes:

> Right in the middle of all these things stands an enormous excep-
> tion. It is quite unlike anything else. It is a thing final like the trump
> of doom, though it is also a piece of good news; or news that seems

36. Webster, *Living in Tension*, vol. 2, 55.

37. Ibid., 198.

38. Metaxas, *Dietrich Bonhoeffer*, 472.

too good to be true. It is nothing less than the loud assertion that this mysterious maker of the world has visited his world in person. It declares that really and even recently or right in the middle of historic times, there did walk into the world this original invisible being; about whom the thinkers make theories and the mythologists hand down myths: The Man Who Made the World.[39]

The reverberation of this truth in worship, witness, and discipleship shapes and strengthens us as resilient saints, even as it did Bonhoeffer, St. Paul, and countless Christian martyrs through the centuries. Worship, witness, and following Jesus Christ can truly become matters of life and death. The positive tension inherent in embracing and proclaiming him develops resilient, reverberant saints.

As we've noted, tone and beautiful sound can emanate from vibrations of something stretched or set in motion: the taut string of a violin, the tight membrane of a kettle drum, the chocks of a marimba, or even the column of air blown through a flute, a trumpet, or human vocal cords. If the string, or membrane, or air column are flaccid, no possibility of producing beautiful sound exists. There must be a positive tension to energize the process. Without the tension, the instrument lies dull and inert. If the string is tightened and tuned by a skilled master, music can be elicited and emerge from it.

Again Webster writes,

> Most approaches in ministry try to reduce tension, solve problems and promote success. The aim . . . is to increase positive tensions and prepare resilient saints. . .Negative tension in ministry is the result of disobedience, ignorance and resistance to the will of God. Positive tension comes from obedience, biblical integrity, faithfulness to the will of God, and costly discipleship.[40]

Like the production of beautiful sound through vibrations from a positive tension, the process of producing resilient Christians is enhanced by the word of God reverberating through worship, witness, and discipleship. Staying with its story and its tensions tethers us day to day to that strengthening power of God for our endurance, patience, and joy.[41]

---

39. Chesterton, *Everlasting Man*, 266–67.
40. Webster, *Living in Tension*, vol. 1, 1
41. Colossians 1:11.

Reverberating Outward

What changes, then, might we hope for or expect through worship that reverberates to clear proclamation of God's word? Whether individually or corporately, our redemption, reconciliation, and all of God's works that comprise our so-great salvation, are intended to bring change both in and through us. Transformation is the name of the game. Paul exhorts the fledgling church in Rome, "Do not conform any longer to the pattern of this world, but be transformed by the renewing of your mind. Then you will be able to test and approve what God's will is—his good, pleasing, and perfect will" (Rom 12:2 NIV). To the Corinthian church he writes, "And we, who with unveiled faces all reflect the Lord's glory, are being transformed into his likeness with ever-increasing glory, which comes from the Lord, who is the Spirit" (2 Cor 3:18 NIV)." Stasis isn't part of the plan, though rest, peace, and the abundance of what the OT calls *shalom* characterize life offered us in Christ, a relationship that should foster vital, dynamic growth for our good and God's glory. Thus writes Charles Wesley,

> Finish, then, thy new creation;
>> Pure and spotless let us be;
> Let us see thy great salvation
>> Perfectly restored in thee;
> Changed from glory into glory,
>> Till in heav'n we take our place,
> Till we cast our crowns before thee,
>> Lost in wonder, love, and praise.[42]

"Changed from glory into glory" in both the Wesleyan and Pauline reckonings isn't merely a private matter between a Christian and the Lord, though personal transformation is certainly part of the picture. It's an inward reality that ultimately focuses outward toward others. This centrifugal trajectory is as integral to God's will for his children as is the inward spiritual reality that prompts and energizes it. Our neighbor is our very great concern if for no other reason than our neighbor is God's very great concern. What's more, from a biblical perspective this impulse is devoid of political overtones or framework, though I've recently somewhat guiltily found William Sloane Coffin's perspective positively troubling, that

---

42. Wesley, "Love Divine, All Loves Excelling," 376.

"the heart is a little to the left."[43] There's something far deeper than politics and social policy at play in the gospel, but those who worship and serve the Bible's God do not have the luxury of living insular, self-absorbed lives. Neither our Lord's own life pattern nor his parting mandate in Matthew 28 will allow it.

Jesus' arresting mid-day conversation with the Samaritan woman at her village water well changed her life and the lives of many of her town folk. His probing exchange in John 4 put her needs in far starker relief than did even the scorching noontime sun or the trudging solitariness of her task. Along with his gracious provision for those needs, he signaled that no status of ethnicity, tradition, or human effort was a sufficient foundation for worship as God intends it to be worshiped.

What our Lord says to the woman in this passage is fundamental to the kind of change he wants for her and us. Whatever else it is, worship "in spirit and in truth," according to Jesus, is the kind of worship we are obliged to offer God. It is consistent with God's character, but also cognizant of and responsive to God's concerns for every constituent of creation.[44] "The urgent, indeed troubling, message of Scripture," says Labberton, "is that everything that matters is at stake in worship."[45] Matters of justice are indicative of the very heart of God.[46] The God of the Bible is a very big God, and a healthy biblical anthropology begins with awareness of our significant but bounded and limited status. A life of true worship is liberated from lesser or misleading pursuits. We're not left alone or to our own devices, but are part of God's sovereign purposes for ourselves, the church, and the world.

Ours is a privileged and responsible position in the created order,[47] and our calling as God's church is likewise pointedly privileged. But

---

43. Coffin, in his book by same title, *Heart*, 9–25.

44. Bruce notes that the important point here in this John 4 conversation is "not *where* people worship God but *how* they worship him" (Bruce, *Gospel of John*, 109). Brown writes, ". . . in proclaiming worship in Spirit and truth, Jesus is not contrasting external worship with internal worship. His statement has nothing to do with worshiping God in the inner recesses of one's own spirit . . . An ideal of purely internal worship ill fits the NT scene. . ." (Brown, *Gospel According to St. John*, 180).

45. Labberton, *Dangerous Act of Worship*, 188.

46. Cf. Micah 6:8.

47. This conviction markedly contrasts with naturalistic assertions (assumptions) that human beings, specifically *homo sapiens*, are of no particular "significance," that "animals much like modern humans first appeared about 2.5 million years ago," but that "for countless generations they did not stand out from the myriad other organisms with which they shared their habitats" (Harari, *Sapiens*, 1–2). Understanding and

Labberton hammers away that such privilege has lulled us to sleep concerning what really matters to God: the seeking and embodiment of justice.[48] This isn't merely blind justice in a jurisprudential sense, but justice born out of gratitude for divine blessing and out of concern that others also are treated well. Insisting on justice only for oneself is narcissistic. Biblical justice is passionate that things also will be set right for others. Such concern moves us to bear witness, to offer care, and to stand for the right, as we engage in these and every form of Christian ministry.[49] The reverberating word thus moves by the power of God's Spirit from inspired text, to illumined text, to transforming text, to commissioning text in our worship and every facet of Christian living.

reconciling this majority view with biblical perspective that human beings are at least unusual (unique) by virtue of being created (Gen 1:27) "in the image of God" (*Imago Dei*) remains a challenge.

48. Labberton's emphasis here does not preclude importance to God of evangelism or service. It's not a question of "either/or" but of "both/and," but we noted earlier God's displeasure with meticulous law keeping, empty, rote ritual, and hypocritical lifestyles evidenced in unconcern for what really matters. God warns, "These things you have done and I kept silent. You thought I was altogether like you. But I will rebuke you to your face" (Ps 50:21). Cf. Malachi railing against corrupt priesthood while Judah profaned God's covenant (Mal 1:6—2:17).

49. PC(USA) constitutional questions asked of those being ordained or installed as teaching elders include, "Will you be a faithful minister, proclaiming the good news in Word and Sacrament, teaching faithfully, and caring for people? Will you be active in government and discipline, serving the governing bodies of the church, and in your ministry will you try to show the love and justice of Jesus Christ?" Office of Theology and Worship for the Presbyterian Church (U.S.A), *Book of Occasional Services*, 95.

4

A Clear Focus

A transforming vision of God is what worship seeks. We begin with the Bible's own categories, neither less nor more than what it says, in touch with its own concerns.

THE CHURCH'S VARIED WORSHIP voice nevertheless heralds a cherished and central message: the universal good news of salvation made known and available through Jesus Christ. We therefore do want Christian worship to be expressive, engaging, and effective. Different people have differing ideas about what makes this so, but these differences shouldn't deter us from asking if there are ways to craft liturgy to better focus on the Holy One we worship. After all, we're soliciting the most tremendous contact possible. It's the Lord God of creation whose presence and blessing we seek. Our benefit is a supernatural part of this exchange. Briefly, then, who is this Holy One?

Some of us arguably have what amounts to an angelic view of God: extraordinary perhaps, otherworldly, powerful and captivating, but sub-biblical. This is unnecessary, for the biblical witness portrays God as far transcending even our loftiest descriptions. The prophet Isaiah recounts the central question: Who is like God?[1] The apostle Paul proffers the same sentiment in paraphrasing the prophet: no eye has seen, no ear has heard, no mind has conceived what God has prepared for those who love him.[2] The God of the Bible is a very big God. Worship that misses this immensity simply misses the point.

1. Isaish 40:18, 25.
2. 1 Corinthians 2:9; cf. Isaiah 64:4; 65:17.

"Blessing" is a key worship word: "Bless the Lord, O my soul, and all that is within me bless his holy name," says the psalmist (103:1 NRSV). The Hebrew verb, *barak,* essentially means "to kneel."[3] When we speak of us blessing God, "bless" points to our kneeling before him. Given God's identity and activity, it's an appropriate gesture. We've already seen that Scripture speaks of worship as "bowing down" or "bowing oneself down low to the ground." Such homage is what's happening when we "bless the Lord." When the Lord blesses us, the gesture, if you will, is just the opposite: God bends to us. We *bow* to bless the Lord even as the Lord *bends* to bless us.[4] Biblical worship consistently affirms these two postures, one primarily an act of obeisance and obedience, the other an act of grace, mercy, and love. What kind of God does this for us, and what kind of God accepts this from us?

Structural Stones

Two facets in the jewel of God's attributes and character are so important that they should capture our attention every time we worship—so much so that they become structural stones undergirding what is built upon them. No matter what else happens in worship, if we haven't gazed in wonder at these, we might justly wonder if we've worshiped at all. These two brilliant facets, these two structural stones, are God's holiness and glory.

There are of course other aspects of God's person and work that qualify as structural for our worship—attributes like grace and mercy, faithfulness and love, righteousness and justice—but we need to start somewhere, and the Bible so persistently characterizes God as holy and glorious that, when our worship persistently points to this, we confidently adopt Scripture's own categories. We remember Isaiah's declaration:

> This is what the high and exalted One says—he who lives forever, whose name is holy: "I live in a high and holy place, but also with the one who is contrite and lowly in spirit, to revive the spirit of the lowly, to revive the heart of the contrite." (Isa 57:15 NIV)

3. Brown et al., *Hebrew and English Lexicon,* 138.

4. Cf. Deuteronomy 8:10 (NRSV), "You shall eat your fill and bless the Lord your God for the good land he has given you," and Genesis 12:2 (NRSV), "I will make of you a great nation, and I will bless you, and make you great, so that you will be a blessing."

Because of their long history of monarchy, the British understand implicitly—even if they disagree with it—the idea of royalty, the "high and lofty" part of the prophet's declaration. I once was privileged to be among the throng on The Mall in London during Queen Elizabeth's official birthday celebration. As she rode by in her ceremonial carriage on the way to Buckingham Palace, I watched many of her adoring subjects stand taller and prouder as she passed by them. It was a deeply ingrained appreciation and connection.

On the other hand, an old story is told of former New York Governor Al Smith addressing a convention dinner in New York City. The wine had been flowing too freely when a stammering emcee finally stood to introduce the governor far too casually and with fawning familiarity as "a really great guy." Smith instinctively sensed a serious affront to his office, so he deliberately rose to the microphone, tersely said, "Gentlemen, the Governor of New York bids you good night," and then walked out. The comparison of course is ludicrous, but if we're listening, we might hear Isaiah's words echoing faintly in our ears: "Thus says the Lord, the One who is high and lifted up, who inhabits eternity, whose name is Holy . . . "

According to Romans 1, in settling for a subbiblical or extrabiblical view of God, we turn things upside down. We create God in our own, or some lesser, image, then wonder why we're disappointed. St. Paul writes,

> For I am not ashamed of the gospel, for it is the power of God for salvation to everyone who believes, to the Jew first and also to the Greek. For in it the righteousness of God is revealed through faith for faith; as it is written, "The righteous shall live by faith." For the wrath of God is revealed from heaven against all ungodliness and unrighteousness of those who by their wickedness suppress the truth. For what can be known about God is plain to them, because God has shown it to them. For his invisible attributes, namely, his eternal power and divine nature, have been clearly perceived, ever since the creation of the world, in the things that have been made. So they are without excuse, for though they knew God, they did not honor him as God or give thanks to him, but they became futile in their thinking, and their foolish hearts were darkened. Claiming to be wise they became fools, and exchanged the glory of the immortal God for images resembling mortal humans or birds and animals and creeping things . . . they exchanged the truth about God for a lie and worshiped and served the creature rather than the Creator, who is blessed forever! Amen. (1:16–23; 25 ESV)

One of the chief and recurring emphases of the OT is that Israel fell into disobedience and idolatry through this kind of dubious exchange. Religion has often departed from biblical revelation. There is a view that perceives, in the development of religions, an evolutionary trajectory from polytheism to monotheism, for example, that the Jews simply evolved in their thinking toward a belief in one true God. We then ask ourselves, "Does the Bible portray itself this way? Does this interpretive model hold up under scrutiny?" Ross writes,

> Many scholars argue that Israel simply borrowed ideas from their pagan neighbors, cleaned them up for their newfound monotheism (which was also borrowed from Egypt), and then attempted to conceal their origin by attributing it all to direct revelation. There is, of course, no evidence for this. In fact, the theory runs contrary to the biblical witness that every time Israel borrowed religious ideas from her pagan neighbors it led them away from monotheism and toward the corruption of idolatry, never away from polytheism to a purer form of worship. But even more critically, it is hard to accept a theory that says the whole religious system of Israel was simply borrowed from the pagan world and then artificially credited to God's revelation at Mt. Sinai. Such a theory not only destroys the idea of revelation, attributing deception to the formation of the faith, but it also makes the true faith pagan in origin, invented for the most part by humans, and thus of no greater value than the false religion.[5]

If our concern is to focus closely on the biblical witness—on neither less nor more than what it says—and to stay in touch with its own concerns, certain emphases emerge.[6]

Holiness

Of all that the Bible reveals about God, the most fundamental characterization is that God is holy. God's holiness is what is principally portrayed in Isaiah 6, in the prophet's vision of worship around the heavenly throne. The seraphim call out antiphonally, "Holy, holy, holy, is the Lord God Almighty; the whole earth is full of his glory." The same magnificent view is recapitulated in John's apocalyptic vision in Revelation 4. Surrounding God's throne

5. Ross, *Recalling the Hope of Glory*, 132–33.

6. Ibid., 41–60. This brief section on "holiness" and "glory" follows Ross's substantive treatment, "Holy God of Glory."

is an array of celestial beings so wonderful as to defy description: crowned elders on thrones of their own, mysterious creatures with multiple wings and eyes, and seven lampstands representing the very fullness of the Spirit of God. From the center of the throne come flashes of lightning and peals of thunder, and the One sitting there has the appearance of precious stones encircled by a rainbow. John writes, "Day and night the assembly cried out, 'Holy, holy, holy!' and joined in chorus giving glory to God." This is striking evidence of God's holiness as the integrating quality of his character, and the centering subject of worship.

We've seen that our word "holy" translates the Hebrew word *kadosh* and the Greek word *hagios*. The basic meaning is "set apart, reserved, distinct, unique."[7] It can refer to something as mundane as cooking pots. Some are set apart by design for really special recipes. Others are simply used for more common, everyday meals. The whole idea of consecration emerges from this meaning. When something or someone is consecrated, it's the result of being set apart from common usage for special purpose. This arguably is the force of 1 Peter 1:15, "Just as he who called you is holy, so be holy in all you do." To say that something is common does not necessarily imply that it's evil; just common, not consecrated. The apostle affirms Christians' consecrated status: God has set us apart for special purposes and use.

But what does it mean to say that *God* is holy? "Holiness," says Ross, "is not one of many descriptions of God; it is the summary designation of all that God is and is known to be in contrast to creation."[8] God's holiness is the ground of his utter uniqueness with respect to being, power, character, knowledge, and presence. God is the Creator (theism not atheism). God is distinct from creation (theism not pantheism). God is not limited, creaturely, physical, fallen, or corrupt (theism not polytheism, syncretism, animism, or other paganism). God is neither human nor angelic (theism not deism or finite godism).[9] God is unlike anyone or anything else in existence, and "holiness" is at the center of his essential character.

---

7. Brown et al., *Hebrew and English Lexicon*, 872; Bauer, *Greek-English Lexicon*, 9.

8. Ross, *Recalling the Hope of Glory*, 45.

9. For a concise review of theism and opposing world views, see Geisler, *Systematic Theology in One Volume*, 17–18.

Glory

If God's holiness captures our attention first, it's God's glory that closely follows. The root idea of the basic OT word for glory is "heaviness."[10] This leads to the idea of importance. If God's holiness points to his utter uniqueness, God's glory points to his ultimate importance. God is the heaviest, most important being, preeminent in everything, and glory is the powerful manifestation of his essence, reality, and presence.

God's reality and presence were sorely tested by the Israelites' sinful idolatry with the golden calf. Only a short time before had some of them accompanied Moses onto the slopes of Mount Sinai, where according to Exodus 24 they actually "saw" (whatever this means) "the God of Israel," and feasted in his company. Apparently, the impact on them from this would be strikingly short lived, but after instructing them to wait until he returned, Moses left them and proceeded further up the mountain:

> The cloud covered it, and the glory of the Lord settled on Mount Sinai. For six days the cloud covered the mountain, and on the seventh day the Lord called to Moses from within the cloud. To the Israelites the glory of the Lord looked like a consuming fire on top of the mountain. Then Moses entered the cloud as he went up the mountain. And he stayed in the mountain forty days and forty nights. (Exod 24:15–18 NIV)

During Moses' audience with the Lord atop the mount, he received detailed instructions about the tabernacle, a sanctuary where God would meet the people and "dwell" with them:

> I will consecrate the Tent of Meeting and the altar and will consecrate Aaron and his sons to serve me as priests. Then I will dwell among the Israelites and be their God. They will know that I am the Lord their God, who brought them out of Egypt so that I may dwell among them. I am the Lord their God. (Exod 29:44–46 NIV)

The tabernacle is a significant focus here in Exodus,[11] implicitly in Leviticus, Numbers, and Deuteronomy, and in the NT book of Hebrews.[12] The latter emphasizes how it prefigured the perfect approach to God through

---

10. *Kavēd,* Brown et al., *Hebrew and English Lexicon,* 457.

11. Exodus 25–31, 35–40.

12. Hebrews 10:19–24; John 1:14: *eskēnoō* (dwelt, made dwelling) from *skēnē* (tent, booth, lodging, dwelling, tabernacle), Bauer, *Greek-English Lexicon,* 754.

the sacrifice and blood of Jesus Christ who, according to the prologue of John's Gospel, tabernacled among us:

> The Word became flesh and made his dwelling among us. We have seen his glory, the glory of the One and Only, who came from the Father, full of grace and truth. (John 1:14 NIV)

The length of Moses' mountaintop sojourn fed the people's fear, impatience, impertinence, and faithlessness:

> When the people saw that Moses was so long in coming down from the mountain, they gathered around Aaron and said, "Come, make us gods who will go before us. As for this fellow Moses who brought us up out of Egypt, we do not know what has happened to him." (Exod 32:1 NIV)[13]

Their idolatrous debauchery that followed incited divine judgment: "I have seen these people," the Lord said to Moses, "and they are a stiff-necked people. Now leave me alone so that my anger may burn against them and that I may destroy them." (Exod 32:9–10 NIV).

Moses pleaded and intervened on their behalf to the Lord, who relented, but Moses also burned with anger when he saw with his own eyes what the Lord told him had happened in his absence. His wrath led to swift retribution and a deadly process of purification, after which Moses again intervened between the people and the Lord:

> So Moses went back to the Lord and said, "Oh, what a great sin these people have committed! They have made themselves gods of gold. But now, please forgive their sin—but if not, then blot me out of the book you have written. (Exod 32:31–32 NIV)

This is an impulse to self-sacrificial, substitutionary atonement on Moses' part. Whatever was his motivation, he had been given a glimpse of God's glory. Even a glimpse had changed him, and had left traces of God's presence on him. God used him to bring the people to repentance and to put them on a pathway to restoration and covenant renewal.[14]

Exodus 33 tells us that, in the aftermath of this upheaval, Moses pitched what he called a "tent of meeting"[15] some distance from the Israelites' camp.

---

13. See Block, *For the Glory of God,* 29–53.

14. Exodus 34.

15. Not a tabernacle.

Anyone inquiring about something would go there to entreat Moses and encounter the Lord:

> As Moses went into the tent, the pillar of cloud would come down
> and stay at the entrance, while the Lord spoke with Moses. Whenev-
> er the people saw the pillar of cloud standing at the entrance to the
> tent, they all stood and worshiped, each at the entrance to his tent.
> The Lord would speak to Moses face to face, as a man speaks with
> his friend. Then Moses would return to the camp. (33:9–11a NIV)

Even after this level of intimacy and interaction had developed between himself and the Lord, Moses sought deeper assurances of divine
favor and of the effectiveness of his own leadership in doing God's will. The
Lord replied, "My Presence will go with you, and I will give you rest . . . I
will do the very thing you have asked, because I am pleased with you and
I know you by name." Moses said, "Now show me your glory." Whatever
Moses had come to know of God, whatever he had learned through meek
and humble obedience and trust, he wanted more. Long before, when God
had called him out of a burning bush, Moses had said, "Who am I, that I
should go to Pharaoh and bring the Israelites out of Egypt?" Even then,
God had said, "I will be with you." Now, even though he has seen the pil-
lar of cloud by day and fire by night, even though he has seen the waters
of the Red Sea parted, even though he has been in God's presence on the
mountaintop, Moses says, "Show me your glory." Show me yourself. Show
me even more of who you really are.[16] God grants Moses' request, but with
a precautionary caveat:

> I will cause all my goodness to pass in front of you, and I will
> proclaim my name, the Lord, in your presence. I will have mercy
> on whom I will have mercy, and I will have compassion on whom
> I will have compassion. But, he said, you cannot see my face, for no
> one may see my face and live. There is a place near me where you
> may stand on a rock. When my glory passes by, I will put you in a
> cleft in the rock and cover you with my hand until I have passed
> by. Then I will remove my hand and you will see my back; but my
> face must not be seen. (Exod 33:19–25 NIV)

---

16. Ross points out that the Septuagint here translates "glory" by use of the personal
pronoun "yourself," "capturing the precise connotation of the word in Moses' request,"
Recalling the Hope of Glory, 47.

In her nineteenth-century devotional hymn, "A Wonderful Savior is Jesus My Lord," the blind but prolific hymn writer Fanny Crosby reflects on this scene:

A wonderful Savior is Jesus my Lord, a wonderful Savior to me;
He hideth my soul in the cleft of the rock, where rivers of pleasure I see.
He hideth my soul in the cleft of the rock that shadows a dry, thirsty land;
He hideth my life in the depth of his love, and covers me there with his hand. [17]

Even glimpses of divine revelation are accommodations to our finiteness and frailty, even to our safety. God isn't to be domesticated. We remember the exchange between the children and Mr. and Mrs. Beaver about Aslan, the Christ-figure lion in C. S. Lewis' *The Lion, the Witch and the Wardrobe:*

"You'll understand when you see him."

"But shall we see him?" asked Susan.

"Why, Daughter of Eve, that's what I brought you here for.

I'm to lead where you shall meet him," said Mr. Beaver.

"Is—is he a man?" asked Lucy.

"Aslan a man!" said Mr. Beaver sternly. "Certainly not. I tell you he is the King of the wood and the son of the great Emperor-Beyond-the Sea. Don't you know who is the King of Beasts? Aslan is a lion—*the* Lion, the great Lion."

"Ooh!" said Susan, "I'd thought he was a man. Is he—quite safe? I shall feel rather nervous about meeting a lion."

"That you will, dearie, and make no mistake," said Mrs. Beaver, "if there's anyone who can appear before Aslan without their knees knocking, they're either braver than most or else just silly."

"Then he isn't safe? said Lucy.

"Safe?" said Mr. Beaver. "Don't you hear what Mrs. Beaver tells you? Who said anything about safe? 'Course he isn't safe. But he's good. . ."[18]

In his *Unspoken Sermons*, George MacDonald approaches this dangerous goodness from a different angle:

He will shake heaven and earth that only the unshakable may remain: he is a consuming fire, that only that which cannot be

17. Crosby, "Wonderful Savior Is Jesus," 175.

18. Lewis, *Lion, the Witch*, 99.

consumed may stand forth eternal. It is the nature of God, so terribly pure that it destroys all that is not pure as fire, which demands like purity in our worship. He will have purity. It is not that the fire will burn us if we do not worship thus; yea, will go on burning within us after all that is foreign to it has yielded to its force, no longer with pain and consuming, but as the highest consciousness of life, the presence of God.[19]

We're simply too small, too bounded to fully grasp what's too great to bear. MacDonald also said, "The miracles of Jesus were the ordinary works of his Father, wrought small and swift that we might take them in."[20] We do not fully understand or even know all that God is doing for us and in us, but we trust his intentions, ability, and care to accomplish his purposes.

We also don't know everything that transpired between the Lord and Moses atop Mount Sinai or in the makeshift tent of meeting, but it was of course no surprise to the Lord. It was only Moses who needed protection from the very thing he devoutly sought: the dangerous goodness of God's holiness and glory, the essence and manifestation of his character and presence.

It was God's holiness and glory that also confronted Isaiah. His vision of the Lord left him "undone," but led to a life filled with courageous proclamation and prophecy. It was God's holiness and glory that arrested Saul of Tarsus. His Damascus Road vision of the risen Jesus transformed him from "persecutor" of the church to *St. Paul*, "apostle of the heart set free."[21] It was God's holiness and glory that overwhelmed John, the disciple "whom Jesus loved." The one who'd leaned on our Lord at the Last Supper fell "as a dead man" before the risen Christ, but his apocalyptic vision led him to write of "the One who is alive forevermore" (Rev 1:17–18).

In the Gospels, what transpired on the Mount of Transfiguration was also no surprise to Jesus, only to those disciples waiting nearby:[22]

> Jesus took with him Peter, James and John the brother of James and led them up a high mountain by themselves. There he was transfigured before them. His face shone like the sun, and his clothes became as white as the light. Just then there appeared before them

19. MacDonald, *Unspoken Sermons: Series One*, 12; also in Lewis, *George MacDonald*, 2.

20. MacDonald, *Unspoken Sermons: Second Series*, 21; also in Lewis, *George MacDonald*, 33.

21. See Bruce, *Paul*, 21.

22. Matthew 17 (NIV); Mark 9 (NIV); Luke 9 (NIV).

> Moses and Elijah, talking with Jesus. Peter said, "Lord, it is good for us to be here. If you wish, I will put up three shelters—one for you, one for Moses and one for Elijah."

Luke's account of this dazzling moment mentions that impulsive Peter "did not know what he was saying." Matthew continues:

> While he was still speaking, a bright cloud enveloped them, and a voice from the cloud said, "This is my Son, whom I love; with him I am well pleased. Listen to him." When the disciples heard this, they fell facedown to the ground, terrified. But Jesus came and touched them. "Get up," he said. "Don't be afraid."

Mark says Peter's impulsiveness was driven by fear, but these three disciples seem to have been too overwhelmed to fully appreciate the dangerous goodness of the holiness and glory being manifested to them. What they were seeing and hearing, like what was shown in Exodus to Moses, was some sort of accommodated awareness of God, but most importantly that God's very presence and person could be found in, and were in fact identified with, Jesus Christ. He had just queried them at Caesarea Philippi about who other people were saying he was, and about who they thought he was.[23] Peter's, "You are the Christ, the Son of the living God" (Matt 16:16), was a strong, spiritually-discerned affirmation that our Lord himself readily blessed and confirmed, even if he later needed to straighten out Peter on some of the ramifications of that statement of faith (16:22–28). What Peter, James and John witnessed was made all the more powerful (and probably dizzying) to them by the confirming voice from the cloud, and by the presence of Moses and Elijah connecting the present vision to powerful and defining times from Israel's past. The holiness and glory they were shown tied together the promise and provision of the old covenant to salvation and restoration in the new thing being brought to pass.

We've noted that holiness and glory are not the only divine characteristics that should regularly pervade our worship. We also worship a gracious and merciful God who is faithful and abounding in love, and who is keen to see our lives match what we profess to believe about righteousness and justice. With respect to the latter, we're too often prone to say, "I'm more important than you," while we worship our Lord who says, "You're more important than I."

---

23. Matthew 16:13–20.

This brings into clear focus another divine core characteristic that comes to bear on how we worship together, how we treat each other, and how we act in our larger community contexts. God is, at heart, a servant.

Servanthood

Nowhere is this more evident than in the deeply personal message of St. Paul's letter to the church at Philippi.[24] The apostle expresses his gratitude for these believers, whom he calls "partners" in the gospel. Yet he gently warns them against any rivalries or personal ambitions coming between them (2:3–4; 4:2–3). He buttresses his plea with an appeal to Christ's own humility and attitude of servanthood: "Let this same mind be in you that was in Christ Jesus." In coming to us, Christ didn't surrender deity, but emptied himself of the privileges and prerogatives of being God.[25] He voluntarily set them aside in favor of becoming fully human on our behalf. Paul writes,

> Have this mind among yourselves which is yours in Christ Jesus, who though he was in the form of God, did not count equality with God a thing to be grasped, but emptied himself, by taking the form of a servant, being born in human likeness. (Phil 2:5–7 ESV)

He might as well have said, "There's something far more important than winning, than being first." Even Jesus didn't strive for it, but gave himself to serving his Father and us.

The same attitude and actions are incumbent on us who worship him. Our Lord demonstrates this another way the day before his crucifixion. John 13 recounts a poignant scene with Jesus and his disciples at their last Passover together:

> Jesus, knowing that God the Father had given all things into his hands, and that he had come from God and was going back to God, rose from supper. He laid aside his outer garments, and taking a towel tied it around his waist. Then he poured water into a basin and began to wash the disciples' feet and to wipe them with that towel that was wrapped around him. . .When he had washed their feet, and put on his outer garments and resumed his place, he said to them, "Do you understand what I have done to you? You call me Teacher and Lord, and you are right, for so I am. If I, then,

24. Philippians 2:1–11.

25. "Kenosis" from the Greek *kenoō*: "to empty" (Bauer, *Greek-English Lexicon*, 428).

your Lord and Teacher, have washed your feet, you also ought to wash one another's feet. For I have given you an example, that you also should do just as I have done to you. (13:3–5; 12–15 ESV)

Jesus wraps up this exchange by reminding them that a servant isn't greater than his master, nor is a messenger greater than the one who sent him. In other words, pay close attention to this mandate. You'll be blessed if you act on what you have heard from me and have seen me demonstrate. Serve each other. Be quick to forgive each other. Put each other's needs above your own.

God's servant heart is also clearly evident in the Holy Spirit's ministry of "coming along side" us in advocacy and support.[26] This ministry stands in stark contrast to any spirit of accusation or any pernicious impulse of competition.[27] Both are simply antithetical to the gospel and to values of Christ's kingdom. "Here," writes George MacDonald, "there is no room for ambition. Ambition is the desire to be above one's neighbor . . . Relative worth is not only unknown—to the children of the Kingdom it is unknowable."[28]

This strikes at the heart of what's become a coarse and adversarial nature of our public discourse. Christians are called, rather, to treat each other with deference and mutual concern—to love each other.[29] We're also called not to accuse, demonize, or excoriate our enemies, but to love them.[30] This begins by being less concerned or even unconcerned with our own rights, and more with those of others. If we insist on fighting a battle over our own rights, then we've already lost the war. It's one thing to stand for the right and to fight for righteousness—even at great personal cost. It's quite another to ostensibly be salt and light against what may be perceived as spiritual and cultural decay, but to do so with tactics and strategies barely distinguishable from those we're called to resist and redeem. We don't really need to overly ponder whether it's better to be in someone's face or at their side.

---

26. Hence a primary designation of the Holy Spirit as "Paraclete" (Greek *paraklētos*), one who is called alongside, to someone's aid, to appeal, urge, exhort, encourage, comfort (Bauer, *Greek-English Lexicon,* 617). Also see Brown, *Introduction to the New Testament,* 353–55; and "Paraclete in the Fourth Gospel," 113–32.

27. For clear articulation of kingdom values see Mark 9:35; 10:37–45; Ephesians 5:21.

28. MacDonald, *Unspoken Sermons: Series One,* 39; also in Lewis, *George MacDonald,* 10.

29. 1 John 4:7; Matthew 22:39.

30. Matthew 5:44; Luke 6:27.

The NT figure Joseph of Cypress is a prime example of this latter mindset and method, so much so that he was known primarily by his nickname, Barnabas, "son of encouragement" (Acts 4:36). Long a hero of mine, he was a leader in the early days of the Jerusalem church. He evidently was a person of discernment, faith, and courage. He apparently was a skilled and convincing advocate, able to instill confidence and build trust through the sincerity and warmth of his personality and service. Luke tells us that Barnabas was "a good man, full of the Holy Spirit" (Acts 11:24).

He went to Syrian Antioch as emissary of the Jerusalem church. Some early Jewish believers had fled there following the martyrdom of Stephen. As Antioch Gentiles also began to come to faith in Jesus, open-hearted and open-handed Barnabas confirmed this development to be a movement of God's grace. At some risk to his own reputation, he also personally confirmed as genuine the conversion of Saul, the feared persecutor, to Paul, God's chosen apostle. They later served together as missionaries.

Wherever they went, Barnabas made a positive impact on and for others through his congenial personality, generous outlook, deep spiritual maturity, and affable spirit. Though they didn't always agree, his persuasiveness on Paul's behalf was so pivotal, one wonders whether Barnabas was initially part of Paul's circle, or the other way around. So engaging was Barnabas's manner that he could easily have worn it heavily. Yet we see in every NT reference to him a consistent picture of a man devoted to Jesus Christ, comfortable in his own skin, and at liberty to give freely of himself. Other than of our Lord himself, it's one of the clearest biblical views available of the coming alongside ministry inherent in the Holy Spirit's activities as *Paraclete*. This alone is a commendable legacy to emulate.

"God's way, always, is to use servants," writes Peterson"[31] Barnabas arguably understood that his natural and commendable gifts of personality and persuasion meant little in any really lasting sense apart from their use in service of Jesus Christ. Worship also means little in any really lasting sense apart from its witness to and service of Jesus Christ. This is why servanthood also qualifies as a structural stone for worship. Peterson continues,

> The core element in a servant identity is *not* being God, not being in charge, not taking the initiative. Or, to put it positively, a servant enters into what has already been decided by another, what is already going on, alert to the gestures and guidance of the Master (Ps 123). The servant doesn't know the whole story, doesn't know

31. Peterson, *Jesus Way,* 174.

the end from the beginning. The servant's task is to be competent in the immediate affairs that have to do with what he knows of the desires of the Master. All the while he is also aware that there is far more going on, both good and evil, than he has knowledge of. He lives, in other words, in a mystery but not in confusion. A good servant is eager to trust and obey and honor God as the sovereign who is always personal and present . . . [32]

This is why we said from the outset that none of us will ever be expert worshipers, and that we come with empty hands to be filled from God's unique and inexhaustible supply. We live under heaven and its authority, and in Christ's service find perfect freedom.[33] This freedom borne of servanthood empowers as will nothing else. Peterson amplifies:

> This is the gospel way to deal with what is wrong in the world . . . whether the wrong is intentional or inadvertent, the servant neither avoids it in revulsion nor attacks it by force of words or arms. Instead, the servant embraces, accepts, *suffers* in the sense of submitting to the conditions and accepting the consequences. The servant personally *takes* the wrongdoer and the wrong to the altar of sacrifice and makes an offering for him or her on it. The servant says to his brothers and sisters, "Only God can save you. You don't think you can go to him? I'll go for you." Or, at least, "Let me go with you."[34]

Servanthood, justice, righteousness, love, faithfulness, mercy, grace, glory, and holiness: all qualify as structural stones of Christian worship. Each is an integral part of the person and work of God. Yet we begin with holiness and glory. Over time, do we portray God as uniquely immense and important? Do we recognize our human, bounded, and sinful status as too limited to fully grasp this? Does our worship offer biblical glimpses of God that in the aggregate can offer a transforming vision?

Do we seek biblically balanced worship that bears gracious witness to who God is and what God does for us? Does our worship affirm both God's transcendence and immanence? God's otherness, in terms of holiness and uniqueness, and God's nearness, in terms of revealing, initiating, covenant-making, and visiting (*Emmanuel*, "God with us")? Do we look to God as a heavenly Father drawing close to us for our identity, security, and destiny,

---

32. Ibid., 174, italics his.
33. See the Episcopal Church, "Collect for Peace," 57.
34. Peterson, *Jesus Way*, 177, italics his.

as well as a sovereign King gathering and ruling an enduring, eternal kingdom? These all are part of the biblical portrait of God available to us in Scripture. The clarity of our focus on what already has been revealed to us will deeply influence what we see and who we become.[35]

35. See Humphrey, *Grand,* 43.

5

An Observant Approach

*It is Scripture that calls and captivates us. If worship is
to convey the message of the biblical text, we must first
learn what it says and means.*

CALVIN'S CONFIDENCE IN THE Word of God proclaimed reminds us that
this great expositor was persuaded by the persuasiveness of holy Scripture.
He did recognize that, in the very use of language and words, God accommodated himself to human limitations of communication, but the tacit
presumption in this is that words and language are sufficient for conveying
what God intends and desires to convey. They arguably are sufficient, even
efficient. One is reminded of Mark Twain's distinction between "the right
word and the nearly right word" being the difference "between lightning
and a lightning bug."[1] It is no accident that John's Gospel calls Jesus Christ
"the Word," and that Scripture is our source of knowledge about his unique
role in revealing and explaining God (John 1:18).

Nobel Laureate Isidor Isaac Rabi discovered nuclear magnetic resonance, which led to development of magnetic resonance imaging. He was
once asked by psychiatrist and philanthropist Arthur Sackler, "Why did
you become a scientist, rather than a doctor, lawyer, or businessman, like all
the other immigrant kids in your neighborhood?" Rabi responded,

> My mother made me a scientist without ever intending it. Every
> other Jewish mother in Brooklyn would ask her child after school,

1. Quoted in October 15, 1888 letter from Twain recounted in Bainton, *Authorship*,
87–88.

"So, did you learn anything today?" But not my mother. She always asked me something different. "Izzy," she would say, "did you ask a good question today?" That difference—asking good questions—is what made me a scientist.[2]

If worship is to convey at least the sense and message of the proclaimed text at hand, we first need to know what it says, what the big idea really is.[3] In this, several questions come to mind: What do we see? How does it fit? What does it mean? So what? These are questions of inductive process: observation, correlation, interpretation, and application. The more time we spend in the first two steps, the more accurate and potentially powerful the last two will be.

Two approaches, of course, in logic and reasoning are deduction and induction. Deductive reasoning begins with a theory, statement, or hypothesis, then works its way to a conclusion based on evidence observed. Inductive reasoning begins with small observations or questions and works its way to a conclusion by examining data. Deduction works from the general to the specific: hypothesis, to observation, to confirmation. Induction moves from the specific to the general: observation, to pattern, to hypothesis, to theory. Each rests on asking good questions.

Another example from science will further illustrate. Years ago I heard the inimitable Christian educator and communicator Howard Hendricks[4] recount a story about Louis Agassiz, the famed nineteenth-century Harvard professor of natural history.[5] A student was given a fish. He didn't know it at the time, but he was going to become very friendly with his fish. At the outset, Agassiz assigned him the task of making simple observations about the fish, just observations. Answer the question, "What do I see?" The same assignment was given repeatedly in each class for months. The student grumbled, but he persevered. At the end of the term, the professor congratulated him that by then no one knew more about his fish than he. He'd become a better ichthyologist, but he'd also received a hands-on introduction to scientific method, to inductive process.

2. Sheff, "Izzy, Did You Ask," lines 1–15.

3. Borden, "Is There Really One Big Idea?," 67–80.

4. See Hendricks, *Teaching to Change Lives*, 21–24, and *Color Outside the Lines*, 19–40. Cf. Lincoln, "Message and Ministry," 34–95.

5. The likeliest first-hand account of this story can be found in Scudder, "In the Laboratory with Agassiz," 369–70. This eventual assistant to Agassiz recalls an early experience with his mentor in an account that is occasionally embellished by others. For further insight into Agassiz, see McCullogh, "American Adventure of Louis Agassiz," 20.

Inductive Bible study is the methodological foundation and touchstone of expositional worship. Expositional preaching and expositional worship begin with some such process with Scripture as we seek to heighten its expression.[6] Asking inductive questions initiates that process of building context and understanding in order to unpack meaning. We get to know a biblical passage better in order to eventually accurately communicate its powerful truth. So we ask:

- What do I see?

- How does it (or does it not) fit?

- What does it mean?

- So what?

Inductive study of Scripture points and leads to an important distinction between a sermon that is expositional and one that may indeed use the Bible or is biblical in its general orientation, but isn't necessarily designed to let the Bible make its own point through attuning its categories, points, or big ideas to those of the actual passage(s) being proclaimed. Widely admired teacher of preachers Haddon Robinson sets the parameters:

> The thought of the biblical writer determines the substance of an expository sermon . . . the expositor searches for the objective meaning of a passage through understanding of language, backgrounds, and the setting of the text . . . Ultimately the authority behind preaching resides not in the preacher but in the biblical text.[7]

Earl Palmer drives home the point:

> I became convinced that the most meaningful preaching and teaching over the long haul would be biblical exposition. If I could get somebody to look at the text, it would sooner or later win their respect . . . If I can get people to consider the text seriously, it will do its own convincing . . . It sometimes takes a little skill to get people to do that. . .the best theology is always theology that begins with the text.[8]

---

6. Traina, *Methodical Bible Study*, 4–6; Bauer, *Inductive Bible Study*, 17–27.

7. Robinson, *Biblical Preaching*, 5.

8. Palmer, "Case for Expositional Preaching," 8–13.

Context always determines meaning. Consider the words, "I love you." Think how even the simplest difference, in context, of tone of voice or word emphasis completely alters meaning:

- I *love* you.

- *I* love *you*.

- *I* (?) love *you* (?)

- Okay, for crying out loud, I *love* you!

This last example reminds me of the doltish husband who declared, "I love my wife so much, it's all I can do to keep from telling her!"

Understanding a passage in its own context helps us articulate its big idea. This is basic operating procedure for anyone interested in crafting worship that is expositional. How helpful it would be if pastors and worship leaders would intentionally and regularly delve into such a process, individually and as a team! We might be tempted to say, "Who has time for that? We're all way too busy!" Well, maybe we are too busy if we can't prioritize some team study and team reflection around Scripture each week that will form the basis and foundation of upcoming sermons and services. What a wonderful way to get on the same page together! What a wonderful way to creatively consider how to build biblically expressive worship together! And if it's done weeks and even months ahead of time, what a wonderful way to ameliorate or avoid altogether the tyranny of approaching deadlines. It may seem at first like a daunting task for a pastoral and worship staff, but it will yield high dividends to long-term investors!

There certainly is more than one way to articulate a big idea, but let's take a few moments and consider a handful of biblical passages and the kinds of things we might discover about them through inductive study— living with them long enough and well enough to be able to say in our own words what they're saying. Our understanding and articulation of big ideas will guide us as we craft worship that orbits around each text. We begin with Exodus 33, with a view to articulating for it at least a possible big idea to inform its proclamation and reverberation.

Exodus 33:12–23 (NIV)

Moses said to the Lord, "You have been telling me, 'Lead these people,' but you have not let me know whom you will send with me. You have said, 'I know you by name and you have found favor with me.' If you are pleased with me, teach me your ways so I may know you and continue to find favor with you. Remember that this nation is your people." The Lord replied, "My Presence will be with you, and I will give you rest." Then Moses said to him, "If your Presence does not go with us, do not send us up from here. How will anyone know that you are pleased with me and with your people unless you go with us? What else will distinguish me and your people from all the other people on the face of the earth" And the Lord said to Moses, "I will do the very thing you have asked, because I am pleased with you and I know you by name." Then Moses said, "Show me your glory." And the Lord said, "I will cause all my goodness to pass in front of you, and I will proclaim my name, the Lord, in your presence. I will have mercy on whom I will have mercy, and I will have compassion on whom I will have compassion. But you cannot see my face, for no one may see me and live." Then the Lord said, "There is a place near me where you may stand on a rock. When my glory passes by, I will put you in the cleft in the rock and cover you with my hand until I have passed by. Then I will remove my hand and you will see my back; but my face must not be seen."

Context

- Mt. Sinai: a rarified time of divine revelation

- Moses' fledgling leadership is uncertain, insecure

- Moses says he has been told God's name (I AM) but knows less about God than he would like to know

- Moses is persistently insistent (this nation is *your* people)

- God offers the assurance of his "Presence" and his "rest"

- Moses recognizes his and the Hebrews' inadequacies

- He needs God's verification and approval

- God says he will be with Moses and will respond to him

- Moses asks for even more (show me your glory/yourself)

- God says that would be too much for Moses to bear but that he would reveal to Moses his goodness and reiterate his name

- God reserves divine prerogatives, but this also is for Moses' own safety

Big Idea

Those who place their faith in the holy God of glory can be assured of his presence and care in their lives, a presence that brings the truest of rest. Such identity, security, and destiny do not, however, abrogate God's sovereignty or mitigate our creaturely status.

Psalm 81 (ESV)

Sing aloud to God our strength; shout for joy to the God of Jacob! Raise a song; sound the tambourine, the sweet lyre with the harp. Blow the trumpet at the new moon, at the full moon, our feast day. For it is a statute for Israel, a rule of the God of Jacob. He made it a decree in Joseph, when he went out over the land of Egypt. I heard a language I had not known: "I relieved your shoulder from the burden; your hands were freed from the basket. In distress you called, and I delivered you; I answered you in the secret place of thunder; I tested you at the waters of Meribah. Hear, O my people, while I admonish you! O Israel, if you would but listen to me! There shall be no strange god among you; you shall not bow down to a foreign god. I am the Lord your God, who brought you out of the land of Egypt. Open your mouth wide, and I will fill it." "But my people did not listen to my voice; Israel would not submit to me. So I gave them over to their stubborn hearts, to follow their own counsels. Oh, that my people would listen to me, that Israel would walk in my ways! I would soon subdue their enemies and turn my hand against their foes. Those who hate the Lord would cringe toward him, and their fate would last forever. But I would feed you with the finest of wheat, and with honey from the rock I would satisfy you."

Context

- Some sort of festival in Israel (new moon, feast, blowing the trumpet)
- Such celebrations were memorials to God's saving acts (exodus, freedom from slavery, sustaining on wilderness sojourn)
- These divine acts called for remembrance and recommitment

- A warning and a corrective are included (no foreign god/if my people would but listen), but also a promise (feed, satisfy)
- See Deuteronomy 32:13 (Song of Moses)

Big Idea

Remembering who God is and what God has done for us is the best guard against the idolatry of seeking meaning and fulfillment elsewhere, and the best reminder that ultimate satisfaction comes only through what God provides.

Daniel 1:1–2 + Jeremiah 29:4–14 (NRSV)

In the third year of the reign of King Jehoiakim of Judah, King Nebuchadnezzar of Babylon came to Jerusalem and besieged it. The Lord let King Jehoiakim of Judah fall into his power, as well as some of the vessels of the house of God. These he brought to the land of Shinar, and placed the vessels in the treasury of his gods. (Dan 1:1–2)

Thus says the Lord of hosts, the God of Israel, to all the exiles whom I have sent into exile from Jerusalem to Babylon: Build houses and live in them; plant gardens and eat what they produce. Take wives and have sons and daughters; take wives for your sons, and give your daughters in marriage, that they may bear sons and daughters; multiply there, and do not decrease. But seek the welfare of the city where I have sent you into exile, and pray to the Lord on its behalf, for in its welfare you will find your welfare. For thus says the Lord of hosts, the God of Israel: Do not let the prophets and the diviners who are among you deceive you, and do not listen to the dreams that they dream, for it is a lie that they are prophesying to you in my name; I did not send them, says the Lord. For thus says the Lord: Only when Babylon's seventy years are completed will I visit you, and I will fulfill to you my promise and bring you back to this place. For surely I know the plans I have for you, says the Lord, plans for your welfare and not for harm, to give you a future with hope. Then when you call upon me and come and pray to me, I will hear you. When you search for me, you will find me; if you seek me with all your heart. I will let you find me, says the Lord, and I will restore your fortunes and gather you from all the nations and all the places where I have driven you, says the Lord, and I will bring you back to the place from which I sent you into exile. (Jer 29:4–14)

Context

- Sixth-century-BCE Babylonian exile of the Hebrews
- Conquest and deportation a result of divine decision (apparently even the desecration of the temple in Jerusalem and removal of its sacred treasures to a foreign, pagan place of worship) at an appointed future time (after the course of divine judgment) the Hebrews will be brought back to their homeland (a place of identity and promise)
- This will be according to God's plan (which has always been to give them a hope and a future)
- They will one day realize that their security is in the Lord
- They will seek the Lord and he will be found by them
- They will pray to him and he will hear them
- In the meantime (surprisingly) they are to settle in the foreign land
- There they are to live productive, helpful, exemplary lives

Big Idea

Even through judgment of sin, God is faithful to his promises and his people, whom he graciously saves and to whom he lovingly gives himself.

Jeremiah 31:33–34 (NKJV)

"But this is the covenant that I will make with the house of Israel after those days, says the Lord: I will put my law in their minds, and write it on their hearts; and I will be their God, and they shall be my people. No more shall every man teach his neighbor, and every man his brother, saying 'Know the Lord,' for they all shall know me, from the least of them to the greatest of them, says the Lord. For I will forgive their iniquity, and their sin I will remember no more."

Context

- Despite disobedience and divine judgment a "new covenant" is coming
- Unlike older ones and transcending what God did for their ancestors
- It will be internal (in their minds, on their hearts)
- It will be universal (all will know me)
- It will be based simply on grace, mercy, and forgiveness (forgive their wickedness, remember their sins no more)
- It will be eternal (an everlasting covenant)
- It will be evident/present/tangible (my dwelling place will be with them, my presence will make my people holy, the nations will know)
- See Ezekiel 37:26–28

Big Idea

Despite our propensity to disobedience and sin, God's faithful and unending promise is to change us from the inside out for his glory, and our good.

Luke 4:14–21 (NIV)

Jesus returned to Galilee in the power of the Spirit, and news about him spread through the whole countryside. He was teaching in their synagogues, and everyone praised him. He went to Nazareth, where he had been brought up, and on the Sabbath day he went into the synagogue, as was his custom. He stood up to read, and the scroll of the prophet Isaiah was handed to him. Unrolling it, he found the place where it is written: The Spirit of the Lord is on me, because he has anointed me to proclaim good news to the poor. He has sent me to proclaim freedom for the prisoners and recovery of sight for the blind, to set the oppressed free, to proclaim the year of the Lord's favor. Then he rolled up the scroll, gave it back to the attendant and sat down. The eyes of everyone in the synagogue were fastened on him. He began by saying to them, "Today this scripture is fulfilled in your hearing." All spoke well of him and were amazed at the gracious words that came from his lips. "Isn't this Joseph's son?" they asked. Jesus said to them, "Surely you will quote this proverb to me: 'Physician, heal yourself!' And you will tell me, 'Do here in your hometown what we have heard that you did in Capernaum.'" "Truly I tell you," he continued, "no prophet is accepted in his hometown. I assure you that there were many widows in Israel in Elijah's time, when the sky was shut for three and a half years and there was a severe famine throughout the land. Yet Elijah was not sent to any of them, but to a widow in Zarephath in the region of Sidon. And there were many in Israel with leprosy in the time of Elisha the prophet, yet not one of them was cleansed— only Naaman the Syrian." All the people in the synagogue were furious when they heard this. They got up, drove him out of the town, and took him to the brow of the hill on which the town was built, in order to throw him off the cliff. But he walked through the crowd and went on his way.

Context

- Early in Jesus' earthly ministry, just after his baptism
- Synagogue was customary Sabbath activity for him and his faithful countrymen
- An abbreviated reading from a messianic passage in Isaiah 61
- Reference to year of Jubilee (favor) (Lev 28:8–55) every 50 years (Isaiah prophesied of the Hebrews' liberation from Babylonian captivity while Jesus proclaimed liberation from sin and its consequences)
- Controversial reference to two non-Israelites (a widow in Zarephath [1 Kgs 17:1–15] and Naaman the Syrian [2 Kgs 5:1–14])
- When Israel rejected God's messenger of redemption (Elijah and Elisha), God sent him to the Gentiles
- Jesus fascinated the people, but was quickly rejected for his claims

Big Idea

Jesus completely fulfills God's word in ways that can excite or disturb us.

Galatians 1:6–9 (ESV)

I am astonished that you are so quickly deserting him who called you in the grace of Christ and are turning to a different gospel— not that there is another one, but there are some who trouble you and want to distort the gospel of Christ. But even if we or an angel from heaven should preach to you a gospel contrary to the one we preached to you, let him be accursed. As we have said before, so now I say again: If anyone is preaching to you a gospel contrary to the one you received, let him be accursed.

Context

- A time after some initial visit by St. Paul to the region of Galatia
- Some disagreed with Paul and characterized him as an inauthentic apostle
- They implied that his teaching was watering down established Jewish religious requirements such as circumcision
- He responded by clearly authenticating his apostleship and clearly articulating the true message of the gospel: justification by grace through faith apart from works of the law
- The apostle deals surgically with what he considered to be heresy

Big Idea

Human tendency is to want to play a role in our own salvation. God's way is always and only by grace through simple faith.

2 Timothy 3:16–17 (NIV)

All Scripture is God-breathed and is useful for teaching, rebuking, correcting, and training in righteousness, so that the servant of God may be thoroughly equipped for every good work.

Context

- St. Paul's last letter
- He was languishing in a Roman prison
- Writing to a trusted and beloved younger colleague who pastored in Ephesus
- Paul was lonely
- Paul was concerned about new churches he had helped establish during his four missionary journeys
- Paul was particularly interested in encouraging and edifying Timothy and his Ephesian congregation
- 2 Timothy is a valedictory word—a heartfelt farewell

Big Idea

God's word is supernaturally enabled to change us in every way we need to please God and to do God's work.

This sort of intentional method can be applied to individual sermons, series of sermons, regular worship services, or what we might call exceptional ones such as those at Christmas, during Holy Week, on Easter, or for Communion of the Saints. It applies equally effectively to exposition for children and youth, whose need of biblical truth we readily acknowledge, but whose interest in it, and capacity to understand and receive it, we may well underestimate. Biblical truth and worship calculated to orbit around it need to be contextualized and crafted age-appropriately, but children and youth are well suited to benefit from careful exegesis, clear exposition, and creative communication. Commitment to and confidence in the text that orients, structures, and calibrates expositional preaching also undergirds expositional worship. Such worship seeks to expressively and artfully convey and heighten that same message by whatever creative means we can faithfully engage, and for the same reason: it's the word of God by the power of God that invigorates—that actually creates new life.[9] Life of the Word made flesh becomes life of the word made fresh through its proclamation and reverberation in all our worship, growth, and service together.

9. See Horton, *People and Place*, 40.

6

An Eye for Detail

Through preaching that stays in Scripture's story, and worship that tells the same story, God's provision and purpose for us become all the more clear.

FROM BUILDING CONTEXTS AND articulating big ideas for biblical passages to be proclaimed, we turn our attention to choosing other possible worship components to complement or reverberate truths conveyed from the pulpit. If this and the previous chapter are the most practical of our study, chapter five was more *process*-oriented, while, chapter six is more *product*-focused.

What follows are four examples from Scripture. For each, a big idea is articulated, sermon titles are offered, prayers are cited, and musical suggestions are made. Since these are drawn from actual National Presbyterian Church worship services, the general layouts used at the time are provided here simply to orient and help visually contextualize the choices made. The fit and flow of worship components is hopefully made clearer in the services as they were conceived and presented. Not every original detail is included, but only information indicating expositional use of the component. Neither the choices nor the layout are meant to be prescriptive, just descriptive of the kinds of things that can be done. We begin with one example of passages from chapter five (where the texts and some observations about them already appear). Here we remind ourselves again of the big idea.

Daniel 1:1–2 + Jeremiah 29:4–14 (NRSV)

Big Idea

Even through judgment of sin, God is faithful to his promises and his people, whom he graciously saves and to whom he lovingly gives himself.

Two sermon titles had actually come to mind: "Lessons from Babylon" and "Promissory Note." The preaching pastor chose the first. For corporate confession we often use prayers of past historical figures. Over time, this helps our contemporary congregation connect with the larger church's great cloud of witnesses. We considered also doing that here, but it seemed appropriate in this instance to use an actual portion of Scripture. We chose part of Psalm 25.

For opening and closing hymns we settled on "O Sing a New Song to the Lord" and "Glorious Things of Thee are Spoken." Rich in OT imagery, they point to God's rule over the whole earth and all its peoples, to God's graciousness (even to those who do not worship him), to the great privilege of being God's own people, and to the blessing of identity, security, and destiny, both in a place like the holy city Jerusalem and in the heavenly city itself. We chose to reprise the tune of this second hymn (*Austria*) for a congregational benediction response at the end of the service, but with some new words rich in imagery from Exodus 3 and Revelation 21.

For choral material we chose "By the Waters of Babylon," a setting of Psalm 137:1 composed as a musical round based on a pensive ancient Jewish melody; a tender setting by Craig Courtney of the actual Jeremiah 29:11–13 text being preached; and a jubilant arrangement by Aaron Copland of an old American song, "Zion's Walls." Together the three offered a balanced biblical, theological, and musical set of reflections and reverberations on the proclaimed texts at hand.

Sample Worship Service One

CALL TO WORSHIP

HYMN   O Sing a New Song to the Lord   *Gonfalon Royal*

> O sing a new song to the Lord; sing, all the earth, and bless his name;
> From day to day God's praise record; the Lord's redeeming grace proclaim.

Tell all the world God's gracious ways; tell heathen nations far and near;
Great is the Lord, and great God's praise; the Lord alone let nations fear.

The heathen gods are idols vain; the shining heav'ns the Lord supports;
Both light and honor lead the train, while strength and beauty fill his courts.

Let every tongue and every tribe give to the Lord due praise and sing:
All glory unto God ascribe; come, throng his courts, and off'rings bring.
Alleluia![1]

PRAYER OF ADORATION

CONFESSION OF SIN

Be mindful of your mercy, O Lord, and your steadfast love, for
they are from of old. Do not remember my sins or my transgres-
sions; according to your steadfast love remember me, for your
goodness' sake. For your name's sake, O Lord, pardon my guilt, for
it is great. Turn to me and be gracious to me; relieve the trouble of
my heart, and bring me out of distress. Consider my affliction and
all my trouble, and forgive all my sin. From Psalm 25

CHORAL MEDITATION

By the waters of Babylon, we sat down and wept for thee, Zion. We
remember thee, Zion.[2]

SILENT CONFESSION AND ASSURANCE OF PARDON

CONGREGATIONAL RESPONSE   *Gloria Patri*

AFFIRMATION OF FAITH

SCRIPTURE   Daniel 1:1–2; Jeremiah 29:4–14

SERMON   Lessons from Babylon

CHORAL RESPONSE   If You Search with All Your Heart   Craig Courtney

If you seek me you will find me, if you search with all your heart.
For I know the plans I have for you, plans of welfare, not of evil.

---

1. McKim, *Presbyterian Hymnal*, 216. Text: C. H. Gabriel. Music: P. C. Buck.
2. Ibid., 245. Text: from Psalm 137; Music: Ancient Jewish melody.

For I know the plans I have for you, plans of hope and a future.

I will bring you out of bondage to a place I have prepared.

I will bring you out of bondage. I will bring you home to me.[3]

PASTORAL PRAYER AND THE LORD'S PRAYER

OFFERTORY   Zion's Walls   Aaron Copland

Come, fathers and mothers, come, sisters and brothers,

Come, join us in singing the praises of Zion!

O fathers, don't you feel determined to meet within the walls of Zion.

We'll shout and go round the walls of Zion![4]

DOXOLOGY   *Old Hundredth*

PRAYER OF DEDICATION

HYMN   Glorious Things of Thee are Spoken   *Austrian Hymn*

Glorious things of thee are spoken, Zion city of our God;

God, whose word cannot be broken, formed thee for a blest abode.

On the Rock of Ages founded, what can shake thy sure repose?

With salvation's walls surrounded, thou may'st smile at all thy foes.

See, the streams of living water, springing from eternal love,

Well supply thy sons and daughters and all fear of want remove.

Who can faint while such a river ever flows thy thirst to assuage?

Grace, which like the Lord the giver, never fails from age to age.

Round each habitation hov'ring, see the cloud of fire appear

For a glory and a cov'ring, showing that the Lord is near.

Thus deriving from their banner light by night and shade by day,

Safe they feed upon the manna which God gives them when they pray.[5]

3. Courtney, *If You Search*, 2–8.

4. Copland, *Old American Songs*, 10–14. Text attributed to J. G. McCurry, and first appeared in *The Social Harp* (1855), a compilation of over 200 southern revivalist-tradition hymns.

5. McKim, *Hymnal*, 446. Text: J. Newton. Music: F. J. Haydn.

From on high the Holy City to God's people will descend;
    There, amidst exultant glory and rejoicing without end:
Hallelujah, Hallelujah—shall we praise the great I AM!
    Hallelujah, Hallelujah—shall we praise the great I AM![6]

Matthew 14:22–33 (NRSV)

Immediately he made the disciples get into the boat and go ahead to the other side, while he dismissed the crowds. And after he had dismissed the crowds, he went up the mountain to by himself to pray. When evening came, he was there alone, but by this time the boat, battered by the waves, was far from land, for the wind was against them. And early in the morning he came walking toward them on the sea. But when the disciples saw him walking on the sea, they were terrified, saying, "It is a ghost!" And they cried out in fear. But immediately Jesus spoke to them and said, "Take heart, it is I; do not be afraid." Peter answered him, "Lord, if it is you, command me to come to you on the water." He said, "Come." So Peter got out of the boat, started walking on the water, and came toward Jesus. But when he noticed the strong wind, he became frightened, and beginning to sink, he cried out, "Lord, save me!" Jesus immediately reached out his hand and caught him, saying to him, "You of little faith, why did you doubt?" When they got into the boat, the wind ceased. And those in the boat worshiped him, saying, "Truly you are the Son of God."

Big Idea

It is only the depth and breadth of our Lord's power and love that can increase our faith and dispel our fear.

The sermon title was "Walking on Water." It focused on human fear, weakness of faith, desire for greater faith, and the true object of faith. For the corporate confession of sin we therefore chose a prayer of Martin Luther for strengthened faith and trust. For congregational hymns we chose "Faith of Our Fathers" and "We Walk by Faith and Not by Sight." For choral

6. Text: M. Denham.

material we chose a verse of the hymn "O Sing a Song of Galilee," "O Lord, Increase My Faith" (an English anthem attributed to Renaissance composer Orlando Gibbons), and "Be Not Afraid," a contemporary setting based on Isaiah 43:1–4, again by Craig Courtney.

I should note that we have neither an agenda, nor any sense of quota, for choosing or blending musical or other components from any particular historical periods or prevailing styles. With respect to each we try to maintain some variety, but our *modus operandi* is to make musical and liturgical choices that help convey the sense of the proclaimed text. Experience has demonstrated that our congregation is quite open to different things if those choices are well contextualized.

Sample Worship Service Two

CALL TO WORSHIP

HYMN   Faith of Our Fathers   *St. Catherine*

Faith of our fathers, living still, in spite of prison, fire, and sword,
    O how our hearts beat high with joy whene'er we hear that glorious Word!
    Faith of our fathers, holy faith, we will be true to thee till death.

Faith of our mothers, we will love both friend and foe in all our strife,
    And preach it, too, as love knows how, by kindly words and virtuous life!
    Faith of our mothers, holy faith, we will be true to thee till death.

Faith of the martyrs who, though bound, were still in heart and conscience true;
    How blest would be their children's fate, if they, like them, should live for you!
    Faith of the martyrs, holy faith, we will be true to you till death.

*Faith of disciples, foll'wing Christ, along his path to Calvary,
    Trusting, obeying the Master's words onward unto eternity
    Faith of disciples, holy faith, we will be true to thee till death.[7]

---

7. Shorney et al., *Worship and Rejoice*, 530, alt. Text: F. W. Faber, alternate Music H. F. Hemy. *Verse 4: M. Denham.

PRAYER OF ADORATION

CHORAL RESPONSE   O Sing a Song of Galilee   *Shepherd's Pipes*

O sing a song of Galilee, of lake and woods and hill,
Of him who walked upon the sea and bade its waves be still.
For though, like waves of Galilee, dark seas of trouble roll,
When faith has heard the Master's word, falls peace upon the soul.[8]

CONFESSION OF SIN

Behold, Lord, an empty vessel that needs to be filled. My Lord, fill it. I am weak in faith; strengthen me. I am cold in love; warm me and make me fervent. I am prone to sin; forgive me. At times I doubt, and am unable to trust you altogether. Help me, O Lord. Strengthen my faith and trust in you.[9]—Martin Luther

SILENT CONFESSION AND ASSURANCE OF PARDON

CONGREGATIONAL RESPONSE   *Gloria Patri*

AFFIRMATION OF FAITH

SCRIPTURE   Matthew 14:22–33

SERMON   Walking on Water

CHORAL RESPONSE   O Lord, Increase My Faith   Orlando Gibbons

O Lord, increase my faith, strengthen me and confirm me in thy true path.
Teach me to follow as thou callest me. In every adversity, teach me to say Amen.[10]

PASTORAL PRAYER AND THE LORD'S PRAYER

OFFERTORY   Be Not Afraid   Craig Courtney

Be not afraid, for I have redeemed you. Be not afraid, I have called you by name.
When you pass through the waters I will be with you.
When you pass through the floods they will not sweep o'er you.

8. McKim, *Presbyterian Hymnal*, 308, v. 3, but to alt. tune of A. M. Gay. Text: L. F. Benson.

9. Counsell, *2000 Years of Prayer*, 179.

10. Gibbons, *O Lord, Increase My Faith*, 284–87.

When you walk through the fire you will not be consumed.
You are mine; you are precious in my sight[11]

DOXOLOGY   *Old Hundredth*

PRAYER OF DEDICATION

HYMN   We Walk by Faith and Not by Sight   *Dunlap's Creek*

We walk by faith and not by sight; no gracious word we hear
    From Christ, who spoke as none e'er spoke, but we believe him near.

We may not touch his hands, his side, nor follow where he trod;
    But in his promise we rejoice, and cry, "My Lord, my God!"

Help then, O Lord, our unbelief; and may our faith abound
    To call on you when you are near, and seek where you are found.[12]

BENEDICTION AND CHORAL AMEN

Luke 15:1–8; 11–24 (NIV)

Now the tax collectors and sinners were all gathering around to
see him. But the Pharisees and the teachers of the law muttered,
"This man welcomes sinners and eats with them." Then Jesus told
them this parable: "Suppose one of you has a hundred sheep and
loses one of them. Does he not leave the ninety-nine in the open
country and go after the lost sheep until he finds it? And when he
finds it, he joyfully puts it on his shoulders and goes home. Then
he calls his friends and neighbors together and says, 'Rejoice with
me; I have found my lost sheep.' I tell you that in the same way
there will be more rejoicing in heaven over one sinner who re-
pents than over ninety-nine righteous persons who do not repent
. . . " Jesus continued: "There was a man who had two sons. The
younger one said to his father, 'Father, give me my share of the
estate.' So he divided his property between them. Not long after
that, the younger brother got together all he had, set off for a distant country and there squandered his wealth in wild living. After

11. Courtney, *Be Not Afraid*, 3–11.

12. McKim, *Presbyterian Hymnal*, 399.Text: H. Alford, alt. Music: S. McFarland, arr.
R. Proulx.

he had spent everything, there was a severe famine in that whole country, and he began to be in need. So he went and hired himself out to a citizen of that country, who sent him to feed the pigs. He longed to fill his stomach with the pods that the pigs were eating, but no one gave him anything. When he came to his senses, he said, 'How many of my father's hired men have food to spare, and here I am starving to death! I will set out and go back to my father and say to him: "Father, I have sinned against heaven and against you. I am no longer worthy to be called your son; make me one of your hired men." So he got up and went to his father. But while he was still a long way off, his father saw him and was filled with compassion for him; he ran to his son, threw his arms around him and kissed him. The son said, "Father, I have sinned against heaven and against you. I am no longer worthy to be called your son." But the father said to his servants, "Quick! Bring the best robe and put it on him. Put a ring on his finger and sandals on his feet. Bring the fatted calf and kill it. Let's have a feast and celebrate. For this son of mine was dead and is alive again; he was lost and is found."

Big Idea

God the Father's persistent, resilient, and complete grace draws and guides us, and welcomes us back to our only true home.

This service actually focused on two things: Luke 15, plus an emphasis on faith, creativity, and art. There was a related exhibit that day of works by artists from the congregation and from the larger community. The preaching pastor wanted to focus both on doctrines of grace, and on beauty as an expression of God's nature and character. He therefore had chosen Luke 15 with the parables of the lost sheep and of the prodigal son to serve both. He called particular attention to Rembrandt's great portrayal of the latter in a painting. The sermon title was thus "The Beauty of Grace: Parables of the Lost and Found."

Because of its reference to creativity and expression, for the confession of sin we chose and amended a prayer associated with St. Anselm's Chapel in Canterbury. For congregational hymns we chose "Let the Whole Creation Cry" (with some additional text), and "The King of Love My Shepherd Is." For a vocal solo reflecting upon the lost sheep parable we chose, "I Love My Master," a new text paired with music of American composer Luigi Zaninelli. For an anthem meditating on the faithfulness and loving forbearance of God the Father, we chose Craig Courtney's setting of

Pamela Martin's text, "In My Father's House." Finally, because of the special emphasis on creativity and art, and the expositional focus on the beauty of God's grace, we chose to include at the end of the morning worship guide a sixteenth-century sonnet attributed to Michelangelo.

Sample Worship Service Three

CALL TO WORSHIP

HYMN   Let the Whole Creation Cry   *Llanfair*

Let the whole creation cry: Alleluia!
   "Glory to the Lord on high!" Alleluia!
   Heav'n and earth awake and sing! Alleluia!
   God is God and therefore King. Alleluia!

Praise God, all you hosts above, Alleluia!
   Ever bright and fair in love! Alleluia!
   Cherubim and Seraphim, Alleluia!
   "Holy!" their eternal hymn: Alleluia!

Poet, singer, come rejoice! Alleluia!
   Here employ your pen and voice! Alleluia!
   Painter, sculptor, lift your heart! Alleluia!
   Bring to God your skillful art! Alleluia!

Through artistic vision bright, Alleluia!
   Let us one and all delight! Alleluia!
   All God made and then called "good," Alleluia!
   We may tend and not exclude. Alleluia!

Men and women, young and old, Alleluia!
   Raise the anthem manifold! Alleluia!
   And let children's happy hearts, Alleluia!
   In God's worship bear their parts! Alleluia![13]

---

13 Ibid., 256 to alternate tune *Llanfair*. Text: S. Brooke, alt.

PRAYER OF ADORATION AND CONFESSION

> O God, by your indwelling Spirit you lead us to seek for truth and to rejoice in beauty. Bring to light the darkness of our hearts that we may cast ourselves upon your grace, and trust your pardon. Through redemption by your own beloved Son, illuminate and inspire us, along with all thinkers, writers, artists, and craftsmen, that whatever is true and pure and lovely may hallow your name and kingdom; through Jesus Christ our Lord. [14]—St. Anselm's Chapel, Canterbury

SILENT CONFESSION AND ASSURANCE OF PARDON

CONGREGATIONAL RESPONSE   *Gloria Patri*

AFFIRMATION OF FAITH

SCRIPTURE   Luke 15

SERMON   The Beauty of Grace: Parables of the Lost and Found

SOLO RESPONSE   I Love My Master   Luigi Zaninelli

> I love my Master, for he is kind; so gentle he, and O so meek!
>> He labors long his own to find; lost, lonely lambs the Shepherd seeks.
> I love my Master, for he is strong; with watchful eye he is our stay.
>> All those he calls to him belong; his helpless lambs the Shepherd saves.
> My Master's love will e'er abide; in pastures green his flock he feeds.
>> His tender hand will be my guide; his little lambs the Shepherd leads. [15]

PASTORAL PRAYER AND THE LORD'S PRAYER

OFFERTORY   In My Father's House   Craig Courtney

> In my Father's house you will find a place in the warm embrace of an open door.
>> In my Father's house leave the past behind, come inside and find what you're longing for.

---

14. Reference to "all thinkers, writers, artists, and craftsmen" found in prayers from various sources. Cf. Panel on Worship in the Church of Scotland, "Prayers from the Book," lines 610–14.

15. Alt. text based on Psalm 23: M. Denham. Music: English folk tune, "O Waly Waly," arr. L. Zaninelli in *Five Folk Songs*, 2–5.

In my Father's house solace can be found, comfort will surround the bruised and broken.

> In my Father's house children live in peace, war and hatred cease and love is spoken.

In my Father's house, pardoned from all sin, free from what has been, life can start again.

> In my Father's house prodigals come home, no one walks alone, come and enter in.[16]

DOXOLOGY AND PRAYER OF DEDICATION

HYMN   The King of Love My Shepherd is   *St. Columba*

The King of love my Shepherd is, whose goodness faileth never.
> I nothing lack if I am his and he is mine forever.

Where streams of living water flow my ransomed soul he leadeth,
> And where the verdant pastures grow, with food celestial feedeth.

Perverse and foolish oft I strayed, but yet in love he sought me,
> And on his shoulder gently laid, and home, rejoicing, brought me.

In death's dark vale I fear no ill with thee, dear Lord, beside me;
> Thy rod and staff my comfort still, they cross before to guide me.

Thou spread'st a table in my sight; thy unction grace bestoweth;
> And O what transport of delight from thy pure chalice floweth.

And so through all the length of days thy goodness faileth never;
> Good Shepherd, may I sing thy praise within thy house forever.[17]

BENEDICTION AND CHORAL RESPONSE

Amazing grace, how sweet the sound that saved a wretch like me;
I once was lost but now am found, was blind but now I see.

---

16. Courtney, *In My Father's House*, 2–7. Text: Pamela Martin.

17. McKim, *Presbyterian Hymnal*, 171, to the tune of *St. Columba*. Text: H. W. Baker on Psalm 23.

The prayers I make will then be sweet indeed,
If thou the Spirit give by which I pray:
My unassisted heart is barren clay,
Which of its native self can nothing feed:
Of good and pious works thou art the seed,
Which quickens only where thou say'st it may;
Unless thou show to us thine own true way,
No man can find it: Father! Thou must lead.
Do thou, then, breathe those thoughts into my mind
By which such virtue may in me be bred
That in thy holy footsteps I may tread;
The fetters of my tongue do thou unbind,
That I may have the power to sing of thee,
And sound thy praises everlastingly.[18]

Michelangelo Buonaroti

Matthew 22:36–40 + Revelation 12:10–12 (ESV)

One of them, a lawyer, asked him, "Teacher, which is the great commandment in the Law?" And he said to them, "You shall love the Lord your God with all your heart and with all your soul and with all your mind. This is the great and first commandment. And a second is like it: You shall love your neighbor as yourself. On these two commandments depend all the Law and Prophets." . . . And I heard a loud voice in heaven saying, "Now the salvation and the power and the kingdom of our God and the authority of his Christ have come, for the accuser of our brothers has been thrown down, who accuses them day and night before our God. And they have conquered him by the blood of the Lamb and by the word of their testimony, for they loved not their lives even unto death. Therefore, rejoice, O heavens and you who dwell in them. But woe to you, O earth and sea, for the devil has come down to you in great wrath, because he knows that his time is short!"

---

18. For this translation see Wordsworth, *Collected Poems of William Wordsworth*, 305. Cf. Linscott, *Complete Poems and Selected Letters*, 162. Also see Waddington, *Sonnets of Europe*, lines 3–19.

Big Idea

The love of God and neighbor fulfills all the commandments of God, who is at work putting all things to right while redeeming us and all his cherished creation.

The sermon was titled "The Day is Coming." It focused on our Lord's own articulation of God's greatest commandment, the coming redemption and recreation of all things, and the ultimate triumph of righteousness, justice, and light. It also happened to be the final Sunday with us of a beloved pastor who counted John Calvin, Karl Barth, Dietrich Bonhoeffer, and C. S. Lewis among key influences in his life.

For an opening hymn we chose "O Christ the Great Foundation" (a reworking of the more familiar "Christ is Made the Sure Foundation"). Originally in Chinese, it powerfully emphasizes God's sovereignty in the face of persecution and evil.

Sample Worship Service Four

CALL TO WORSHIP

HYMN   O Christ, the Great Foundation   *Aurelia*

O Christ, the great foundation on which your people stand
    To preach your true salvation in every age and land;
    Pour out your Holy Spirit to make us strong and pure,
    To keep the faith unbroken as long as worlds endure.

Baptized in one confession, one church in all the earth,
    We bear our Lord's impression: the sign of second birth.
    One holy people gathered in love beyond our own,
    By grace we were invited, by grace we make you known.

Where tyrants' hold is tightened, where strong devour the weak,
    Where innocents are frightened, the righteous fear to speak,
    There let your church awaking attack the powers of sin
    And, all their ramparts breaking, with you the victory win.

This is the moment glorious when he who once was dead
  Shall lead his church victorious, their champion and their head.
  The Lord of all creation his heav'nly kingdom brings,
  The final consummation, the glory of all things.[19]

PRAYER OF ADORATION

For a choral introit we chose John Rutter's setting of Lancelot Andrewes "Open Thou Mine Eyes" to reflect on the centering nature of God's commandments.

CHORAL INTROIT   Open Thou Mine Eyes   John Rutter

> Open thou mine eyes and I shall see, incline my heart and I shall desire. Order my steps and I shall walk in the way of thy commandments. O Lord God, be thou to me a God, and beside thee let there be none else, no other, naught else with thee. Vouchsafe to me to worship thee and serve thee according to thy commandments, in truth of spirit, in rev'rence of body, in blessing of lips, in private and in public.[20]—Lancelot Andrewes

We chose a prayer of confession by Calvin that emphasizes faithfulness to the end and everlasting life.

CONFESSION OF SIN

> Almighty God our heavenly Father, you have extended your tender love toward us sinners and have given us your Son, that believing in him we may have everlasting life. Forgive our manifold sins and strengthen us for righteous living. Grant us your Holy Spirit that we may continue steadfast in the faith to the end, and may come to everlasting life through Jesus Christ, your Son our Savior.[21]—John Calvin

19. Lew, "O Christ, the Great Foundation," 273. Removed in 2006 edition, but readily available in McKim, *Presbyterian Hymnal*, 443, and in Eicher, "O Christ, the Great Foundation," 361.

20. Andrewes, "Open Thou Mine Eyes," 71–72. Rutter, *Open Thou Mine Eyes*, 2–3.

21. Adapted from Collins, *2000 Years of Classic Christian Prayers*, 94.

Silent Confession and Assurance of Pardon

Congregational Response   *Gloria Patri*

Affirmation of Faith

Scripture   Matthew 22:36–40; Revelation 12:10–12

For an anthem we chose "How Can I Keep from Singing," a recent setting of an old gospel hymn text by Robert Lowery, to be a meditation on the ongoing and undeterred nature of God's kingdom in the face of evident evil.

Anthem   How Can I Keep from Singing?   Taylor Davis

My life flows on in endless song amidst earth's lamentations.
I hear the real, the far-off hymn that hails a new creation.
Through all the tumult and the strife I hear its music ringing.
It finds an echo in my soul: How can I keep from singing?
While though the tempest loudly roars, I hear the truth: it liveth;
And though the darkness round me close, songs in the night it giveth.
No storm can shake my inmost calm while to that Rock I'm clinging.
Since Christ is Lord of heav'n and earth, how can I keep from singing?
When tyrants tremble, sick with fear, and hear their death knell ringing,
When friends rejoice both far and near, how can I keep from singing?
In prison cell and dungeon vile, our thoughts to them are winging,
When friends by shame are undefiled, how can I keep from singing?[22]

For a hymn of response after the sermon we chose "By Gracious Powers So Wonderfully Sheltered." A recent translation of Bonhoeffer's poignant prison text, it emphasizes God's sovereign and recompensing hand in the midst of and beyond trials and suffering.

Sermon   The Day is Coming

Hymn of Response   By Gracious Powers   *O Perfect Love*

By gracious powers so wonderfully sheltered,
And confidently waiting, come what may,
We know that God is with us night and morning,

---

22. Davis, *How Can I Keep from Singing?*, 3–14. For a slightly altered text in hymn form, see Eicher, *Glory to God*, 821.

And never fails to greet us each new day.

Yet is this heart by its old foe tormented,
    Still, evil days bring burdens hard to bear;
    O give our frightened souls the sure salvation
    For which, O Lord, you taught us to prepare.

And when this cup you give is filled to brimming
    With bitter suff'ring hard to understand,
    We take it thankfully and without trembling
    Out of so good and so beloved a hand.

Yet when again in this same world you give us
    The joy we had, the brightness of your sun,
    We shall remember all the days we lived through,
    And our whole life shall then be yours alone.[23]

PASTORAL PRAYER AND THE LORD'S PRAYER

For the offertory we chose Richard Proulx's "O God, Beyond All Praising," a beautiful text also conveying a sense of God's sovereignty, ultimate victory, and our part in it.

OFFERTORY   O God Beyond All Praising   *Thaxted*

O God, beyond all praising, we worship you today
    And sing the love amazing that songs cannot repay;
For we can only wonder at ev'ry gift you send,
    At blessings without number and mercies without end.
We lift our hearts before you and wait upon your word,
    We honor and adore you, our great and mighty Lord.
The flow'r of earthly splendor in time must surely die,
    Its fragile bloom surrender to you, the Lord most high;
But hidden from all nature the eternal seed is sown—
    Through small in mortal stature, to heaven's garden grow:

---

23. McKim, *Presbyterial Hymnal*, 342, to "O Perfect Love." Text: Original German, D. Bonhoeffer. English translation, F. P. Green.

The depth of night is passing, the dawn is nearly come,
And nearer our salvation than when we first began;
So lay aside the works of deep darkness for the right,
*And let us then be girded with armor of the light:**

For Christ, the man from heaven, from death has set us free,
And we through him are given the final victory.

Then hear, O gracious Savior! Accept the love we bring
That we who know your favor may serve you as our King.
And whether our tomorrows be filled with good or ill,
We'll triumph through our sorrows and rise to bless you still:
To marvel at your beauty and glory in your ways,
And make a joyful duty our sacrifice of praise.[24]

DOXOLOGY

PRAYER OF DEDICATION

The final hymn was "O Lord, You are My God and King," a paraphrase of Psalm 145, emphasizing the inexorableness of God's coming kingdom.

HYMN   O Lord, You are My God and King   *Jerusalem*

O Lord, you are my God and King, and I will ever bless your name;
I will extol you every day, and evermore your praise proclaim.
You, Lord, are greatly to be praised, your greatness is beyond our thoughts;
All generations shall tell forth the mighty wonders you have wrought.

How rich in grace are you, O Lord, full of compassion, merciful,
Your anger always slow to rise; your steadfast love you show to all,
For you are good in all your ways, your creatures know your constant care.
To all your works your love extends, all souls your tender mercies share.

24. Proulx, *O God, Beyond All Praising*, to Holst's stirring tune, "Thaxted." Text: M. Perry, with possible alternative text M. Denham (see italicized text between asterisks*).

Your works will give you thanks, O Lord, your saints your mighty acts will show,
  Till all the peoples of the earth your kingdom, power, glory know.
  Eternal is your kingdom, Lord, forever strong, forever sure;
  While generations rise and die, your high dominion will endure.[25]

Benediction and Choral Amen

All these choices were made with an eye toward holy Scripture, but also to our congregation and its own worship proclivities and sense of ministry niche. It's important to remember that there really are no wrong answers or solutions in making these kinds of choices, except those that pay no attention to the biblical text, those that deal inaccurately with it, or those that discount it in favor of something else. Choices suggested here are offered primarily to spark interest in interacting with Scripture in and for worship. The next step is yours: making your own choices to heighten the expression, meaning, and impact of God's living word in expressive and powerful expositional worship.

25. McKim, *Presbyterian Hymnal*, 252. Text: *The Psalter*, 1912, alt. Music: C. H. H. Perry.

7

A View Ahead

The impact of all biblical worship follows solely the Holy Spirit's power to mediate, illuminate, and inculcate in us the life of God's Son through the message of God's written word.

WE BEGAN BY SAYING that a rich worship life is a commendable desire that insight and skill can fan. If we cannot give away something we don't possess, then we also will want to be impacted for God's glory and our own good by worship we plan and lead. For leaders it's not just a matter of Christian formation, it's also a matter of personal integrity.

In my earlier days of ministry, a well-meaning parishioner offered me what I immediately considered to be ill-conceived advice. He said, "In your job you don't have the luxury of being a worshiper. You're too busy leading the choir and the congregation." I do think what he meant was that there always are so many details to attend to that, if our focus falters, things might unravel. While it's true that commitment to anything close to excellence in ministry requires sustained attention to many details,[1] suggesting that they themselves are the desired end is like saying a ship's captain ultimately chooses his profession for reasons other than sheer love of the open sea. To arrive at an intended port he certainly must navigate rightly, but he always must keep in mind the big picture, and find joy in the journey itself.

---

1. See Jones and Armstrong, *Resurrecting Excellence*, 84.

Transforming Vision

Proverbs 29:18 says, "Where there is no vison the people perish." For those planning and leading worship that vision is revelation of the holy God of glory, and like Isaiah, if we ourselves are not undone by it, we have little to offer the people we purport to lead. This is why we seek a renewed, reformed, and ever being reformed personal perspective and practice of worship.

The defining and driving force for such perspective and practice is God revealed in holy Scripture. The richness of this revelation includes glimpses of God such as the majestic and sovereign king, loving and loyal Father, good and great shepherd, humble suffering servant, obedient paschal lamb, and comforting encouraging advocate. If these and other biblical pictures of God aren't part of our own perspective and practice, and aren't regularly appearing in the worship we plan and present, then we're aiming too low. That lack of vision will undernourish us, and could eventually cause us to falter.

At a recent men's breakfast, a colleague of mine offered some brief reflections on the book of Revelation that captured an essential emphasis, both of that letter, and tacitly of expositional worship: a sustained and transforming vision of Jesus Christ. According to the book's epistolary prologue, he is "the faithful witness, the firstborn from the dead, and ruler of the kings of the earth" (1:5). Reading Revelation can sometimes leave us lost in the weeds, as various schools of thought and interpretive models share a burden of proof to present a complete or comprehensive picture.[2] Yet from the beginning it's clear that our Lord's person and work are central to the letter's message, to our place and role in God's kingdom, and to history itself:

> To him who loves us and has freed us from our sins by his blood, and has made us a kingdom, priests to his God and Father, to him be glory and dominion forever and ever. Amen. Behold, he is coming with the clouds, and every eye will see him, even those who pierced him, and all the tribes of the earth will wail on account of him. Even so. Amen. "I am the Alpha and Omega," says the Lord, "who is and who was and who is to come, the Almighty." (1:5–8 ESV)[3]

---

2. For helpful comments about exposition, see Palmer, "Revelation," 89–99; Webster, *Follow*, 5–11.

3. See Wesley's great Second Advent hymn, "Jesus," McKim, *Presbyterian Hymnal*, 6.

Prevailing popular thoughts and comments about Revelation range widely, but tend to focus on things such as the apocalypse, judgment, Armageddon, and the end of the world. Less often do we hear hopeful comments about rejoicing in heaven, healing the nations, the river of life, and wiping away all tears. All of these elements and more are also integral to John's vision. The one overarching and centering thing that captures us is worship—unbounded, ceaseless worship.[4]

Worship is the corrective and antidote to the troubles and ills of the seven churches to whom John is writing: representative believers facing persecution, in danger of cultural assimilation, or mired and lost in complacency. True worship is indicative of real faith, deep love, and sincere obedience. All the exhortations and commands in this portion of the letter easily fit within it: "remember" (2:5; 3:3), "repent" (2:5, 16, 22; 3:3, 10), "be faithful" (1:10), "hold fast" (2:25; 3:11), "wake up" (3:2), and "he who has ears, let him hear what the Spirit says" (2:7, 11, 17, 29; 3:6, 13, 22). Every challenge facing the seven churches of Asia Minor—and us today—is placed, in the next portion of the letter, in proper perspective by a vision of God made known in Jesus Christ. If we're struggling under persecution or assault, look to Jesus. If we're diluted or falling away under cultural pressure, look to Jesus Christ. If we're apathetic or complacent about the truth or power of the faith, look to Jesus. That vision alone is the clarifying factor and catalyst we need.

Supernatural Resource

The impact of expositional worship must follow solely the Holy Spirit's power to mediate, illuminate, and inculcate in us the life of God's Son through the message of God's written word. Rejuvenated and reenergized commitment to that compelling spiritual process is our bedrock touchstone.

It's indeed a supernatural process to which God graciously calls us. Jesus didn't say, "Without me you can do more than you thought you could." He said, "Without me you can do nothing."[5] The God of the Bible is powerful and influential to speak to and act on behalf of those who acknowledge their need. We can trust the reverberating word of God in worship to move by the power of God's Spirit from inspired text, to proclaimed text, to transforming text, to commissioning text. We're not left alone to our own de-

---

4. See Revelation 4:1–11; 5:8–14; 11:15–17; 15:2–4; 19:1–8; 22:8–9.

5. John 15:5.

vices, but are part of God's sovereign and gracious purposes for ourselves, the church, and the world.

Team Effort

Implementing this week to week is predicated on good working relationships and interaction between pastors and any other worship planners and leaders. If a worship service as a whole is to be expositional to any degree, it must reflect the preacher's choice, correct understanding, and proclamation of the biblical text for the day. The possibility of expositional worship orbiting at least in part around that text presupposes that sufficient time for study and collegial interaction has been taken to enable and coordinate a consistent response to it. The potential impact of expositional worship decreases proportionally the less time and effort are spent in this inductive process. Yet, expositional worship doesn't call for rigid planning rules, but for a straightforward procedure that can ground and guide pastors and other planners in both biblical and creative ways.

I cannot emphasize this point strongly enough. If good communication and exchange of ideas is not occurring between the preaching pastor and supporting planners, a tremendous opportunity will have been missed, and worship will be impoverished. It doesn't matter whether a church is served by a solo pastor and a single song leader, or is blessed with resources of many talented and trained staff. Setting a clear goal and course informed by a mutual understanding of and orientation around a central biblical message, and planning together in advance, will reap great benefits.

There are occasional biases that can negatively impact this procedure. At a worship conference a number of years ago, a former pastoral colleague and I were asked to talk about how we planned worship. He told them how he typically went away for a week during the summer months to cap a year-long time of study by planning all the sermons he'd be preaching in the coming eleven months. By week's end he'd have chosen his biblical texts, his sermon titles, and some hymns, and he'd have have written a paragraph *précis* for each one of those projected sermons.

Someone asked him, "Doesn't the way you work leave little room for the Holy Spirit?" Amidst chuckles and some nervous laughter around the room, my colleague answered, "Good question, but might it not presuppose that the Holy Spirit can't also work through good planning?"

This allowed me opportunity as a supporting planner to emphasize how liberating such an approach was year in and year out. It offered decisive direction resulting from detailed exegetical, hermeneutical, and expositional spade work that would help guide the rest of us in planning, crafting, and implementing suitable and expressive worship services. It also helped relieve potential "tyranny of the moment" scrambling around by providing a well-conceived roadmap. This is keenly important to worship musicians, who need sufficient lead time (sometimes several weeks or longer) to prepare and rehearse whatever supporting and surrounding music is chosen. It was striking how little deviation from the plan was needed (or taken) in the course of any given year, and how timely and fitting the well-planned sermons and services ended up being.

Music as "Surround"

While we've not presented expositional worship solely or even primarily as a music of worship issue, music *in* worship is a crucial one. How music is conceived and what role it plays are vital issues. We don't mean every worshiper's opinion about it—we all have a right to our own thoughts—but rather the *guiding* view (if there is one) about music in any given congregation.

Language in our own denomination's book of order refers primarily to music as the voice of the congregation to God in prayer. It's certainly that. We cannot imagine anyone finding fault with such a notion:

> Prayer is the heart of worship. In prayer, through the Holy Spirit, people seek after and are found by the one true God who has been revealed in Jesus Christ. They listen and wait upon God, call God by name, remember God's gracious acts, and offer themselves to God. Prayer may be spoken, sung, offered in silence, or enacted. Prayer grows out of the center of a person's life in response to the Spirit. Prayer is shaped by the Word of God in Scripture and by the life of the community of faith. Prayer issues in commitment to join God's work in the world.[6]

This guidance is carefully conceived and communicated. Music is also described as another form of "proclamation."[7] Both of these characterizations are correct and helpful, and they may well resonate with views throughout the church, but one wonders if music is not more typically thought of as func-

6. General Assembly Directory, "W-2.1001," 87.
7. Ibid., "W-2.2008," 89.

tioning in isolation, rather than "in surround," reverberantly heightening proclamation, celebration, confession, sacrifice, and witness.

Many congregations are earnestly trying to define and decide what worship should mean in their own ministry niche. There are, of course, demographic, cultural, and theological factors uniquely coming to bear upon each. No church is exactly like another. Some have multiple worship services, and embrace a single, common approach or style of worship for each. The rationale is that congregational unity will be strengthened if parishioners share the ethos and environment of identical worship services, despite attending at different times. Others adopt a different model that embraces a variety of approaches or styles for different services predicated on the presumption of differing tastes and desires among worshipers. The rationale is that, in the interest of church growth and reaching currently unchurched or marginally-churched people, a variety of services is desirable and commendable. Our chief concerns are essentially neutral relative to different music vocabularies, and styles of varying services (to which, for the lack of better terminology, "contemporary" and "traditional" are too often applied).

My own interests and tastes for our discernibly traditional American congregation favor music that reflects the broad, historical sweep of repertoire as it has developed in Western culture and in the bosom of the church. Why? Even over time, we have limited and precious little opportunity to introduce to or remind worshipers of music sung and played by some in the great cloud of witnesses that has preceded us, as well as to incorporate significant musical worship voices from more recent times, and even our own day. This not only seems incumbent upon us, but it also helps guard us against myopia and insularity, as if Christian history began with our own generation. One is reminded of the aphorism often attributed to the great composer and conductor Gustav Mahler: "Tradition is not the worship of ashes, but the preservation of fire."[8] Whatever music finds greatest currency in any given congregation, our weightier concern here is that any and all musical vocabularies also serve biblically expositional communication ends.

Most vital is the concern that music not be confused with worship itself, as if worship were what happens only during various forms of congregational singing before the sermon. This simply is to misunderstand worship as much as it is to freight music with more responsibility than it

---

8. Mahler: "Tradition is not the worship," lines 1–4; for original German, *Tradition ist nicht die Anbetung der Asche, sondern die Weitergabe des Feuers*, see Mahler, "Tradition ist nicht die Anbetung," lines 1–2.

can bear. The Reformation rightly returned biblical proclamation to the heart of worship. Spectacle and ceremony were eschewed in favor of clear and systematic preaching. As our entertainment-oriented and image-driven culture augurs against this emphasis, preachers sometimes look warily at worship planners and musicians as interlopers. The way music is sometimes used in worship arguably can cross boundaries.[9] What too often is missed is that music does not have to compete with preaching when it effectively correlates with it. Music can well serve an expositional role in worship, but it requires considerable commitment and planning to help this happen. Otherwise we're potentially left with confusing the nature of music with its function, and perpetuating false and unnecessary dichotomies.

Authentic preaching is central to Christian worship, but its centrality is not threatened by a proper supporting and surrounding role for music through what is sung or played by the congregation or its representative ensembles or soloists. The need for the larger church is to find a positive and objective way to proceed. We believe that focusing on worship which intentionally exposits holy Scripture is that objective way.

Personality and Personhood

Another factor potentially coming to bear on us as we seek a positive, objective, and mutual way for worship, can be inferred from Susan Cain's insightful study of introversion.[10] She argues that, to our detriment, contemporary culture prevailingly equates extroversion with leadership, and that this has striking implications for ministry and worship. She offers balanced and irenic evidence of entities as different as Harvard Business School (HBS) and Saddleback Community Church in California being shaped and driven by this equation. Introverted personality traits, she observes, and leadership styles, and the kinds of organizations they foster, are generally less understood, valued, esteemed, or embraced.

While expositional worship is not chiefly concerned with this, it's noteworthy that Saddleback is viewed in some quarters as a model (perhaps even *the* model) to be admired and emulated. Without in the least calling into question that congregation's ministry motivation, vision, trajectory, or

9. Mistrust can flow both ways, as evidenced in treatments of the subject such as Guenther, *Rivals or a Team*, 10–18. For patterns in the early days of Reformed worship, see McKee, "Reformed Worship in the Sixteenth Century," 3–31.

10. Cain, *Quiet*, 64–70.

accomplishments, it's not unfair to delicately ask to what extent some of these might be predicated, less on biblical models, and more on the "extroversion equals leadership" equation even now being called into question by people like Cain. Nor is it uncharitable to wonder whether the impulse there (and other places) toward offering a variety of worship venues is less informed by St. Paul's comment "I have become all things to all people so that by all possible means I might save some,"[11] than merely by church growth marketing techniques that attract consumers to having their felt needs met.[12] Cain suggests that, in some ways, evangelicalism has taken the "Extrovert Ideal" to its "logical conclusion," having become "a religious culture viewing extroversion not only as a personality trait but also as an indicator of virtue." She writes,

> Righteous behavior is not so much the good we do behind closed doors when no one is there to praise us; it is what we "put out into the world" . . . Aggressive selling . . . is OK . . . because spreading helpful ideas is part of being a good person, and just as HBS expects its students to be good talkers because this is seen as a prerequisite of leadership, so have many evangelicals come to associate godliness with sociability."[13]

Not to put too fine a point on it, but commitment to biblical exposition-oriented methodologies of worship planning can help redefine and if necessary ameliorate the favoring or overindulgence of personality-based preferences or, worse, religious-flavored entertainment.

In worship, the medium must never be the message. The message is the message.[14] That message is powerful in its own historicity and its own spiritual vitality. It will validate itself. Whether or not we like it, and whether or not it makes us feel good, are immaterial. These may be byproducts of worship engaging us at the center of intellect, emotion, aesthetics, and will, but at its core, worship has a different purpose leading to God's glory and our good.

---

11. 1 Corinthians 9:22.

12. Barna, *America at the Crossroads,* 110, and *Grow Your Church,* 109; Cf. Webster, *Selling Jesus,* 74–93; Gallup and Lindsay, *Surveying the Religious Landscape,* 65–96; Nelson, "At Ease with Our Own Kind," 45–68; Spinks, *Worship Mall,* 63–89; and Atchinson, "Developing a Practice of Worship," 171–92.

13. Cain, *Quiet,* 70.

14. Cf. Postman, *Amusing Ourselves to Death,* 83.

In all of this, two qualifying disclaimers are likely in order. First, this investigation into expositional worship makes no claim to be a theology of music or of worship. Any such study would be more comprehensive in scope.[15] Our concerns here are more specific and limited. Second, lest anyone think that what expositional worship offers and emphasizes is too idealistic or overly narrow, we're more than aware that wide swaths of Christ's church today suffer under mounting pressure or even intense persecution, and that many Christians struggle daily in the face of poverty, political unrest, and even mortal dangers. They and their families are simply focused on survival (or martyrdom), and have little time to dwell on liberties or luxuries of theology and practice that safer, more stable environments afford. Yet even the vilest and most burdensome circumstances do not abrogate the divine ordination and acceptance of our praise, and every provision that sustains it.

One is reminded of the way that clandestine readings of Scripture spoke quietly but powerfully through the lives of Corrie ten Boom and her sister Betsie to their fellow prisoners in Ravensbruck, the wretched World War II Nazi extermination camp for women. Into the misery of that terrible and notorious crucible the word of God brought comfort and hope to many, and, even to those who would not survive, the rawest, most primal impetus to worship.

> It grew harder and harder . . . there was too much misery, too much seemingly pointless suffering. Every day something else failed to make sense, something else grew too heavy. *"Will you carry this, too, Lord Jesus?"* But as the rest of the world grew stranger, one thing became increasingly clear. And that was the reason the two of us were here. Why others should suffer we were not shown. As for us, from morning until lights-out, whenever we were not in ranks for roll call, our Bible was the center of an ever-widening circle of help and hope. Like waifs clustered around a blazing fire,

---

15. See Bateman, *Authentic Worship,* 23–52; Block, *For the Glory of God,* 1–27; Bradley, *From Memory to Imagination,* 31–47; Carson, *Worship by the Book,* 193–249; Chapell, *Christ-Centered Preaching,* 125–44; Duncan, "Foudations for Biblically Directed Worship," 51–73; Dyrness, *Primer on Christian Worship,* 1–16; Frame, *Worship in Spirit,* 1–13; Johnson, *Conviction of Things Not Seen,* 67–81; Johnson, *Worshipping with Calvin,* 44–46; Nelson, "Voicing God's Praise," 145–69; Peterson, *Engaging God,* 15–22; Ross, *Recalling the Hope of Glory,* 31–40; Ryken, *Give Praise to God,* 94–106; Smith, *Desiring the Kingdom,* 131–54; *Imagining the Kingdom,* 101–50. Also see Begbie, *Resounding Truth,* 211–76; Best, *Music through the Eyes of Faith,* 138–216; *Unceasing Worship,* 17–108; Aniol, *Worship in Song,* 173–221.

we gathered about it, holding out our hearts to its warmth and light. The blacker the night around us grew, the brighter and truer and more beautiful burned the word of God.[16]

After the war, ten Boom proclaimed widely her martyred sister's prison vision to bear witness that Jesus was the real victor in that concentration camp. "Tell people what we have learned here," Betsie had implored Corrie, "that there is no pit so deep that He is not deeper still."[17]

Nor are we unaware, in the face of striking evidence of cultural, demographic, and spiritual shifts, of obituaries being written for much of Christianity's influence and impact in America and the West. It's true that what has long been considered and depended on as solid ground is trembling beneath us.[18] Yet our Lord said, "I will build my church."[19] It's flourishing even now in fresh and powerful ways around the world, and God is being worshiped.

A life of Christian worship and service today is no less centering or rewarding than it ever has been, as we're reminded by Archbishop of Canterbury William Temple's widely admired definition:

> Worship is the submission of our nature to God. It is the quickening of conscience by His holiness; the nourishment of mind with His truth; the purifying of imagination by His beauty; the opening of the heart to His love; the surrender of will to His purpose—and all of this gathered up in adoration, the most selfless emotion of which our nature is capable and therefore the chief remedy for that self-centeredness which is our original sin and the source of all actual sin."[20]

Nor is it less challenging. Alternative voices have always intruded upon what the Bible purports to say that God says. Social and cultural forces have always impinged upon the message of the Gospel; but Jesus said that it would be upon the revelation that he is the Christ, the Son of the living God, and upon profession of faith in that revelation, that he would build his church to withstand even the greatest of counter forces.[21]

In his great work of religious satire, *The Screwtape Letters*, C. S. Lewis writes of spiritual warfare seen through the eyes of Screwtape and

---

16. ten Boom, *Hiding Place*, 206.

17. Ibid., 235.

18. Jones, *End of White Christian America*, 45–78.

19. Matthew 16:18.

20. Temple, *Readings in St. John's Gospel*, 68.

21. Matthew 16:15–18.

Wormwood, two conniving and sometimes comical minions of the Devil. By their pernicious bumbling Lewis cleverly stands everything on its head: Good is bad and bad is good. God is "the Enemy Above," while Satan is "Our Father Below." In one letter to his junior assistant, Screwtape effectively sums it all up:

> To us a human is primarily food; our aim is the absorption of its will into ours, the increase of our area of selfhood at its expense. But the obedience which the Enemy demands of men is quite a different thing. One must face the fact that all the talk about His love for men, and His service being perfect freedom, is not (as one would gladly believe) mere propaganda, but an appalling truth. He really *does* want to fill the universe with a lot of loathsome little replicas of Himself—creatures whose life, on its miniature scale, will be qualitatively like His own, not because he has absorbed them but because their wills freely conform to His. We want cattle who can finally become food; He wants servants who can finally become sons.[22]

This gracious adoptive process on God's part wonderfully complements what St. Paul appeals for on our part at the beginning of Romans 12: that we be living sacrifices freely offered as acts of spiritual worship. Offering ourselves wholeheartedly to God will appropriately follow what we've come to know and trust about God revealed in holy Scripture. Worship that clearly and winsomely conveys that revelation—portraying clear and consistent glimpses of the holy God of glory—will help make that choice even more compelling. Worship that intentionally heightens expression of what the Bible says about who God is and what God has done for us best points to that identity, security, and destiny that are integral to God's gracious plans for his children.

---

22. Lewis, *Screwtape Letters*, 38–39. Cf. Ephesians 1:5.

Conversation with Earl Palmer

EARL F. PALMER IS a longtime pastor-theologian-preacher-author in the Presbyterian Church.[1] He served just after seminary as Minister to Students at University Presbyterian Church (UPC) in Seattle, then for several years as Senior Pastor at the Union Church in Manila, Philippines, for many years as Senior Pastor of First Presbyterian Church, Berkeley, CA, and finally returning to Seattle for many years as Senior Pastor at UPC. Following his retirement and designated emeritus status there, he became minister-at large with Earl Palmer Ministries, where he serves to encourage and build others up in Christian faith. His first assignment in this international preaching, teaching, and writing ministry was as Preaching-Pastor-in-Residence at The National Presbyterian Church in Washington, DC. I first heard Earl preach while I was a college student. His influence on my life was immediate and has been sustained through my own thirty-five years in ministry.

MICHAEL DENHAM (MD): Earl, as we begin our conversation, would you please reflect on what you think expositional preaching and expositional worship are, and what they have to offer Christian worship.

EARL PALMER (EP): Exposition involves making content accessible; intellectual content and emotional content, though the latter isn't controllable. It's more subjective. Though there is a subjective element to intellectual content as well. Sometimes you have to win a hearing so that people are willing and ready to hear what you have to say. For example, there are hard

---

1. See Old, "A 'New Breed' of Presbyterians," 87–169. Palmer is cited as one of the twentieth century's most influential expositional preachers and Presbyterian communicators.

truths in a text that must be made accessible in a way that a person is able and willing to hear them. Think about judgment language. How can they be made willing to hear it? How can it be made accessible so that someone continues to listen, so that they don't just automatically start defending themselves against it and don't hear it?

The art of preaching expositionally involves bringing people along (nonconfrontationally). They may be thinking, "We don't particularly like to hear this. It's a hard statement. It's confusing, difficult." We don't like to hear it because it seems to be calling something, or us, into question, challenging us on some point or at some level. The expositor then faces a huge task in making difficult or hard texts accessible to people.

But this can also happen with softer texts, for example passages about love. The problem is people think they know what they mean when they say love. We think everybody knows what it means, but do they? Maybe the Bible has something more (or different, or better, or richer, or fuller) to say. So we also need to win a hearing for these kinds of texts and truths—good truths—to win a hearing by helping people to think of them in a way they may not have thought before.

For example, in 2 Timothy 1:8–10, Paul uses a kind of rare word choice where he urges Timothy to get involved in the hardship Paul is experiencing in the gospel. The NRSV says "suffering," but in the passage it's not the Greek word for suffering that's used. There's another word Paul would ordinarily use for that. Here, he uses a word for "hardship" (*sugkakopatheō*) as in enduring hardship together as soldiers. Get involved with me in the hardship of it. Don't be ashamed of me, and get involved in the hardship with me (not the suffering or agony).

As expositors this is something with which we can help people, making sure they know what the text is really saying. If they hear "suffering" they may well think one thing. If they hear "hardship" they will think another. Something goes through their mind . . . and we want to make sure it's the right thing, not an unnecessary thing. It's like a football player. He wants to get into the game. He's willing to endure its hardships. But the game's not easy. He's going to get scuffed up. This is what Paul is trying to convey. Get into and stay in the game and its hardships with me.

Rely on the power of God and his enabling and gifting. Remember, Paul had just said that God did not give Timothy a spirit of fear, but of power, of love, and a healthy mind. It's immediately after that reminder that he urges Timothy to get involved with him in the hardship of the gospel.

Rely on the power of God who saved us, and called us (not according to our own works [*erga*] but according to his purpose out of love and grace). It's actually God's love and grace that have called us into the hardship.

This grace (*charis*), this surprise "gift love," was given in Christ Jesus before the ages began. . .before I was even born. . .God decided before. . .but this whole provision has now been revealed. . .is now here and present . . . through the appearing of our Savior Christ Jesus. . .who *abolished* (NRSV) (*katargēsantos*) death, and brought life and immortality to light through the gospel. . .this word *abolished* likely at root actually means "made not workable" (*katargeō* . . . literally, *against*-work). Death is made inoperative, inoperable. It doesn't *work* anymore (See 2 Tim 1:10).

Remember, Paul wrote to Timothy at a time when persecution was intense. Nero was emperor. It was close to the time of the burning of Rome, when Christians were accused of setting the fires, and were thrown to the lions. Paul later said he himself had twice been spared from the lions, so we know that stresses were high all around. But also remember this grace was given to us in Christ Jesus, who *abolished* death. Paul's use of this word is rare, not quite but almost a *hapax legomenon* (something written only once). He uses it four times, but only one other time in the same way in 1 Corinthians 15 (25–26), where he says that Christ must reign until he has put all his enemies under his feet, and the last enemy to be *destroyed* (*katargeitai* from *katargeō*) is death.

In both cases, he does not use a more neutral "a-" prefix, but the stronger "kata-" (against). It's the same basic word in these two places, but translated differently in the NRSV and other translations. But at its root, death becomes inoperable. It's "*kata-erg*," against-work. It doesn't work anymore. I think that's a much more powerful point to preach than that it has been abrogated, abolished, or even destroyed.

The other two times Paul uses the word in any corollary way are in 1 Corinthians 13 (8–10), where he says, while love never *ends* (*piptō*), prophecy (and knowledge) become *inoperative* (*katargēthēsontai*). When everything is fulfilled, prophecies and knowledge become inoperative. They are unworkable. I frankly don't remember any commentators pointing this out.

What a great and humbling thing this is for prophets, and for prophetic movements that orient themselves around highly detailed and codified theological and historical schemes. We know this is true because Paul immediately says that we now know only in part and prophesy in part. But when the final, ultimate, perfect thing (*teleion*) comes, the thing in part will cease, or will not even be operable. Expositionally, the best thing we can say about our prophecies and knowledge is that they're never the whole story or the last word.

These passages may be more extreme examples of what we mean when we talk about helping to make accessible what Scripture is actually saying, but Paul is so precise, and so wise. Death has become inoperable because of Jesus Christ. It's real, but now because of him it doesn't work as it once did. So why should we be overly concerned about it? The last word belongs to Christ, the word that finally does become operative, the word that will endure. This is Paul's point to Timothy.

The challenge for expositors is to enable the hard words to become acceptable, and the good words to be understood as they're meant to be. C. S. Lewis said, "Tell me what the hard words mean and you've done more for me than a thousand commentaries." It seems to me that expositional preaching and therefore expositional worship are focused on the following questions: What do the words mean? How can I understand them? When I leave this worship service can they then become mine? Can I take them with me? For expositors, these are accessibility concerns.

Then, suppose an anthem, or hymn, or song, or some other component of a worship service helps make whatever that point is or those points are, for example, that the last word is Christ's, and it's the one that endures. This is where what you call the reverberation comes in. Knowledge becomes personal. Worshipers not only hear God's word, but they feel it. They can experience it, and act on it. If a truth can become accessible, that's the great goal.

As we've said, this also works with hard truths, on the judgment side of things. We have to be careful how we preach judgment passages, which can be so difficult and harsh. We can't dismiss them or dodge them, but we want to exposit them in such a way that worshipers can say, "I accept this because I know it's not the last word." The Judge has the last word, and he's good. He's loving. If he were only truth, we'd certainly be in trouble. But he's also good and loving.

The good news in the Sermon on the Mount is the teacher. The words of the sermon are so hard, so heavy. One might have to say, "Well, then, who can be saved?" But those words are from the same teacher who says, "Ask . . . seek . . . knock . . ." And it is he who ends the sermon with that comparison, "If you being evil know how to give good gifts to your children, how much more will your Father in heaven give good things to those who ask him!" (Matt 5:7–11).

Jesus reserves the last word for himself, and judgment passages have to be seen in this light. They must be resolved in view of the goodness and love of the Judge. If he were only true, then we could expect the worst, but he's also good and loving and gracious and merciful. This is where the worship experience can try to pull together these grand themes expositionally.

MD: Worship interfacing accurately and artfully with the proclaimed biblical text, and seeking to heighten its expression, can better communicate God's word and better convey a sense of its power to comfort, to confront, and to conform us to the Holy One who ordains our praise. We are thereby edified—built up in Christian faith. With respect to this enriching and maturing process, we receive apostolic advice in Colossians 3:16 where St. Paul writes, "Let the word of Christ dwell in you richly, teaching and admonishing one another in all wisdom, singing psalms and hymns and spiritual songs with thankfulness in your hearts to God." It's not surprising that the apostle characterizes this as a wise undertaking. The psalter itself begins by pointing to the wisdom of "delighting in the law of the Lord," and "meditating on it day and night" (Ps 1:1–3).

EP: I like how you tie together "dwelling richly" in Colossians 3 with the picture of a tree planted by rivers of water in Psalm 1. Believers are nurtured by Scripture—here in Psalm 1 it's the Torah—like a tree is nourished by abundant water through its root. But there is a concrete result to dwelling richly in God's word in worship. There is growth, maturity, fruitfulness, and benefit to others. The tree's leaves or fruit are not just for its own enjoyment, nor is the fruit of the Spirit intended only for personal benefit. If it were just the word of God dwelling richly in *me*, I would be in danger of missing the point that God means for his word dwelling richly in *us* to have good effect on others. We are not just to be enriched inwardly, but to outward benefit.

Think again of Timothy. As a young pastor he was facing pressures from outside and inside his congregation. Stresses from persecution of Christians under Nero were continuing unabated, and stresses brought on by false teachers among the body were encroaching and challenging. What was Paul's strategy for Timothy? He first reminds him that Jesus Christ is the faithful one (2:11–13). He knows his own (2:19).

Paul then counsels by way of a contrast. "Shun youthful passions and pursue righteousness, faith, love, and peace" (2:22). Later he writes, "Proclaim the message; be persistent whether the time is favorable or unfavorable; convince, rebuke, and encourage, with the utmost patience in teaching" (4:2).

When Paul speaks of "youthful passions" (*epithumias*), he's not concerned about Timothy's moral character, but self-control. In other words, don't be a youthful radical, with runaway zeal. This is evident because when Paul later (4:2) says teach with "utmost patience" (*makrothumia*), the contrast is clear. It's a play on words. And why should Timothy do this? Because, who knows? Through it God may bring some people to repentance (2:25). There may be stresses coming to bear from every direction, but don't sweat it. Just teach faithfully.

Right in the middle of this overall passage is 3:16, "All scripture is inspired by God and is useful for teaching, for reproof, for correction, and for training in righteousness, so that everyone who belongs to God may be proficient, equipped for every good work." In other words, don't get blown off course by quarrelsome arguing. Don't let your youthful zeal get the best of you. Keep a cool head. Do exposition. Fulfill your ministry. Trust Jesus Christ to know his own. Teach faithfully. Endeavor to make the gospel, the word of God, accessible. In the meantime, in teaching and in worship, we need to trust that God will validate himself, that truth will validate itself.[2]

MD: What a wonderful resting place that is! I do remember in one of your sermons on Luke 2 at National Presbyterian that you affirmed essentially the same thing. You were unpacking for us the song of the angelic host, "Glory to God in the highest, and on earth peace, goodwill to men." In it you said we see the gospel in a nutshell, the universal, eternal gospel that does not change, that is the result of God's "good decision" (*eudokias*) toward us, and that from that moment until now has become the basis and content of our Christian witness. Something, you reminded us, as Barth said, that a "mere four-year old" can grasp: "The world was lost. Christ has come. Rejoice!"

You reminded us that God gets the revelation of all this "just right" and you paraphrased Blaise Pascal from his *Pensées* when he said something like,

> A peasant might speak about wealth, but what does he know about wealth? A lawyer might speak about war, but what does he know about war? A scribe might speak about royalty, but what does he know about royalty? But a rich man can speak about wealth, and

---

2. For a more complete treatment of Paul's letter to his young friend, see Palmer, *To Run the Race*.

a king can speak indifferently about what it's like to be a king and to give a great kingly gift. God knows how to speak about God.[3]

He does it just right. As you say, God will validate himself.

EP: It may not be today. It may not be tomorrow. One worship service will never capture everyone. But, like Timothy, we're going to work hard, but wait it out. Take the long view (*makrothumia*), not the short one (*epithumia*). Don't let runaway desires to make it all happen today take over. Take time. Don't panic.

Obviously, it isn't a monastic solution that Paul is urging. He's not telling Timothy to withdraw. But he is advising him not to be deceived (3:13) by false teachers and teaching.

The word for deceiver (*planos*) comes from the Greek verb that means "to wander" or "lead astray." The Greeks didn't know what Copernicus knew, but they did recognize that some stars twinkled and some didn't. The ones that didn't twinkle, however, wandered. They moved across the sky. These were the planets, and the Greeks knew that if you tried to navigate by them at sea, you'd be lost. If you set your sights on Venus or Mars you wouldn't get where you wanted. John uses the same word in his first letter. "If we say we have no sin, we deceive ourselves" (*planaō*) (1:8). We're detoured. We're adrift. We're vectored. It's not the truth.

In a way, we have to help people who are adrift, who've vectored off course, who've lost their way. But we don't do this by condemning them. We help them by teaching through whatever the difficulty is, and showing them how material the Scriptures are. This is why Paul tells Timothy to hold fast to what he has learned, even from childhood: the sacred writings, that is, the text, the OT and by implication the NT. As Calvin emphasized, the OT by anticipation will always bring us to its living center Jesus Christ. The NT by witness will always bring us to its living center: Jesus Christ. The text is not a *planos* (planet). It's not a wandering star. It's a twinkling star. We can navigate safely and securely by it.

This is why Paul's advice to Timothy is so important, and so important to the thrust of what you're urging for worship: trust the text to bring the people to God, not the community, not the church. I love the church. I love its fellowship, but the church can be a *planos*. Remember what Karl Barth says, "The church moves through history in understanding and in

---

3. Cf. Pascal, "Theology & Philosophy," 236.

misunderstanding, in obedience and in disobedience, to the lofty good that has been given to it."[4] The text, the gospel, can still break through.

For example, in China you can still find the gospel in the officially sanctioned Three-Self Church, and you can find it in an unregistered church. Those who think that unaffiliated or unregistered churches are the only pure ones . . . Give me a break! Sin can be found in every one. There is no perfect church. The gospel can still break through anywhere. Remember, Bonhoeffer didn't want the confessing churches to leave the German church. They got kicked out, but they didn't leave. He wanted the young men to join the army. Even he joined the army for his own reasons. In the Finkenwalde School he did not urge his students to leave the German church. The German church was filled with error, but he wanted them to stay.

MD: The Barmen Declaration didn't encourage separation, did it?

EP: No. To stay faithfully, and to witness faithfully against the errors. This gets back to Paul and Timothy. Paul didn't tell Timothy not to teach, but to do so with a view to the long haul, not the quick trip.

MD: As I see it, this isn't just about faithful teaching against error, but faithful teaching over the long haul about the faith as a whole. If we live in a culture inured by instant gratification and intellectually truncated by sound-bite communication and, more importantly, if we embrace this as a normative methodology for how we do church, how we do worship, we're just tossing aside the expositional value you're talking about. If we use (misuse) worship for the sake of evangelism (or worse, for the sake of church growth), are we not susceptible to merely scratching felt or perceived-need itches? I'm not talking about being pedantic, or resisting fresh ideas or vocabularies. Nor am I talking about any particular style of worship.

EP: It could be relative to any style.

MD: Yes, it's more a matter of what those felt needs are perceived to be, and that they need to be instantly gratified. If this is what drives our methodology for preaching or worship planning, I think we're in serious trouble. I

---

4. Here Palmer paraphrases Barth's original: "The Christian Church lives on earth and it lives in history, with the lofty good entrusted to it by God. In the possession and administration of this lofty good it passes on its way through history, in strength and weakness, in faithfulness and in unfaithfulness, in obedience and in disobedience, in understanding and in misunderstanding of what is said to it." See also, Barth, *Dogmatics in Outline*, 10–11.

think we run a risk of getting to a point where, as Gertrude Stein pejoratively said of Oakland, "When you get there, there isn't any there, there."[5]

EP: What we really do have going for us—and some pastors don't realize it—is that we're here every week. It's back to taking the long view and teaching for the long haul. We made a real point of this during my years in Berkeley. Through all the days of student unrest, protests, and riots . . .

MD: . . . all the youthful zeal . . .

EP: . . . yes, we never closed shop at First Presbyterian Church. Unlike some other schools around the country, through it all Cal-Berkeley never lost a single day of instruction. Turmoil and tear gas may have been all around, some students may have been anywhere but in class, but we continued to show up at church. You know, there's something to that: to continue showing up for worship, showing up to teach, showing up to serve and care, to remaining faithful.

MD: It's like a ministry of presence.

EP: I remember your story about the Buddhist woman who came to faith after many conversations with you. You didn't pressure her with the gospel. You let it take effect. That just takes time.

When I was a young youth pastor in Seattle, there was a teenager who was a leader in our youth group. His father was a professor at the University of Washington. He was not a Christian, and was fairly arrogant about it, so the young man had little spiritual support at home. One day he came up to me and said, "You know, I don't believe all this stuff anymore, so I'm going to quit coming." Now, he liked me well enough. He wasn't mad at me. He was just honest enough to say what he thought, and that he felt like it would be hypocritical to stay. So he said goodbye. I was really sad. I figured we'd lost him. But we just kept doing what we could with the young people still there.

Fifteen or twenty years later I saw him one morning in the congregation in Berkeley. After worship he greeted me like a long-lost friend. Along the way, he'd earned a PhD in history, had been married, and had come to faith in Christ. He said something I'll never forget. "You know, Earl, I couldn't get away from Jesus Christ. If I dismissed him as an idea, he bothered me as a fact of history, as a person. If I dismissed him as a person, he bothered me as an idea."

---

5. Stein, *Everybody's Autobiography*, 289.

I can't really say I'd given him all these great truths, or mentored him, or spent a long time discipling him. But at least I'd introduced him to Jesus Christ. He didn't say, "Oh, your wonderful teaching on this or that always stuck with me." He just said, "When I dismissed Jesus as an idea or a person, he still haunted me."

So, yes, I believe we have to take the long view. In his final letter, it was a mature St. Paul who near the end of his life wasn't desperate or frantic. He just told Timothy, "Fulfill your ministry. God will show you." I like that. Arrogant teachers don't say that. They say, "I've shown you!" Not Paul. Now, he wasn't shy to say, "Timothy, you've learned some important things from me, by watching me." After all, the young man was from Lystra. Paul had been pretty well beaten up there. Timothy knew that, as well as Paul's steadiness and faithfulness. So, after fifty-five years of ministry, the more I like this model, this day-to-day, week-to-week steadiness and faithfulness.

MD: Let's shift direction a bit. What about the so-called "New Homiletic?" As I understand it, it's related to a sense of preaching only as shared story. Might it involve suspicion about objective (much less propositional) truth being contained in the biblical witness? We can only trust our own sense about it, what we think about it, or what we share in it. If this is so, it seems to me that an objective ground of reality and authority is lost, or at least has shifted, or is elusive. The best a preacher can hope to do is preach in a way that everyone can recognize their own story in what's being said, and share in it with others.

EP: While helpful in other ways, some aspects of critical scholarship contribute to this mistrust by suggesting that the message of the text shouldn't be taken at face value, or that what it purports to mean is not appropriate for us today because it was framed at a time when the church just needed to teach about one thing or another, and came up with a helpful story.

For example, think of Bultmann's conjectures[6] about John's gospel account of Jesus' first miracle turning water to wine at a wedding in Galilee. He suggests that the early church needed to validate the practice of the Lord's Supper, or that it needed to counter views at the time about wine and Greek gods, to offer some sort of Christian response or reinterpretation. So this water to wine story was concocted. This so affects the way we read this passage! It's form criticism gone crazy. When they ask, "What was the setting in the church that generated this story?" then say, "Oh the water

6. Bultmann, *Gospel of John*, 118.

to wine story obviously justifies the Lord's Supper." Give me a break! That miracle baffled everyone at Cana in John's account just as much as everyone since. This kind of approach eviscerates preaching. How can you take the text seriously? You can't preach on that.

Or, for example, Dibelius suggests,[7] that certain second- or third-century pseudo-Pauline authors wrote in 2 Timothy about Lois and Eunice, Timothy's supposed grandmother and mother, in order somehow to show the importance of the church's role in cultivating the faith of young Christians. These women are written off as mere fabrications. These supposed Jewish mothers and their care for Timothy are only acknowledgements that the church has Jewish roots. So an elaborate handling of Lois and Eunice as symbols of this Jewish root system is concocted.

Now, you're a preacher and are supposed to preach this? I'm glad for more recent scholars like Luke Timothy Johnson, who've basically said, "No, this isn't what happened. This makes no sense at all. This is just silliness. The letter was written by St. Paul about real people." Of course, this is my own view.

Or think of how Helmut Thielicke, in his theological ethics, contrasts Paul Tillich and Karl Barth. Tillich raises his "correlation questions" and goes to the so-called "Easter Faith" of the church for answers. Barth, on the other hand, starts with the text then moves to the world. Then the collisions occur. For example, the Barmen Declaration, which he largely wrote, doesn't even mention Nazism or the Aryan Paragraph. But it moves indirectly to and collides with the premises behind them to state the faith of the confessing church in World War II Germany.

Thielicke calls this the biblical theological model of Barth versus the theoretical speculative model of Tillich. Guess which one of these theologians has been more durable? Tillich is so stylized, so stuck in a certain frame of reference. It didn't ring true to begin with, and still doesn't ring true. James McCord, who was president of Princeton Seminary, said, "Today's relevance is tomorrow's irrelevance."

Where Tillich begs the question, as do some modern approaches to preaching, is in the essential method, that more or less says, "I get to ask the questions. I only ask the questions to which I want answers." This amounts to controlling the story. Compare Paul as we've already seen in 1 Corinthians 15. He essentially is saying, "No, there is a concrete truth. We may prophesy, but our word is not final."

7. Dibelius and Conzelmann, *Pastoral Epistles*, 98.

MD: Modesty before the text is not the same thing as mistrust of the text.

EP: Yes, that's exactly right. Remember how, in an earlier conversation, we made a distinction between "revelation" and "experience." Revelation moves *downward*, if you will, from God to us. Experience moves *upward*, from us to God. The latter never controls the former. This is where the modesty and humility enter in.

I remember in my own seminary days at Princeton, each year we had some sort of theological colloquium for students who were nearing the end of their training there. My last year, we had an opportunity to interact with Hans Hoffman[8] specifically over the question, "What is a Christian?"

Several perspectives were evident in the various answers given. Those in a more evangelical camp tended to say one sort of thing. Those holding more liberal positions tended to say other sorts of things. I posed the question, "Is a Christian a Christian only when he is awake? Does he cease to be a Christian when he is asleep?" In other words, is there anything about a Christian and Christianity that remains essentially (even propositionally) true at all times? Is there something about revelation that remains true whether or not I experience it or affirm it? For example, is the statement "Jesus is Lord" true only if I affirm or experience it, or is it propositionally true even if I don't or if I'm asleep? I think this may be getting at what you're asking about the "New Homiletic."

MD: Influences such as demand for story in narrative preaching, doctrinal relativism, and therapeutic concerns of western culture seem to have shifted us away from starting with the biblical text, toward beginning with modern questions and concerns, then working backward to Scripture. There seems to be a notion this is actually what gives the biblical message meaning. Any comment?

EP: Only a small one. I think it's important to maintain for preaching and its effect the same freedom that our Lord maintained for himself and those who listened to him. This is summarized in his familiar statement, "Let those who have ears to hear, hear" (Matt 11:15; 13:9, 43; Luke 8:8; 14:35). With Jesus there was always freedom for the listener to consider what he was saying to them. He preserved that for them, and he preserves this for us. He invites. He does not impose. Preachers don't preach with

---

8. Hoffman served on the faculties of Princeton Theological Seminary and Harvard Divinity School. He is the author of *Theology of Reinhold Niebuhr* (New York: Scribner, 1956).

authority so people will obey, but so they will consider. Scripture is true, authoritative, and good, but it invites people to attend to it. It's no different in Deuteronomy 6:4 in the great Shema, "Hear, O Israel . . ." Of course God is calling them to obey, but because they have seen his mighty acts and loyal love in action. It's not obedience out of a vacuum. It's a reasonable thing they're being called or even commanded to do, but not without due consideration. St. Paul speaks similarly in Philippians 2:12, "Therefore, my beloved, just as you have always obeyed me, not only in my presence, but now much more in my absence . . ." Here, "obey" is better translated "listen to" (*hupēkousate*). The element of careful consideration before response is inherent.

Human agency is never cancelled. Paul (or Moses, for that matter) is not an authoritarian. There's a wonderful freedom in the gospel. This doesn't take away certitude or authority, but it calls people to consider and freely believe. It's like Billy Graham saying, "You're in the hour of decision, and you can decide to come."

MD: Let's chat briefly about music relative to preaching and worship. We agree that authentic preaching of God's word is and should be central to Christian worship. I would like to add that preaching's central role is not threatened by a proper supporting, heightening role for music. I also would like to add that this seemingly utilitarian function is not the only role for music in worship. Music is not valuable only as it helps convey meaning and power of a biblical text (though this can be and is a key role). What about untexted music, or music that makes no allusion (in a programmatic way) to a tacitly understood biblical text or hymn text? Is there value for worship in music offered abstractly as its own language, as its own expression? My own sense is that this is where the biblical theology of a "sacrifice of praise" comes to bear. These of course are important questions to consider. Jeremy Begbie has recently done wonderful work in the area of music as a paradigm for actually doing theology.[9]

All of this gets to the meat of the distinction between making what some refer to as "Christian music," in contrast simply to Christians making music. Music that is well contextualized in Christian worship—either by heightening the spoken and proclaimed word, or by being offered to God as its own discreet expression—has a higher chance of being perceived as authentic.

9. Begbie and Guthrie, *Resonant Witness*, 83–108.

EP: Young people today do seem to be more attuned to factors of authenticity than I remember from my younger years. Their radar just seems to be more sensitive to it. If something doesn't feel authentic they automatically devalue it.

This is not to denigrate technology *per se*, but "slick" has got to be really good not to become offensive. Even something as innocuous as PowerPoint can be intrusive. Some speakers and preachers use it and other technologies ostensibly to reinforce communication, but I'm not so sure it always aids in ways they hope, or even helps get or keep people's attention. Such things can put a buffer or barrier between speaker and audience. The argument that multi-sensory presentation heightens communication may carry some weight, but it also can simply lead to sensory overload. In public speaking or preaching it can derail any expectation or onus of imagination on the part of sermon-hearers. Despite this, the human mind is still enormously capable of imagination.

MD: First and foremost, is a biblical vision of God our focus in worship today? Does our worship help make clearer who God is? Does our pattern of worship testify to the character of God? Would our worship offer a visiting observer a consistent portrayal of the God of the Bible? Would we or that visitor recognize our need to respond to God's initiatives in our lives, or are we so focused on how we worship that we have forgotten who we worship?

EP: Helpful distinctions.

MD: Earl is there anything you'd like to reiterate or add to our conversation?

EP: Well, for us to remember that worship always has two aspects: a downward, revelatory one, and an upward, experiential and responsive one. Revelation always informs experience, and not the other way around, but we continually do need to ask ourselves as leaders how to better connect with people, to be in tune with what draws them to worship in the first place. What made you want to believe, to trust in the trustworthiness of Christ? What makes you want to worship, to grow, to serve? How does worship address and help fulfill these goals?

Part of a pastor's opportunity (responsibility) is to get to know parishioners' "journey stories," their joys and concerns, their challenges and fears—what's happening to them and around them inside and outside of church. The best teachers all believe that their students won't survive in the world without learning their subject matter. It's that important to them.

Would that preachers consistently thought the same way about the Bible! That what it says is so vitally important. But beyond this, we must trust its power to validate itself. We don't have to do that for it. Over time, the text will do that for itself, as will the Lord of the text, God's Living Word. We don't need to tamper with the freedom of the listener. We need to offer the Scriptures a chance to make their mark. In the end, we preachers and worship planners must ask if we ourselves are meek, that is, teachable, before the text. If we are, our congregations stand a much higher chance of becoming the same way.

Bibliography

Abba, Raymond. *Principles of Christian Worship*. New York: Oxford University Press, 1957.

Abbington, James, ed. *Readings in African American Church Music and Worship*, Vol. 1. Chicago: GIA, 2009.

———. *Readings in African American Church Music and Worship*, Vol. 2. Chicago: GIA, 2014.

Abraham, Gerald. *The Concise Oxford History of Music*. New York: Oxford University Press, 1979.

Achtemeier, Elizabeth. *Preaching from the Old Testament*. Louisville: Westminster John Knox, 1989.

———. *Preaching Hard Texts of the Old Testament*. Peabody, MA: Hendrickson, 1998.

Adam, P. J. H. "The Relationship of Biblical Theology and Preaching." In *New Dictionary of Biblical Theology*, edited by Desmond Alexander et al., 104–8. Downers Grove, IL: InterVarsity, 2000.

Adams, Doug. *Meeting House to Camp Meeting: Toward a History of American Free Church Worship*. Austin: Sharing, 1981.

Adler, Samuel. "Sacred Music in a Secular Age." In *Sacred Sound and Social Change: Liturgical Music in Jewish and Christian Experience*, edited by Lawrence A. Hoffman and John R. Walton, 289–99. South Bend, IN: Notre Dame University Press, 1992.

Akin, Daniel L. *A Theology for the Church*. Rev. ed. Nashville: B&H Academic, 2014.

Akin, Daniel L., et al. *Engaging Exposition*. Nashville: B&H, 2011.

Akin, Daniel L., et al., eds. *Text-Driven Preaching: God's Word at the Heart of Every Sermon*. Nashville: B&H, 2010.

Alexander, T. Desmond, and Brian S. Rosner. *New Dictionary of Biblical Theology*. Downers Grove, IL: InterVarsity, 2000.

Allen, Leslie C. "Zākhar." In *New International Dictionary of the Old Testament*, Vol. 1, edited by Willem A. Vangemeren, 1100–6. Grand Rapids: Zondervan, 1997.

Allen, Ronald J. *Contemporary Biblical Interpretation for Preaching*. Valley Forge, PA: Judson, 1984.

———. *Preaching is Believing: The Sermon as Theological Reflection*. Louisville: Westminster John Knox, 2002.

———. "Shaping Sermons by the Language of the Text." In *Preaching Biblically: Creating Sermons in the Shape of Scripture*, edited by Don M. Wardlaw, 29–59. Philadelphia: Westminster, 1983.

Allen, Ronald J., and Gilbert L. Bartholomew. *Preaching Verse by Verse*. Louisville: Westminster John Knox, 2000.

Allen, Ronald J., and Gordon Borror. *Worship: Rediscovering the Missing Jewel*. Portland: Multnomah, 1982.

Allen, Ronald J., and Thomas J. Herin. "Moving from the Story to Our Story." In *Preaching the Story*, edited by Edmund A. Steimle, et al., 151–61. Philadelphia: Fortress, 1980.

Alter, Robert. *The Art of Biblical Narrative*. 2nd ed. New York: Basic, 2011.

———. *The World of Biblical Literature*. New York: Basic, 1992.

Anderson, Bernard W. *Out of the Depths: The Psalms Speak for Us Today*. Philadelphia: Westminster, 1983.

———. *Understanding the Old Testament*. 4th ed. Englewood Cliffs, NJ: Prentice-Hall, 1986.

Anderson, Kenton C. *Preaching with Integrity*. Grand Rapids: Kregel Academic, 2003.

Anderson, Marvin. "John Calvin: Biblical Preacher (1539–1564)." *Scottish Journal of Theology* 42 (1989) 167–81.

Andreason, Niels-Erik A. *The Old Testament Sabbath: A Traditional-Historical Investigation*. Society of Biblical Literature Series 7. Missoula, MT: Society of Biblical Literature, 1972.

Andrewes, Lancelot. "Open Thou Mine Eyes." In *Private Devotions*, edited by Alexander Whyte, 71–2. Reprint. Nashotah, WI: Nashotah House, 2012.

Aniol, Scott. *Sound Worship: A Guide to Making Musical Choices in a Noisy World*. Simpsonville, SC: Religious Affections, 2010.

——— *Worship in Song: A Biblical Approach to Music and Worship*. Winona Lake, IN: BMH, 2009.

Apostolos-Cappadona, Diane, ed. *Art, Creativity, and the Sacred: An Anthology in Religion and Art*. Rev. ed. New York: Continuum, 1995.

Appleby, David P. "Our Changing Music: Early Expressions of Faith." *Decision* 37 (July 1996) 10–12.

Arnold, Jonathan. *Sacred Music in Secular Society*. Farnham, UK: Ashgate, 2014.

Arnold, Richard. *The English Hymn: Studies in a Genre*. New York: Lang, 1995.

Arzola, Fernando Jr. *Exploring Worship: Catholic, Evangelical, and Orthodox Perspectives*. Eugene, OR: Wipf & Stock, 2011.

Atchinson, Thomas. "Developing a Practice of Worship that Unites." In *Authentic Worship: Hearing Scripture's Voice, Applying its Truths*, edited by Herbert Bateman, 171–92. Grand Rapids: Kregel, 2002.

Awbrey, Ben E. "A Critical Examination of the Theory and Practice of John F. MacArthur's Expository Preaching." ThD diss., New Orleans Baptist Theological Seminary, 1990.

Ayer, William W. "The Art of Effective Preaching." *Bibliotheca Sacra* 124 (January–March 1967) 30–41.

Bacchiocchi, Samuele. *From Sabbath to Sunday: A Historical Investigation of the Rise of Sunday Observance in Early Christianity*. Rome: Pontifical Gregorian University, 1977.

Bailey, Albert E. *Choral Music: A Research and Information Guide*. New York: Routledge, 2002.

———. *The Gospel in Hymns*. New York: Scribner's, 1950.

Bailey, E. K., and Warren W. Wiersbe. *Preaching in Black and White*. Grand Rapids: Zondervan, 2003.

Bailey, Ivor. "The Challenge of Change: A Study of Relevance Versus Authority in the Victorian Pulpit." *Expository Times* 86 (1974) 18–22.

Bainton, George, ed. *The Art of Authorship: Literary Reminiscences, Methods of Work, and Advice to Young Beginners, Personally Contributed by Leading Authors of the Day.* New York: D. Appleton, 1890.

Baird, Charles. *Presbyterian Liturgies.* 1855. Reprint, Grand Rapids: Baker, 1957.

Baird, J. S. "Preaching in the Bible." In *Evangelical Dictionary of Theology,* 2nd ed., edited by Walter A. Elwell, 948–49. Grand Rapids: Baker Academic, 2001.

Balmer, Randall. *Mine Eyes Have Seen the Glory: A Journey into the Evangelical Subculture in America.* Rev. ed. New York: Oxford University Press, 2014.

———. Review of *Religious Literacy: What Every American Needs to Know—And Doesn't,* by Stephen Prothero. *Washington Monthly* (May 2007) 66–67.

Balmer, Randall, and John R. Fitzmeier. *The Presbyterians.* Westport, CT: Praeger, 1994.

Balthasar, Hans Urs von. *The Glory of the Lord: A Theological Aesthetics.* Vol. 1. Translated by Erasmo Leiva-Merikaksi. Edinburgh: Ignatius, 1982.

Barclay, William. "A Comparison of Paul's Missionary Preaching and Preaching to the Church." In *Apostolic History and the Gospels: Biblical and Historical Essays Presented to F. F. Bruce,* edited by W. Ward Gasque and Ralph P. Martin, 165–75. Grand Rapids: Eerdmans, 1970.

Barker, William S., and Samuel T. Logan, eds. *Sermons that Shaped America: Reformed Preaching from 1630–2001.* Phillipsburg, NJ: P&R, 2003.

Barlow, Jerry A. "Timely Preaching—Timely Worship." http://www.preaching.com/resources/pastissues/11549330/.

Barna, George. *America at the Crossroads: Explosive Trends Shaping America's Future.* Grand Rapids: Baker, 2016.

———. *Grow Your Church from the Inside Out: The Unchurched and How to Reach Them.* Ventura, CA: Regal, 2002.

Barnes, M. Craig. *Body & Soul: Reclaiming the Heidelberg Catechism.* Grand Rapids: Faith Alive, 2012.

———. "Doubtful Disciples." *Theology Matters* 5, (July/August 1999) 7–9.

———. *The Pastor as Minor Poet: Texts and Subtexts of the Ministerial Life.* Grand Rapids: Eerdmans, 2009.

———. "Proclaiming the Word: Voice in the Wilderness." In *What Is Christian Worship?,* edited by Mary Holder Naegeli, 17–21. Louisville: Presbyterians for Renewal, 2000.

Barnhouse, Donald G. *Teaching the Word of Truth.* Grand Rapids: Eerdmans, 1940.

Barth, Karl. *The Christian Life.* Translated by Geoffrey W. Bromiley. Grand Rapids: Eerdmans, 1981.

———. *Church Dogmatics.* Translated by G. W. Bromiley. Edited by G. W. Bromiley and T. F. Torrance, 1936. Reprint, Edinburgh: T. & T. Clark, 1975.

———. *Dogmatics in Outline.* Translated by G. T. Thomson. New York: Harper Perennial, 1959.

———. *Homiletics.* Translated by Geoffrey W. Bromiley and Donald E. Daniels. Louisville: Westminster John Knox, 1991.

———. *The Preaching of the Gospel.* Translated by B. E. Hooke. Philadelphia: Westminster, 1963.

———. *The Word of God and the Word of Man.* Translated by Douglas Horton. New York: Harper & Row, 1957.

Bartholemew, Craig G., and Michael W. Goheen. *The Drama of Scripture: Finding Our Place in the Biblical Story*. 2nd ed. Grand Rapids: Baker Academic, 2014.

Bartow, Charles L. *God's Human Speech: A Practical Theology of Proclamation*. Grand Rapids: Eerdmans, 1997.

Basden, Paul A, ed. *Six Views on Exploring the Worship Spectrum*. Grand Rapids: Zondervan, 2004.

———. *The Worship Maze: Finding a Style to Fit Your Church*. Downers Grove, IL: InterVarsity, 1999.

Bateman, Christian Henry. "Come, Christians, Join to Sing." In *The Presbyterian Hymnal*, edited by LindaJo McKim, 150. Louisville: Westminster John Knox, 1990.

Bateman, Herbert, IV. *Authentic Worship: Hearing Scripture's Voice, Applying Its Truth*. Grand Rapids: Kregel Academic & Professional, 2002.

Battles, Ford Lewis. "God was Accommodating Himself to Human Capacity." *Interpretation* 31 (1997) 19–38.

———. *The Piety of John Calvin: An Anthology Illustrative of the Spirituality of the Reformer*. Grand Rapids: Baker, 1978.

Bauckham, R. J. "The Lord's Day." In *From Sabbath to Lord's Day*, edited by D. A. Carson, 221–50. Grand Rapids: Zondervan, 1982.

Bauer, David R., and Robert A. Traina. *Inductive Bible Study: A Comprehensive Guide to The Practice of Hermeneutics*. Grand Rapids: Baker Academic, 2011.

Bauer, Walter, et al. *A Greek-English Lexicon of the New Testament and Other Christian Literature*. 2nd ed. Chicago: University of Chicago Press, 1979.

Bayly, Albert F. "When the Morning Stars Together." In *The Presbyterian Hymnal*, edited by LindJo McKim, 486. Louisville: Westminster John Knox, 1990.

Bean, Lydia. *The Politics of Evangelical Identity: Local Churches and Partisan Divides in the United States and Canada*. Princeton, NJ: Princeton University Press, 2014.

Begbie, Jeremy S. *Resounding Truth: Christian Wisdom in the World of Music*. Grand Rapids: Baker, 2007.

———. "Theology and the Arts: Music." In *The Modern Theologians: An Introduction to Christian Theology in the Twentieth Century*, edited by David F. Ford, 686–99. Oxford: Blackwell, 1997.

———. *Theology, Music and Time*. Cambridge: Cambridge University Press, 2000.

Begbie, Jeremy S., ed. *Beholding the Glory: Incarnation through the Arts*. Grand Rapids: Baker, 2001.

Begbie, Jeremy S., and Steven R. Guthrie, eds. *Resonant Witness: Conversations Between Music and Theology*. Grand Rapids: Eerdmans, 2011.

Begg, Alistair. *Preaching for God's Glory*. Wheaton, IL: Crossway, 2010.

Bell, John L. *The Singing Thing: A Case for Congregational Song*. Chicago: GIA, 2000.

Bem, Kazimirez. "Christianity Cannot Survive the Decline in Worship." http://www.faithstreet.com/onfaith/2015/01/23/2015/christianity-cannot-survive-the-decline-in-worship/35932.

Benson, Luis F. *The English Hymn: Its Development and Use in Worship*. New York: Hodder and Stoughton, 1913.

———. "John Calvin and the Psalmody of the Reformed Churches." *Journal of the Presbyterian Historical Society* 5 (1909) 55–87.

Benedict, Daniel T., Jr. *Patterned by Grace: How Liturgy Shapes Us*. Nashville: Upper Room, 2007.

Benko, Stephen. *Pagan Rome and the Early Christians.* Bloomington, IN: Indiana University Press, 1984.

Berglund, Brad. *Reinventing Sunday: Breakthrough Ideas for Transforming Worship.* Valley Forge, PA: Judson, 2001.

Berkhof, Louis. *A History of Christian Doctrines.* Grand Rapids: Baker, 1937.

Best, Harold M. "Music: Offerings of Creativity, An Interview with Harold Best." *Christianity Today* 21.15 (May 6, 1977) 12–15.

———. *Music through the Eyes of Faith.* New York: HarperCollins, 1993.

———. "A Stirring Charge." *Theology, News and Notes* 52 (2006) 4–5.

———. *Unceasing Worship: Biblical Perspectives on Worship and the Arts.* Downers Grove, IL: InterVarsity, 2003.

Bird, Bryan. "Biblical Exposition: Becoming a Lost Art?" *Christianity Today* 30.7 (April 18, 1986) 34–37.

Bisgrove, Mildred E. "Sacred Choral Music in the Calvinist Tradition of the Protestant Reformation in Switzerland and France from 1541–1600." PhD diss., New York University, 1969.

Bishop, Selma L. *Isaac Watts Hymns and Spiritual Songs (1707).* Ann Arbor, MI: Pierian, 1974.

Black, Barry C. "Persuasive Preaching." *Ministry Magazine* 79 (2006) 6–8.

Black, Kathy. *Worship Across Cultures.* Nashville: Abingdon, 1998.

Blackwell, Albert L. *The Sacred in Music.* Louisville: Westminster John Knox, 1999.

Blaising, Craig, and Carmen S. Hardin, eds. "Psalms 1–50." In *Ancient Christian Commentary on Scripture,* Vol. 7, edited by Thomas C. Oden, 384–92. Downers Grove, IL: IVP Academic, 2008.

Block, Daniel I. *For the Glory of God: Recovering a Biblical Theology of Worship.* Grand Rapids: Baker Academic, 2014.

Blocker, Robert. "Preaching the Gospel (of the Arts)." In *The Robert Shaw Reader,* edited by Robert Blocker, 335–411. New Haven: Yale University Press, 2004.

Bloesch, Donald G. *Essentials of Evangelical Theology.* Peabody, MA: Hendrickson, 1998.

Blomberg, Craig L. *Preaching the Parables: From Responsible Interpretation to Powerful Proclamation.* Grand Rapids: Baker Academic, 2004.

Bloom, Allan. *The Closing of the American Mind: How Higher Education has Failed Democracy and Impoverished the Souls of Today's Students.* New York: Simon and Schuster, 1987.

Blume, Friedrich. *Protestant Church Music: A History.* New York: Norton, 1974.

———. *Renaissance and Baroque Music: A Comprehensive Survey.* New York: Norton, 1967.

Boa, Kenneth D. "What is Behind Morality?" *Bibliotheca Sacra* 133 (1976) 153–64.

Bobrick, Benson. *Wide as the Waters: The Story of the English Bible and the Revolution It Inspired.* New York: Penguin, 2001.

Bock, Darrell L., and Buist M. Fanning III. *Interpreting the New Testament Text: Introduction to the Art and Science of Biblical Exegesis.* Wheaton, IL: Crossway, 2006.

Boice, James Montgomery. *Foundations of the Christian Faith: A Comprehensive and Readable Theology.* Downers Grove, IL: InterVarsity, 1986.

Bonhoeffer, Dietrich. *Christ the Center.* New York: Harper & Row, 1978.

———. *Psalms: The Prayer Book of the Bible.* Minneapolis: Augsburg, 1970.

———. *Worldly Preaching.* 2nd ed. Translated by Clyde E. Fant. New York: Crossroad, 1991.

Borden, Paul. "Is there Really One Big Idea?" In *The Big Idea of Biblical Preaching*, edited by Keith Wilhite and Scott M. Gibson, 67–80. Grand Rapids: Baker, 1998.

Borgen, Ole E. *John Wesley on the Sacraments: A Definitive Study of John Wesley's Theology of Worship*. Grand Rapids: Zondervan, 1972.

Bousma, William J. "Calvinism as Renaissance Artifact." In *John Calvin & the Church: Prism of Reform*, edited by Timothy George, 28–41. Louisville: Westminster John Knox, 1990.

———. *John Calvin: A Sixteenth Century Portrait*. New York: Oxford University Press, 1988.

Bower, Peter C., ed. *The Companion to the Book of Common Worship*. Louisville: Geneva, 2003.

Boyce, Greer W. "A Plea for Expository Preaching." *Canadian Journal of Theology* 8 (1962) 18–19.

Boyer, Horace Clarence. "An Analysis of Black Church Music with Examples Drawn from Services in Rochester, New York." PhD diss., Eastman School of Music, 1973.

Bradley, C. Randall. *From Memory to Imagination: Reforming the Church's Music*. Grand Rapids: Eerdmans, 2012.

Bradshaw, Paul F. *Reconstructing Early Christian Worship*. London: SPCK, 2009.

———. *The Search for the Origin of Christian Worship: Sources and Methods for the Study of Early Liturgy*. New York: Oxford University Press, 1992.

Bradshaw, Paul F., ed. *The New Westminster Dictionary of Liturgy and Worship*. Louisville: Westminster John Knox, 2003.

Bradshaw, Paul F., and Maxwell E. Johnson. *The Origins of Feasts, Fasts, and Seasons in Early Christianity*. Collegeville, MN: Liturgical, 2011.

Braga, James. *How to Prepare Biblical Messages*. Portland: Multnomah, 1981.

Brainard, Paul. "Bach as Theologian?" *Yale Studies in Sacred Music, Worship and the Arts, Reflections on the Sacred* (1994) 1–7.

Bray, Gerald, ed. "Galatians, Ephesians." In *Reformation Commentary on Scripture*, Vol. 10, edited by Timothy F. George, 235–74. Downers Grove, IL: IVP Academic, 2011.

Breen, Quirinius. *John Calvin: A Study in French Humanism*. Grand Rapids: Eerdmans, 1931.

Breidenbaugh, Joel. *Preaching for Bodybuilding: Doctrinal and Expository Preaching in a Postmodern World*. Bloomington, IN: CrossBooks/LifeWay, 2010.

Brink, Emily R. "When the Doxology Brings a Yawn, It's Time for a Change." *Reformed Liturgy and Music* 31 (1997) 216.

British Council of Churches. *The Forgotten Trinity: The BCC Study Commission on Trinitarian Doctrine Today*, 2nd ed. London: CTBI, 2011.

Broadus, John A. *On the Preparation and Delivery of Sermons*. 4th ed. Revised by Vernon C. Stanfield. San Francisco: Harper & Row, 1979.

Bromiley, Geoffrey W. *Historical Theology: An Introduction*. Grand Rapids: Eerdmans, 1978.

———. "The Interpretation of the Bible." In *The Expositor's Bible Commentary*, Vol. 1, edited by Frank E. Gaebelein, 61–80. Grand Rapids: Zondervan, 1979.

———. *Introduction to the Theology of Karl Barth*. Grand Rapids: Eerdmans, 1979.

———. *Theological Dictionary of the New Testament: Abridged in One Volume*. Grand Rapids: Eerdmans, 1985.

Brooks, David. *The Road to Character*. New York: Random House, 2015.

Brooks, Phillips. *On Preaching*. New York: Seabury, 1964.

Brown, Colin, ed. *The New International Theological Dictionary of the New Testament.* Grand Rapids: Zondervan, 1975.

Brown, Francis, et al., eds. *A Hebrew and English Lexicon of the Old Testament.* Oxford: Clarendon, 1951.

Brown, Frank Burch. *Inclusive Yet Discerning: Navigating Worship Artfully.* Grand Rapids: Eerdmans, 2009.

———. "Religious Aesthetics: A Theological Study of Making and Meaning." In *Theological Aesthetics: A Reader,* edited by Gesa Elsbeth Thiessen, 266–69. Grand Rapids: Eerdmans, 2005.

Brown, Howard M. *Music in the Renaissance.* Englewood Cliffs, NJ: Prentice-Hall, 1976.

Brown, Montague. *Restoration of Reason: The Eclipse of Truth, Goodness, and Beauty.* Grand Rapids: Baker, 2006.

Brown, Raymond E. *The Gospel According to St. John, I–XIII.* The Anchor Bible Commentary Series. Vol. 29, edited by William F. Albright and David N. Freedman. Garden City, NJ: Doubleday, 1966.

———. *An Introduction to the New Testament.* New York: Doubleday, 1997.

———. "The Paraclete in the Fourth Gospel." *New Testament Studies* 13 (1996–7) 113–32.

Bruce, F. F. *The Canon of Scripture.* Downers Grove, IL: InterVarsity, 1988.

———. "The 'Christ Hymn' of Colossians 1:15–20." *Bibliotheca Sacra* 141 (1984) 99–111.

———. *The Epistle to the Hebrews.* The New International Commentary on the New Testament Series. Grand Rapids: Eerdmans, 1964.

———. *The Gospel of John.* London: Pickering, 1983.

———. *The Message of the New Testament.* Grand Rapids: Eerdmans, 1973.

———. *The New Testament Documents: Are They Reliable?* Grand Rapids: Eerdmans, 2003.

———. *New Testament History.* New York: Doubleday, 1980.

———. *Paul: Apostle of the Heart Set Free.* Grand Rapids: Eerdmans, 1977.

———. *The Pauline Circle.* Grand Rapids: Eerdmans, 1985.

———. *The Spreading Flame: The Rise and Progress of Christianity from its First Beginnings to the Conversion of the English.* Grand Rapids: Eerdmans, 1958.

Bruce, F. F., ed. *The International Bible Commentary.* Grand Rapids: Zondervan, 1986.

Brueggemann, Walter. *Finally Comes the Poet: Daring Speech for Proclamation.* Minneapolis: Augsburg, 1989.

———. *From Whom No Secrets are Hid: Introducing the Psalms.* Princeton, NJ: Princeton University Press, 2014.

———. *Israel's Praise: Doxology against Idolatry and Ideology.* Philadelphia: Fortress, 1988.

———. *The Message of the Psalms.* Minneapolis: Augsburg, 1984.

———. *Spirituality of the Psalms.* Minneapolis: Augsburg, 2002.

———. *The Word Militant: Preaching a Decentering Word.* Minneapolis: Fortress, 2007.

Bruner, Frederick Dale. *A Theology of the Holy Spirit: The Pentecostal Experience and the New Testament Witness.* Eugene, OR: Wipf & Stock, 1997.

Bryson, Harold T. *Expository Preaching: The Art of Preaching through the Bible.* Nashville: B&H, 1995.

Bultmann, Rudolf. *The Gospel of John: A Commentary.* Translated by G. R. Beasley-Murray, et al. Philadelphia: Westminster, 1971.

Burge, Gary. "Are Evangelicals Missing God at Church?" *Christianity Today* 41 (1997) 21–27.

————. "Missing God at Church." In *Worship at the Next Level: Insight from Contemporary Voices*, edited by Tim A. Dearborn and Scott Coil, 147–55. Grand Rapids: Baker, 2004.

Burge, Gary M., et al. *The New Testament in Antiquity: A Survey of the New Testament within its Cultural Context*. Grand Rapids: Zondervan, 2009.

Burns, J. Lanier. *The Nearness of God: His Presence with His People*. Phillipsburg, NJ: P&R, 2009.

Buszin, Walter E. "Luther on Music." *The Musical Quarterly* 32 (1946) 80–97.

Buttrick, David. *Homiletic: Moves and Structures*. Philadelphia: Fortress, 1986.

————. *Preaching the New and the Now*. Louisville: Westminster John Knox, 1998.

Buttrick, George. *Jesus Came Preaching: Christian Preaching in the New Age*. New York: Scribner's, 1931.

Byars, Ronald P. *Christian Worship: Glorifying and Enjoying God*. Louisville: Geneva, 2000.

————. *The Future of Protestant Worship: Beyond the Worship Wars*. Louisville: Westminster John Knox, 2002.

————. *What Language Shall I Borrow?: The Bible and Christian Worship*. Grand Rapids: Eerdmans, 2008.

Cabaniss, Allen. *Pattern in Early Christian Worship*. Macon, GA: Mercer University Press, 1989.

Cahill, Dennis M. "Can Expository Preaching be Relevant to Both Believers and Seekers?" http://www.preaching.com/resources/articles/11565835/.

Cain, Susan. *Quiet: The Power of Introverts in a World that Can't Stop Talking*. New York: Broadway, 2012.

Caldecott, Stratford. *Beauty for Truth's Sake: On the Re-Enchantment of Education*. Grand Rapids: Brazos, 2009.

Callen, Barry L. *Sharing Heaven's Music: The Heart of Christian Preaching*. Nashville: Abingdon, 1995.

Calvin, John. *Commentary on the Book of Psalms*, vol. 1. Translated by James Anderson. Edinburgh: Calvin Translation Society, 1845.

————. "Foreword to the *Geneva Psalter of 1543*." In *John Calvin: Writings on Pastoral Piety*, edited by Elsie Anne McKee, 91–97. New York: Paulist, 2001.

————. *A Harmony of the Gospels: Matthew, Mark, and Luke*. 3 vols. Translated by David W. and Thomas F. Torrance. Grand Rapids: Eerdmans, 1972.

————. *Institutes of the Christian Religion*. Translated by Ford Lewis Battles. Louisville: Westminster John Knox, 1965.

————. *Tracts and Treatises on the Doctrine and Worship of the Church*. Tranlsted by Henry Beveridge. Grand Rapids: Eerdmans, 1958.

Cantalamessa, Raniero. *The Mystery of God's Word*. Collegeville, MN: Liturgical, 1991.

Carl, William J., III. "Music, Rhetoric, and Preaching." *Reformed Liturgy and Music* 17 (1983) 23–26.

————. "Shaping Sermons by the Structure of the Text." In *Preaching Biblically: Creating Sermons in the Shape of Scripture*, edited by Don M. Wardlaw, 121–36. Philadelphia: Westminster, 1983.

Carl, William J., III, ed. *Graying Gracefully: Preaching to Older Adults*. Louisville: Westminster John Knox, 1997.

Carlson, Timothy L. *Transforming Worship*. St. Louis: Chalice, 2003.

Carpenter, Joel A. *Revive Us Again: The Reawakening of American Fundamentalism*. New York: Oxford University Press, 1997.

Carrick, John. *The Imperative of Preaching: A Theology of Sacred Rhetoric.* Carlisle, PA: Banner of Truth, 2002.

Carson, Donald A. "Challenges for 21st Century Preaching." *Preaching* 23 (2008) 20–24.

————. *Christ and Culture Revisited.* Grand Rapids: Eerdmans, 2008.

————. *New Testament Commentary Survey.* 2nd ed. Grand Rapids: Baker Academic, 2007.

————. *Worship: Adoration and Action.* Grand Rapids: Baker, 1993.

————. *Worship by the Book.* Grand Rapids: Zondervan, 2002.

Carson, Donald A., and John Woodbridge. *Scripture and Truth.* Grand Rapids: Zondervan, 1983.

Carson, Donald A., et al. *An Introduction to the New Testament.* Grand Rapids: Zondervan, 1992.

Cassuto, Umberto. *A Commentary on the Book of Exodus.* Translated by Israel Abrahams. Jerusalem: Magnes Press of Hebrew University, 1967.

Chapell, Bryan. *Christ-Centered Preaching: Redeeming the Expository Sermon.* Grand Rapids: Baker Academic, 2005.

————. *Christ-Centered Worship: Letting the Gospel Shape Our Practice.* Grand Rapids: Baker Academic, 2009.

————. "Components of Expository Preaching." http://www.preaching.com/ sermons/11563760/.

————. "The Future of Expository Preaching." *Presbyterion* 30 (2004) 65–80.

————. *Using Illustrations to Preach with Power.* Rev. ed. Wheaton, IL: Crossway, 2001.

————. *The Wonder of it All: Rediscovering the Treasure of Your Faith.* Wheaton, IL: Crossway, 1999.

Chatham, James O. *Enacting the Word: Using Drama in Worship.* Louisville: Westminster John Knox, 2002.

Cherry, Constance M. *The Worship Architect: Designing Culturally Relevant and Biblically Faithful Services.* Grand Rapids: Baker, 2010.

Chesterton, G. K. *The Everlasting Man.* 1925. Reprint, San Francisco: Ignatius, 2008.

————. *Orthodoxy.* New York: Doubleday, 1959.

Childs, Brevard S. *Biblical Theology in Crisis.* Philadelphia: Westminster, 1970.

————. *The Book of Exodus: A Critical, Theological Commentary.* Philadelphia: Westminster, 1974.

————. *Introduction to the Old Testament as Scripture.* Philadelphia: Fortress, 1979.

————. *Memory and Tradition in Israel.* Naperville, IL: Alec R. Allenson, 1962.

Childs, David T. "Our Changing Music: New Trends of the Reformation." *Decision* 37 (1996) 16–18.

Chisholm, Robert B., Jr. "A Theology of the Psalms." In *A Biblical Theology of the Old Testament,* edited by Roy B. Zuck et al., 257–304. Chicago: Moody, 1991.

Christ-Janer, Albert, et al., eds. *American Hymns Old and New.* New York: Columbia University Press, 1980.

Clancy, Robert A. D. "The Old Testament Roots of Remembrance in the Lord's Supper." *Concordia Journal* 19 (1993) 35–50.

————. *Preaching Christ in All of Scripture.* Wheaton, IL: Crossway, 2003.

Clark, Keith C. "A Bibliography of Handbooks to Hymnals: American, Canadian, and English." *The Hymn* 30 (July 1979) 205–9; *The Hymn* 30 (October 1979) 269–72; *The Hymn* 31 (January 1980) 41–47, 73–74; *The Hymn* 31 (April 1980) 120–26.

BIBLIOGRAPHY

————. *A Selective Bibliography for the Study of Hymns, 1980*. Springfield, VA: Hymn Society of America, 1980.

Clark, Linda J. *Music in Churches: Nourishing Your Congregation's Musical Life*. Herndon, VA: Alban, 1994.

Clive, H. P. "The Calvinist Attitude to Music, and its Literary Aspects and Sources." *Bibliotheque d'Humanisme et Renaissance* 19 (1957) 294–319; *Bibliotheque d'Humanisme et Renaissance* 20 (1958) 29–107.

Clowney, Edmund P. *The Unfolding Mystery: Discovering Christ in the Old Testament*. Phillipsburg, NJ: P&R, 1988.

Coalter, Milton J., et al, eds. *The Presbyterian Predicament: Six Perspectives*. Louisville: Westminster John Knox, 1990.

Coffin, Henry Sloane. *The Public Worship of God: A Source Book*. Philadelphia: Westminster, 1946.

Coffin, William Sloane. *The Heart is a Little to the Left*. Lebanon, NH: Dartmouth College University Press of New England, 1999.

Coggan, Donald. *The Sacrament of the Word*. New York: Crossroad, 1988.

Collins, Owen, ed. *2000 Years of Classic Christian Prayers: A Collection for Public and Private Use*. Maryknoll, NY: Orbis, 1999.

Cope, David H. *New Directions in Music*. 4th ed. Dubuque, IA: Brown, 1984.

Copland, Aaron. *Old American Songs*. Set Two. London: Boosey & Hawkes, 1954.

Costen, Melva Wilson. *In Spirit and in Truth: The Music of African American Worship*. Louisville: Westminster John Knox, 2004.

Counsell, Michael, ed. *2000 Years of Prayer*. Harrisburg, PA: Morehouse, 1999.

Courtney, Craig. *Be Not Afraid*. Columbus, OH: Beckenhorst, 1992.

————. *If You Search with All Your Heart*. Columbus, OH: Beckenhorst, 1994.

————. *In My Father's House*. Columbus, OH: Beckenhorst, 2006.

Covey, Cyclone. "Religion and Music in Colonial America." PhD diss., Stanford University Press, 1949.

Craddock, Fred B. *As One Without Authority*. St. Louis: Chalice, 2001.

————. *Overhearing the Gospel*. Nashville: Abingdon, 1978.

————. *Preaching*. Nashville: Abingdon, 1985.

Cranfield. C. E. B. *The Apostle's Creed: A Faith to Live by*. Edinburgh: T. & T. Clark, 1993.

————. *Romans: A Shorter Commentary*. Grand Rapids: Eerdmans, 1985.

Crenshaw, James C. *Trembling at the Threshold of a Biblical Text*. Grand Rapids: Eerdmans, 1994.

Crosby, Fanny Jane. "A Wonderful Savior is Jesus My Lord." In *Trinity Hymnal*, edited by Lawrence C. Roff, 175. Philadelphia: Great Commission, 1990.

Cross, F. L., ed. *The Oxford Dictionary of the Christian Church*. 3rd ed. Edited by E. A. Livingston. New York: Oxford University Press, 1997.

Crouch, Andy. *Culture Making: Recovering Our Creative Calling*. Downers Grove, IL: IVP, 2008.

————. *Playing God: Redeeming the Gift of Power*. Downers Grove, IL: IVP, 2013.

Crow, Loren D. *The Songs of Ascent (Psalms 120–134): Their Place in Israelite History and Religion*. SBL Dissertation Series 148. Atlanta: Scholars, 1996.

Cullman, Oscar. *Early Christian Worship*. Philadelphia: Westminster, 1978.

Cunningham, Lawrence S. *The Catholic Faith: An Introduction*. New York: Paulist, 1987.

Curtis, Edward M. "Ancient Psalms and Modern Worship." *Bibliotheca Sacra* 154 (1997) 285–96.

D. Martin Luthers Werke: Kritische Gesamtausgabe, Weimar, Germany: Harmann Boehlaus Nachfolger, 1883.

Daane, James. *Preaching with Confidence: A Theological Essay on the Power of the Pulpit*. Grand Rapids: Eerdmans, 1980.

D'Amico, John F. "Humanism and Pre-Reformation Theology." In *Renaissance Humanism: Foundations, Forms, and Legacy*, edited by Albert Rabil, Jr., vol. 3, 349–79. Philadelphia: Pennsylvania, 1988.

Daniels, Harold. "The Sign of the Cross." *Reformed Liturgy and Music* 21 (1987) 39–44.

Davidman, Joy. *Smoke on the Mountain*. London: Hodder & Stoughton, 1955.

Davidson, James Robert. *A Dictionary of Protestant Church Music*. Metuchen, NJ: Scarecrow, 1975.

Davidson, Robert. *The Vitality of Worship: A Commentary on the Book of Psalms*. Grand Rapids: Eerdmans, 2000.

Davie, Donald. *The Eighteenth-Century Hymn in England*. New York: Cambridge University Press, 1993.

Davies, Horton. *Christian Worship: Its History and Meaning*. New York: Abingdon, 1957.

———. *Worship and Theology in England: The Ecumenical Century, 1900–1965*. Princeton, NJ: Princeton University Press, 1965.

———. *The Worship of the American Puritans, 1629–1730*. New York: Peter Lang, 1990.

———. *The Worship of the English Puritans*. London: Dacre, 1948.

Davies, J. G., ed. *The New Westminster Dictionary of Liturgy and Worship*. Philadelphia: Westminster, 1986.

Davis, Taylor. *How Can I Keep from Singing?* St. Louis: MorningStar, 2010.

Davis, Thomas J. "Preaching and Presence: Constructing Calvin's Homiletical Legacy." In *The Legacy of John Calvin*, edited by David Foxgrover, 84–106. Grand Rapids: CRC, 2000.

Dawkins, Richard. *The God Delusion*. New York: First Mariner, 2006.

Dawn, Marva J. *How Shall We Worship: Biblical Guidelines for the Worship Wars*. Carol Stream, IL: Tyndale House, 2003.

———. *Keeping the Sabbath Wholly: Ceasing, Resting, Embracing, Feasting*. Grand Rapids: Eerdmans, 1989.

———. *Reaching Out Without Dumbing Down: A Theology of Worship for the Turn-of-the-Century Culture*. Grand Rapids: Eerdmans, 1995.

———. *A Royal "Waste" of Time: The Splendor of Worshiping God and Being the Church for the World*. Grand Rapids: Eerdmans, 1999.

———. *Talking the Walk: Letting Christian Language Live Again*. Grand Rapids: Brazos, 2005.

Day, Thomas. *Why Catholics Can't Sing: The Culture of Catholicism and the Triumph of Bad Taste*. New York: Crossroad, 1990.

Dean, Talmage. *A Survey of Twentieth Century Protestant Church Music in America*. Nashville: Broadman, 1988.

Dearborn, Tim A., and Scott Coil. *Worship at the Next Level: Insight from Contemporary Voices*. Grand Rapids: Baker, 2004.

deClaisse-Walford, Nancy, ed. *The Shape and Shaping of the Book of Psalms: The Current State of Scholarship*. Atlanta: Society of Biblical Literature, 2014.

Delling, Gerhard D. *Worship in the New Testament*. Philadelphia: Westminster, 1962.

Denham, Michael. "Music in Worship." *Bel Canto—Maryland/District of Columbia Newsletter of the American Choral Directors Association* 13 (2002) 4–5.

———. "Reverberating Word: The Concept and Role of Expository Worship at The National Presbyterian Church." DMin diss., Samford University, 2015.

Dennert, Brian C. "John Calvin's Movement from the Bible to Theology and Practice." *Journal of the Evangelical Theological Society* 54 (2011) 345–65.

Detterman, Paul. "It's a Matter of Faith." *Reformed Liturgy & Music* 33 (1999) 1.

———. "The Strong Name of the Trinity." In *What Is Christian Worship?*, edited by Mary Holder Naegeli, 57–62. Louisville: Presbyterians for Renewal, 2000.

Detweiler, David F. "Church Music and Colossians 3:16." *Bibliotheca Sacra* 158 (2001) 347–70.

Dever, Mark. *The Message of the Old Testament.* Wheaton, IL: Crossway, 2006.

Dever, Mark, and Sinclair Ferguson. *The Westminster Dictionary of Public Worship Discussed by Mark Dever and Sinclair Ferguson.* Fearn, Scotland: Christian Focus Publications, 2009.

Dibble, Jeremy. *John Stainer: A Life in Music.* Rochester, NY: Boydell, 2007.

Dibelius, Martin, and Hans Conzelmann. *The Pastoral Epistles.* Translated by Philip Buttolph and Adela Yarboro. Philadelphia. Fortress, 1972.

Dillard, Annie. *Teaching a Stone to Talk.* New York: HarperCollins, 1982.

Dollar, George. "The Lord's Supper in the Fourth and Fifth Centuries." *Bibliotheca Sacra* 117 (1960) 342–49.

———. "The Lord's Supper in the Second Century." *Bibliotheca Sacra* 117 (1960) 144–54.

———. "The Lord's Supper in the Third Century." *Bibliotheca Sacra* 117 (1960) 249–57.

Doran, Carol, and Thomas H. Troeger. *Open to Glory: Renewing Worship in the Congregation.* Valley Forge, PA: Judson, 1983.

———. *Trouble at the Table: Gathering the Tribes for Worship.* Nashville: Abingdon, 1992.

Doriani, Daniel M. *Getting the Message: A Plan for Interpreting and Applying the Bible.* Phillipsburg, NJ: P&R, 1996.

———. *Putting the Truth to Work: The Theory and Practice of Biblical Application.* Phillipsburg, NJ: P&R, 2001.

Dorrien, Gary. *The Remaking of Evangelical Theology.* Louisville: Westminster John Knox, 1988.

Douglas, J. D., ed. *The New International Dictionary of the Christian Church.* Rev. ed. Grand Rapids: Zondervan, 1978.

Douglas, Winfred. *Church Music in History and Practice: Studies in the Praise of God.* New York: Scribner's, 1937.

Dowley, Tim. *Christian Music: A Global History.* Minneapolis: Augsburg/Fortress, 2011.

Driver, S. R. *Deuteronomy: A Critical Commentary.* Edinburgh: T. & T. Clark, 1901.

Duba, Arlo D. "The Psalter in Reformed Worship." *Reformed Liturgy and Music* 26 (1992) 67–69.

Dudley-Smith, Timothy. "Why Wesley still Dominates Our Hymnbook." *Christian History* 10 (1991) 9–13.

Duduit, Michael "Expository Preaching in a Narrative World: An Interview with Haddon Robinson." http://www.preaching.com/resources/articles/11565763/.

———. "Preaching and Worship: An Interview with Michael Quicke." http://www.preaching.com/resources/articles/11605337/.

Duduit, Michael, ed. *Handbook of Contemporary Preaching.* Nashville: Broadman, 1993.

Duguid, Barbara, and Wayne Duguid Houk. *Prone to Wander: Prayers of Confession and Celebration.* Phillipsburg, NJ: P&R, 2014.

Duguid, Ian M. *Hero of Heroes: Seeing Christ in the Beatitudes.* Phillipsburg, NJ: P&R, 2001.

———. *Living in the Gap Between Promise and Reality: The Gospel According to Abraham.* Phillipsburg, NJ: P&R, 1999.

———. *Themes in Old Testament Theology.* Downers Grove, IL: InterVarsity, 1979.

Duncan, J. Ligon, III. "Foudations for Biblically Directed Worship." In *Give Glory to God,* edited by Philip Graham Ryken et al., 51–74. Phillipsburg, NJ: P&R, 2003.

Dunston, Alan, "Hymnody in Christian Worship." In *The Study of Liturgy,* edited by Chelsyn Jones et al., 507–18. New York: Oxford University Press, 1978.

Dyck, John T. "Calvin and Worship." *Western Reformed Seminary Journal* 16 (2009) 33–40.

Dyrness, William A. "Aesthetics in the Old Testament: Beauty in Context." *Journal of the Evangelical Theological Society* 28 (1985) 421–32.

———. "The Imago Dei and Christian Aesthetics." *Journal of the Evangelical Theological Society* 15 (1972) 161–72.

———. *Poetic Theology: God and the Poetics of Everyday Life.* Grand Rapids: Eerdmans, 2011.

———. *A Primer on Christian Worship: Where We've Been, Where We Are, Where We Can Go.* Grand Rapids: Eerdmans, 2009.

———. "Reclaiming Art for Worship." *Theology, News and Notes* 48 (2001) 9–12.

———. *Visual Faith: Art, Theology, and Worship in Dialogue.* Grand Rapids: Baker Academic, 2001.

Eaton, J. H. "Music's Place in Worship: A Contribution from the Psalms." *Old Testament Studies* 23 (1984) 85–107.

Edersheim, Alfred. *The Temple: Its Ministry and Services as They Were at the Time of Christ.* 1908. Reprint. Grand Rapids: Eerdmans, 1987.

Edgar, William. "Calvin's Impact on the Arts" In *Tributes to John Calvin: A Celebration of His Quincentenary,* edited by David. W. Hall, 464–86. Philipsburg, NJ: P&R, 2010.

———. *In Spirit & In Truth: Ten Bible Studies on Worship.* Downers Grove, IL: InterVarsity, 1976.

Editorial Committee. *Hymns of Universal Praise,* New Revised Edition. Hong Kong: Chinese Christian Literature Council, Ltd. 2006.

Ehrman, Bart D. *God's Problem: How the Bible Fails to Answer Our Most Important Question—Why We Suffer.* New York: HarperCollins, 2008.

Eicher, David, ed. *Glory to God: The Presbyterian Hymnal.* Louisville: Westminster John Knox, 2013.

———. "O Christ, the Great Foundation." In *Glory to God: The Presbyterian Hymnal,* edited by David Eicher, 361. Louisville: Westminster John Knox, 2013.

Eichrodt, Walther. *Theology of the Old Testament,* vol. 1. Translated by J. A. Baker. Philadelphia: Westminster, 1987.

———. *Theology of the Old Testament,* vol. 2. Translated by J. A. Baker. Philadelphia: Westminster, 1987.

Eising, H. "Zākhar." In *Theological Dictionary of the Old Testament,* vol. 4, edited by G. Johannes Botterweck and Helmer Ringgren, 64–81. Grand Rapids: Eerdmans, 1980.

Eliot, T. S. *Christianity and Culture.* New York: Harcourt, Brace and World, 1949.

Ellis, William Preston. "A Study of the Nature of the Expository Sermon in the United States from 1940–1968." ThD diss., New Orleans Baptist Theological Seminary, 1971.

Ellison, H. L. "Theophany." In *The Zondervan Pictorial Encyclopedia of the Bible,* vol. 5, edited by Merrill C. Tenney, 719–21. Grand Rapids: Zondervan, 1976.

Emerton, John. "The Etymology of Hištaḥăwāh." *Old Testament Studies* 20 (1977) 41–55.

The Episcopal Church. "A Collect for Peace." In *The Book of Common Prayer*, 57. New York: Seabury, 1979.

Erickson, Craig Douglas. *Participating in Worship: History, Theory, and Practice*. Louisville: Westminster John Knox, 1989.

Eskew, Harry, and Hugh T. McGrath. *Sing with Understanding: An Introduction to Christian Hymnology*. 2nd ed. Nashville: Church Street, 1995.

Eswine, Zack. *Preaching to a Post-Everything World*. Grand Rapids: Baker, 2008.

Evans, Craig A. *From Jesus to the Church: The First Christian Generation*. Louisville: Westminster John Knox, 2014.

Fabarez, Michael. *Preaching that Changes Lives*. Nashville: Thomas Nelson, 2002.

Fanning, Buist M., III. "God's Word and God's People." In *New Dictionary of Biblical Theology*, edited by Desmond Alexander et al., 848–50. Downers Grove, IL: InterVarsity, 2000.

Farhadian, Charles E., ed. *Christian Worship Worldwide: Expanding Horizons, Deepening Practices*. Grand Rapids: Eerdmans, 2007.

Farmer, H. H. *The Servant of the Word*. Philadelphia: Fortress, 1964.

Faulkner, Quentin. *Wiser than Despair: The Evolution of Ideas in the Relationship of Music and the Christian Church*. Westport, CT: Greenwood, 1996.

Faure-Doursaz, André. *Calvin et Loyola: Deux Reformes*. Bruxelles: Editions Universitaires, 1951.

Feinberg, John S., ed. *Continuity and Discontinuity: Perspectives on the Relationship Between the Old and New Testaments, Essays in Honor of S. Lewis Johnson*. Wheaton, IL: Crossway, 1988.

Ferrell, Lori Anne. *The Bible and the People*. New Haven: Yale University Press, 2008.

Finesinger, S. B. "Musical Instruments in the Old Testament." *Hebrew Union College Annual* 3 (1926) 21–76.

Fitch, David E. *The Great Giveaway: Reclaiming the Mission of the Church from Big Business, Parachurch Organizations, Psychotherapy, Consumer Capitalism, and Other Modern Maladies*. Grand Rapids: Baker, 2005.

Flint, Peter W., and Patrick D. Miller, Jr., eds. *The Book of Psalms: Composition and Reception*. Vetus Testamentum Supplementum Series. Leiden, the Netherlands: Brill, 2003.

Flusser, David. "Jewish Roots of the Liturgical Trisagion." *Immanuel* 3 (1973–74) 37–43.

Flynn, William T. "Liturgical Music." In *The Oxford History of Christian Worship*, edited by Geoffrey Wainwright and Karen B. Westerfield Tucker, 769–92. New York: Oxford University Press, 2006.

Foley, Edward. "Liturgical Music: A Bibliographic Essay." In *Liturgy and Music: Lifetime Learning*, edited by Robin A. Leaver and Joyce Ann Zimmerman, 411–45. Collegeville, MN: Liturgical, 1998.

Foley, Edward, ed. *Worship Music: A Concise Dictionary*. Collegeville, MN: Liturgical, 2000.

Foote, Henry Wilder. *Three Centuries of American Hymnody*. Cambridge: Harvard University Press, 1940.

Foraler, Steve Allen. "A Layman's Guide for Preparing Expository Messages from Epistolary Literature." DMin diss., Liberty University, 1995.

Forbes, James. *The Holy Spirit in Preaching*. Nashville: Abingdon, 1989.

Ford, James Thomas. "Preaching in the Reformed Tradition." In *Preachers and People in the Reformation and Early Modern Period*, edited by Larissa Taylor, 65–90. Leiden, the Netherlands: Brill, 2001.

Forell, George W., et al. *Luther and Culture*. Decorah, IA: Luther College Press, 1960.

Fosdick, Harry Emerson. "What Is the Matter with Preaching?" *Harper's Magazine* 47 (1928) 133–41.

Foster, Richard. "The Discipline of Worship." *Theology, News and Notes* 48 (2001) 6–8.

Foy, Felician, and Rose M. Avato. *A Concise Guide to the Catholic Church*. Huntington, CA: Our Sunday Visitor, 1984.

Frame, John M. *Contemporary Worship Music: A Biblical Defense*. Phillipsburg, NJ: P&R, 1997.

———. "In Defense of Something Close to Biblicism: Reflections on *Sola Scriptura* and History in Theological Method." *Westminster Theological Journal* 59 (1997) 269–91.

———. *Worship in Spirit and in Truth: A Refreshing Study of the Principles and Practices of Biblical Worship*. Phillipsburg, NJ: P&R, 1996.

Frankforter, A. Daniel. *Stones for Bread: A Critique of Contemporary Worship*. Louisville: Westminster John Knox, 2001.

Frost, Maurice, ed. *Historical Companion to Hymns Ancient and Modern*. London: William Clowes & Sons, 1962.

Fuller, Charles W. "The Pulpit at the Precipice of Heresy: Incarnational Preaching as a Theological Misnomer." Lecture at annual meeting of the Evangelical Homiletics Society, Deerfield, IL, October 14–16, 2010.

Furr, Gary, and Milburn Price. *The Dialogue of Worship: Creating Space for Revelation and Response*. Macon, GA: Smith and Helwys, 1998.

Gaebelein, Frank E. *The Christian, the Arts, and Truth*. Edited by D. Bruce Lockerbie. Portland: Multnomah, 1985.

Gallup, George, Jr., and Michael D. Lindsay. *Surveying the Religious Landscape: Trends in U. S. Beliefs*. New York: Morehouse, 1999.

Gane, Erwin. "Exegetical Methods of Some Sixteenth-Century Puritan Preachers." *Andrews University Seminary Series* 19 (1981) 32–33.

Gardiner, John Elliot. *Bach: Music in the Castle of Heaven*. New York: Knopf, 2013.

Garner, Stephen Chapin. *Getting into Character: The Art of First-Person Narrative Preaching*. Grand Rapids: Brazos, 2008.

Garside, Charles, Jr. "Calvin's Preface to the Psalter." *Musical Quarterly* 37 (1951) 566–77.

———. *The Origin of Calvin's Theology of Music, 1536–1543*. Philadelphia: American Philosophical Society, 1979.

———. "Some Attitudes of the Major Reformers toward the Role of Music in the Liturgy." *McCormick Quarterly* 21 (1967) 151–68.

Geisler, Norman L. *Systematic Theology in One Volume*. Minneapolis: Bethany House, 2011.

George, Timothy. "The Eternity of God." http://firstthings.com/web-exclusives/2016/10/the-eternity-of-God/.

———. "The Nature of God: Being, Attributes, and Acts." In *A Theology for the Church*, edited by David L. Aiken, 157–204. Nashville: B&H Academic, 2014.

———. *Reading Scripture with the Reformers*. Downers Grove, IL: InterVarsity, 2011.

———. *Theology of the Reformers*. Nashville: Broadman, 1988.

George, Timothy, ed. *God the Holy Trinity: Reflections on Faith and Practice*. Grand Rapids: Baker Academic, 2006.

———. *John Calvin & the Church: A Prism of Reform*. Louisville: Westminster John Knox, 1990.

George, Timothy, et al. *Our Suffering God: Essays on Preaching in Honor of Gardner C. Taylor*. Macon, GA: Mercer, 2010.

Gerrish, Brian A., ed. *The Faith of Christendom: A Sourcebook of Creeds, and Confessions*. Cleveland: World, 1963.

———. *Grace and Gratitude: The Eucharistic Theology of John Calvin*. 1993. Reprint, Eugene, OR: Wipf & Stock, 2002.

Gibbons, Orlando. *O Lord, Increase My Faith*. New York: H. W. Gray, n. d.

Gibson, Scott M., ed. *Preaching the Old Testament*. Grand Rapids: Baker, 2006.

———. *Preaching to a Shifting Culture: 12 Perspectives on Communicating that Connects* Grand Rapids: Baker, 2004.

Gignilliat, Mark S. *A Brief History of Old Testament Criticism: From Benedict Spinoza to Brevard Childs*. Grand Rapids: Zondervan, 2012.

Gillespie, George, ed. *A Dispute against English Popish Ceremonies Obtruded on the Church of Scotland*. 1642. Reprint, Dallas: Naphtali, 1993.

Glynn, John. *Commentary and Reference Survey: A Comprehensive Guide to Biblical and Theological Resources*. 10th ed. Grand Rapids: Kregel Academic & Professional, 2007.

Godfrey, Robert W. "Calvin, Worship, and Sacraments." In *A Theological Guide to Calvin's Institutes: Essays & Analysis*, edited by David. W. Hall, 368–89. Philipsburg, NJ: P&R, 2008.

Goheen, Michael W. "Nourishing Our Missional Identity: Worship and the Mission of God's People." In *In Praise of Worship: An Exploration of Text and Practice*, edited by David J. Cohen and Michael Parsons, 32–53. Eugene, OR: Pickwick, 2010.

Goldberg, Louis. "Preaching with Power the Word Correctly Handled to Transform Man and His World." *Journal of the Evangelical Theological Society* 27 (1984) 4–5.

Goldingay, John. *Old Testament Theology*, vol. 1, *Israel's Gospel*. Downers Grove, IL: IVP Academic, 2003.

———. *Old Testament Theology*, vol. 2, *Israel's Faith*. Downers Grove, IL: IVP Academic, 2006.

———. *Old Testament Theology*, vol. 3, *Israel's Life*. Downers Grove, IL: IVP Academic, 2009.

———. *Psalms*, vol. 1, *Psalms 1–41*. Baker Commentary on the Old Testament Wisdom and Psalms, edited by Tremper Longman, III. Grand Rapids: Baker, 2006.

———. *Psalms*, vol. 2, *Psalms 42–89*. Baker Commentary on the Old Testament Wisdom and Psalms, edited by Tremper Longman III. Grand Rapids: Baker, 2007.

———. *Psalms*, vol. 3, *Psalms 90–150*. Baker Commentary on the Old Testament Wisdom and Psalms, edited by Tremper Longman III. Grand Rapids: Baker, 2015.

Goldsworthy, Graeme. *Gospel and Kingdom: A Christian Interpretation of the Old Testament*. Carlisle, UK: Paternoster, 1994.

———. *Preaching the Whole Bible as Scripture*. Grand Rapids: Eerdmans, 2000.

Gomes, Peter J. *Sermons: Biblical Wisdom for Daily Living*. New York: William Morrow, 1998.

Gonzales, Justo L. *A History of Christian Thought*, vol. 2, *From Augustine to the Eve of the Reformation*. Nashville: Abingdon, 1971.

———. *A History of Christian Thought*, vol. 3, *From the Reformation to the Twentieth Century*. Nashville: Abingdon, 1975.

Gordon, Bruce. *John Calvin*. New Haven, CT: Yale University Press, 2009.

Gordon, T. David. *Why Johnny Can't Sing Hymns: How Pop Culture Rewrote the Hymnal.* Phillipsburg, NJ: P&R, 2010.

Gore, R. J. "Covenantal Worship: Reconsidering the Critics." *Westminster Journal of Theology* 67 (2005) 363–79.

———. *Covenantal Worship: Reconsidering the Puritan Regulative Principle.* Phillipsburg, NJ: P&R, 2002.

Gowen, Donald E. *Bridge Between the Testaments: A Reappraisal of Judaism from the Exile to the Birth of Christianity.* Pittsburgh: Pickwick, 1980.

Graves, Mike. *The Sermon as Symphony.* Valley Forge, PA: Judson, 1997.

Graves, Mike, and David J. Schlafer, eds. *What's the Shape of Narrative Preaching?* St. Louis: Chalice, 2008.

Gray, S. W. "Useless Fires: Worship in the Time of Malachi." *Southwestern Journal of Theology* 38 (1987) 35–41.

Gray, Thomas. "Music in the Reformed Tradition." *Theology News & Notes* 29 (1982) 3–5, 20–21.

Green, Joel B., and Michael Pasquarello III. *Narrative Reading, Narrative Preaching.* Grand Rapids: Baker Academic, 2003.

Greenhaw, David M., and Ronald J. Allen. *Preaching in the Context of Worship.* St. Louis: Chalice, 2000.

Gregory, Joel C. *Baptist Preaching: A Global Anthology.* Waco, TX: Baylor University Press, 2014.

Greidanus, Sidney. *The Modern Preacher and the Ancient Text: Interpreting and Preaching Biblical Literature.* Grand Rapids: Eerdmans, 1988.

———. *Preaching Christ from the Old Testament: A Contemporary Hermeneutical Model.* Grand Rapids: Eerdmans, 1999.

Grenz, Stanley J. *A Primer on Postmodernism.* Grand Rapids: Eerdmans, 1996.

———. "Star Trek and the Next Generation: Postmodernism and the Future of Evangelical Theology." In *The Challenge of Postmodernism: An Evangelical Engagement,* edited by David S. Dockery, 89–103. Wheaton, IL: Bridgepoint, 1985.

Griffin, Emory A. *The Mind Changers: The Art of Christian Persuasion.* Wheaton, IL: Tyndale, 1976.

Griffith, Sidney H. *The Church in the Shadow of the Mosque: Christians and Muslims in the World of Islam.* Princeton, NJ: Princeton University Press, 2014.

Griffith-Thomas, W. H. *St. Paul's Epistle to the Romans: A Devotional Commentary.* Grand Rapids: Eerdmans, 1946.

Griffiths, Paul. *The Thames and Hudson Encyclopedia of 20th Century Music.* London: Thames and Hudson, 1996.

Groothius, Douglas. *Truth Decay: Defending Christianity against the Challenges of Postmodernism.* Downers Grove, IL: InterVarsity, 2000.

Grout, Donald J., and Claude V. Palisca. *A History of Western Music.* 4th ed. New York: Norton, 1988.

Guelich, Robert A. *The Sermon on the Mount: A Foundation for Understanding.* Waco, TX: Word, 1982.

Guenther, Eileen. *One Bread, One Body: Exploring Cultural Diversity in Worship.* Herndon, VA: Alban, 2003.

———. *Rivals or a Team: Clergy-Musician Relationships in the Twenty-First Century.* St. Louis: Morning Star, 2012.

Guinness, Os. *Prophetic Untimeliness: A Challenge to the Idol of Relevance.* Grand Rapids: Baker, 2003.

Guthrie, Donald. *New Testament Introduction.* Downers Grove, IL: InterVarsity, 1970.

———. *New Testament Theology.* Downers Grove, IL: InterVarsity, 1981.

Hackel, Sergei. "Orthodox Worship." In *The New Westminster Dictionary of Liturgy & Worship*, edited by J. G. Davies, 423. Philadelphia: Westminster, 1986.

Hagner, Donald. "Biblical Theology and Preaching." *Expository Times* 96 (1985) 137–41.

Hahn, Ferdinand. *The Worship of the Early Church.* Translated by D. E. Green. Philadelphia: Fortress, 1973.

Hall, Basil. *Humanists and Protestants, 1500–1900.* Edinburgh: T. & T. Clark, 1900.

———. *John Calvin: Humanist and Theologian.* London: Historical Association, 1967.

Hall, Christopher A. *Worshipping with the Church Fathers.* Downers Grove, IL: InterVarsity, 2009.

Hall, David W. *The Legacy of John Calvin: His Influence on the Modern World.* Phillipsburg, NJ: P&R, 2009.

Hall, David W., ed. *Tributes to John Calvin: A Celebration of His Quincentenary.* Phillipsburg, NJ: P&R, 2010.

Hamilton, James M. "Biblical Theology and Preaching." In *Text-Driven Preaching: God's Word at the Heart of Every Sermon*, edited by Daniel L. Akin et al., 193–220. Nashville: B&H, 2010.

Hamstra, Sam, Jr. *Principled Worship.* Eugene, OR: Wipf & Stock, 2006.

Harari, Yuval Noah. *Sapiens: A Brief History of Humankind.* New York: HarperCollins, 2015.

Hardin, H. Grady, et al. *The Celebration of the Gospel: A Study of Christian Worship.* Nashville: Abingdon, 1964.

Harper, John. *The Forms and Orders of Western Liturgy from the Tenth to the Eighteenth Century: A Historical Introduction and Guide for Students and Musicians.* Oxford: Clarendon, 1991.

Harris, James Henry. *The Word Made Plain: The Power and Promise of Preaching.* Minneapolis: Fortress, 2004.

Harrison, R. K., et al. *Biblical Criticism: Historical, Literary, and Textual.* Grand Rapids: Zondervan, 1978.

Hart, D. G., and John R. Meuther. *With Reverence and Awe: Returning to the Basics of Reformed Worship.* Phillipsburg, NJ: P&R, 2002.

Hart, David Bentley. *The Beauty of the Infinite: The Aesthetics of Christian Truth.* Grand Rapids: Eerdmans, 2003.

Hart, Trevor. *Making Good: Creation, Creativity, and Artistry.* Waco, TX: Baylor University Press, 2014.

Hartog, Paul, ed. *The Contemporary Church and the Early Church: Case Studies in Ressourcement.* Evangelical Theological Society Monograph Series 9. Eugene, OR: Wipf & Stock, 2010.

Harvey, John. "A New Look at the Christ Hymn in Phil. 2:6–11." *Expository Times* 76 (1965) 337–39.

Hasel, Gerhard. *New Testament Theology: Basic Issues in the Current Debate.* Grand Rapids: Eerdmans, 1978.

———. *Old Testament Theology: Basic Issues in the Current Debate.* 4th ed. Grand Rapids: Eerdmans, 1972.

Haslan, Greg, ed. *Preach the Word! The Call and Challenge of Preaching Today.* Lancaster, UK: Sovereign World, 2006.

Hatch, Edwin. *The Influence of Greek Ideas and Usages upon the Christian Church.* London: Williams and Norgate, 1914.

Hauerwas, Stanley, and William H. Willimon. *Resident Aliens: Life in the Christian Colony—A Provocative Christian Assessment of Culture and Ministry for People Who Know that Something is Wrong.* Nashville: Abingdon, 1989.

Hauerwas, Stanley, and L. Gregory Jones. *Why Narrative? Readings in Narrative Theology.* Eugene, OR: Wipf & Stock, 1997.

Hawn, C. Michael, ed. *New Songs of Celebration Render: Congregational Singing in the 21st Century.* Chicago: GIA, 2013.

Hayford, Jack. *Worship His Majesty.* Glendale Heights, CA: Gospel Light, 2000.

Hayford, Jack, et al. *Mastering Worship.* Portland: Multnomah, 1990.

Healy-Wedsworth, Kathleen. "Ministry or Performance." *Reformed Liturgy & Music* 33 (1999) 8–12.

Hendricks, Howard. *Color Outside the Lines: A Revolutionary Approach to Creative Leadership.* Nashville: Word, 1998.

———. *Teaching to Change Lives.* Portland: Multnomah, 1987.

Hendrix, Scott H. *Early Protestant Spirituality.* New York: Paulist, 2000.

Hengel, Martin. "Hymns and Christology." In *Between Jesus and Paul: Studies in the Earliest History of Christianity,* edited by Martin Hengel, 78–96. Philadelphia: Fortress, 1983.

Henry, Carl F. H. "American Evangelicals in a Turning Time." *Christian Century* 97.35 (November 5, 1980) 1058–62.

———. *The Uneasy Conscience of American Fundamentalism.* Grand Rapids: Eerdmans, 1947.

Herbert, A. S. *Worship in Ancient Israel.* Richmond, VA: John Knox, 1959.

Hickman, Lisa Nichols. *The Worshiping Life: Meditations on the Order of Worship.* Louisville: Westminster John Knox, 2005.

Hitchcock, H. Wiley. *Music in the United States.* 3rd ed. Englewood Cliffs, NJ: Prentice-Hall, 1988.

Hitchens, Christopher. *god is not Great: How Religion Poisons Everything.* New York: Hatchette, 2007.

Hodges, John Mason. "Aesthetics and the Place of Beauty in Worship." *Reformation and Revival* 9 (2000) 59–75.

Holladay, William L. *The Psalms through Three Thousand Years: Prayerbook of a Cloud of Witnesses.* Minneapolis: Fortress, 1993.

Holmes, Arthur, ed. *The Making of a Christian Mind: A Christian World View & the Academic Enterprise.* Downers Grove, IL: InterVarsity, 1985.

Honeycutt, Frank G. *The Truth Shall Make You Odd: Speaking with Pastoral Integrity in Awkward Situations.* Grand Rapids: Baker, 2010.

Hoon, Paul W. *The Integrity of Worship.* Nashville: Abingdon, 1971.

Hoppin, Richard. *Medieval Music.* New York: Norton, 1978.

Horton, Michael. *A Better Way: Rediscovering the Drama of Christ-Centered Worship.* Grand Rapids: Baker, 2002.

———. *Christ-less Christianity: The Alternative Gospel of the American Church.* Grand Rapids: Baker, 2008.

———. *People and Place: A Covenant Eschatology.* Louisville: Westminster John Knox, 2008.

BIBLIOGRAPHY

House, Paul R. *Old Testament Theology.* Downers Grove, IL: InterVarsity, 1998.

Howell, James C. *The Beauty of the Word: The Challenge and Wonder of Preaching.* Louisville: Westminster John Knox, 2011.

Hughes, Anselm. *Liturgical Terms for Music Students: A Dictionary.* Boston: Scholarly 1972.

Hughes, Charles W. *American Hymns Old and New: Notes on the Hymns and Biographies of the Authors and Composers.* New York: Columbia University Press, 1980.

Hughes, R. Kent. *The Sermon on the Mount: The Message of the Kingdom.* Wheaton, IL: Crossway, 2001.

Hull, William E. "Preaching on the Synoptic Gospels." In *Biblical Preaching: An Expositor's Treasury,* edited by James W. Cox, 169–94. Philadelphia: Westminster, 1983.

Humphrey, Edith M. *Grand Entrance: Worship on Earth as in Heaven.* Grand Rapids: Brazos, 2011.

Hunsberger, George, and Craig Van Galder. *The Church between Gospel & Culture.* Grand Rapids: Eerdmans, 1996.

Hunt, Arthur W., III. *The Vanishing Word: The Veneration of Visual Imagery in the Postmodern World.* Wheaton, IL: Crossway, 2003.

Hurtado, Larry W. *At the Origins of Christian Worship: The Context and Character of Earliest Christian Devotion.* Grand Rapids: Eerdmans, 1999.

Hustad, Donald P. "Developing a Biblical Philosophy of Church Music." *Bibliotheca Sacra* 117 (1960) 108–22.

———. *Jubilate II: Church Music in Worship and Renewal.* Carol Stream, IL: Hope, 1993.

———. *True Worship: Reclaiming the Wonder & Majesty.* Wheaton, IL: Harold Shaw, 1998.

Hutchinson, William R. *Between the Times: The Travail of the Protestant Establishment in America: 1900–1960.* Cambridge: Cambridge University Press, 1989.

Inch, Morris, and C. Hassell Bullock. *The Literature and Meaning of Scripture.* Grand Rapids: Baker, 1981.

Irwin, Joyce, ed. *Sacred Sound: Music in Religious Thought and Practice.* New York: Oxford University Press, 1984.

Jackman, David. "Hermeneutical Distinctives of Expository Preaching." In *Preach the Word: Essays on Expositional Preaching in Honor of R. Kent Hughes,* edited by Leland Ryken and Todd A. Wilson, 9–21. Wheaton, IL: Crossway, 2007.

Jacks, G. Robert. *Getting the Word Across: Speech Communication for Pastors and Lay Leaders.* Grand Rapids: Eerdmans, 1995.

Jacobs, Alan. *The Book of Common Prayer: A Biography.* Princeton, NJ: Princeton University Press, 2014.

Jacobsen, Rolf A., and Karl N. Jacobsen. *A Reader's Guide for Discovery and Engagement.* Grand Rapids: Baker Academic, 2013.

Jeter, Joseph R., III, and Ronald J. Allen. *One Gospel, Many Ears.* St. Louis: Chalice, 2002.

Johansson, Calvin M. *Discipling Music Ministry: Twenty-first Century Directions.* Peabody, MA: Hendrickson, 1992.

———. *Music & Ministry: A Biblical Counterpoint.* 2nd ed. Peabody, MA: Hendrickson, 1984.

John, Julian. *A Dictionary of Hymnology: Setting Forth the Origin and History of Christian Hymns of All Ages and Nations.* 2nd ed. Grand Rapids: Kregel, 1985.

Johnson, Darrell W. *The Glory of Preaching: Participating in God's Transformation of the World.* Downers Grove, IL: InterVarsity, 2009.

Johnson, Earl S., Jr. *Witness without Parallel: Eight Biblical Texts that make Us Presbyterian.* Louisville: Westminster John Knox, 2003.

Johnson, Terry L. "Calvin the Liturgist." In *Tributes to John Calvin: A Celebration of His Quincentenary*, edited by David W. Hall, 118–52. Phillipsburg, NJ: P&R, 2010.

———. *Worshipping with Calvin: Recovering the Historic Ministry and Worship of Reformed Protestantism.* North Darlington, UK: EP, 2014.

Johnson, Todd E., ed. *The Conviction of Things Not Seen: Worship and Ministry in the 21st Century.* Grand Rapids: Brazos, 2002.

Johnston, Graham. *Preaching to a Postmodern World: A Guide to Reaching Twenty-first Century Listeners.* Grand Rapids: Baker, 2001.

Jones, Arthur C. *Wade in the Water: The Wisdom of Spirituals.* Maryknoll, NY: Orbis, 1993.

Jones, Cheslyn, et al., eds. *The Study of Liturgy.* New York: Oxford University Press, 1978.

Jones, Joseph. *Why We Do What We Do: Christian Worship in the African-American Tradition.* Nashville: Boyd, 2006.

Jones, L. Gregory and Kevin R. Armstrong. *Resurrecting Excellence.* Grand Rapids, Eerdmans, 2006.

Jones, Paul H. "We Are *How* We Worship: Corporate Worship as a Matrix for Christian Identity Formation." *Worship* 69 (1995) 346–60.

Jones, Paul S. *Singing and Making Music: Issues in Church Music Today.* Phillipsburg, NJ: P&R, 2006.

Jones, Robert P. *The End of White Christian America.* New York: Simon & Schuster, 2016.

Juengst, Sara Covin. *Sharing Faith with Children: Rethinking the Children's Sermon.* Philadelphia: Westminster John Knox, 1994.

Kaiser, Walter C., Jr. *The Old Testament in Contemporary Preaching.* Grand Rapids: Baker, 1973.

———. *Preaching and Teaching from the Old Testament: A Guide for the Church.* Grand Rapids: Baker Academic, 2003.

———. *Rediscovering the Unity of the Bible: One Continuous Story, Plan, and Purpose.* Grand Rapids: Zondervan, 2009.

———. *Toward an Exegetical Theology.* Grand Rapids: Baker, 1981.

———. *Toward an Old Testament Theology.* Grand Rapids: Zondervan, 1978.

Kamien, Roger. *Music: An Appreciation.* 10th ed. New York: McGraw-Hill, 2010.

Kauflin, Bob. *Worship Matters: Leading Others to Encounter the Greatness of God.* Wheaton, IL: Crossway, 2008.

Kavanaugh, Patrick. *The Music of Angels: A Listener's Guide to Sacred Music from Chant to Christian Rock.* Chicago: Loyola University Press, 1999.

———. *Spiritual Lives of Great Composers.* Nashville: Sparrow, 1992.

Kay, James F. "Worship in the Reformed Tradition." In *What IS Christian Worship?*, edited by Mary Holder Naegeli, 42–46. Louisville: Presbyterians for Renewal, 2000.

Keck, Leander. *The Bible in the Pulpit: The Renewal of Biblical Preaching.* Nashville: Abingdon, 1978.

Keith, James Melvin. "The Concept of Expository Preaching as Represented by Alexander Maclaren, George Campbell Morgan, and David Martyn Lloyd-Jones." ThD diss., Southwestern Baptist Theological Seminary, 1975.

Kelderman, Duane K., et al. *Authentic Worship in a Changing Culture.* Grand Rapids: Faith Alive, 1997.

Keller, Timothy. "Post-Everythings." *By Faith* 1 (2003) 29–30.

————. *Prayer: Experiencing Awe and Intimacy with God.* New York: Dutton, 2014.

————. *Preaching: Communicating Faith in an Age of Skepticism.* New York: Penguin, 2015.

————. *The Prodigal God: Recovering the Heart of the Christian Faith.* New York: Dutton, 2008.

————. *The Reason for God: Belief in an Age of Skepticism.* New York: Dutton, 2008.

Kelly, Douglas F. "The Catholicity of Calvin's Theology." In *Tributes to John Calvin: A Celebration of His Quincentenary,* edited by David W. Hall, 189–216. Phillipsburg, NJ: P&R, 2010.

Kelly, J. N. D. *Early Christian Creeds.* New York: Longmans, 1950.

Kenneson, Philip D., and James C. Street. *Selling Out the Church: The Danger of Church Marketing.* Nashville: Abingdon, 1997.

Kent, Grenville, et al., eds. *Reclaiming the Old Testament for Christian Preaching.* Downers Grove, IL: IVP Academic, 2010.

Ker, Ian, ed. *The Everyman Chesterton.* New York: Knopf, 2011.

Kidd, Reggie M. *With One Voice: Discovering Christ's Song in Our Worship.* Grand Rapids: Baker, 2005.

Kidner, Derek. *Psalms 75–150.* Tyndale Old Testament Commentaries. Downers Grove, IL: InterVarsity, 1975.

Kierkegaard, Søren. *Purity of Heart Is to Will One Thing.* Translated by Douglas Steere. New York: Harper, 1948.

Kilby, Clyde S. *Christianity and Aesthetics.* Chicago: InterVarsity, 1961.

Kilde, Jeanne Halgren. *When Church Became Theater: The Transformation of Evangelical Architecture and Worship in Nineteenth-Century America.* New York: Oxford University Press, 2002.

Killinger, John. *The Centrality of Preaching in the Total Task of Ministry.* Waco, TX: Word, 1969.

————. *Fundamentals of Preaching.* Philadelphia: Fortress, 1985.

Kim, Hyun An. *Humanism and the Reform of Sacred Music in Early Modern England.* Aldershot, UK: Ashgate, 2008.

Kimball, Dan. *The Emerging Church.* Grand Rapids: Zondervan, 2003.

King, Roberta R. "The Impact of Global Christian Music in Worship." *Theology, News and Notes* 53 (2006) 6–8.

————. "The Ministry Bridges of World Church Music." *Theology, News and Notes* 48 (2001) 13.

Kingdon, Robert. "The Genevan Revolution in Public Worship." *The Princeton Seminary Bulletin* 20 (1999) 264–80.

Kinnaman, David, and Gabe Lyons. *Unchristian: What a New Generation Really Thinks About Christianity . . . and Why It Matters.* Grand Rapids: Baker, 2007.

Kirkland, Bryant M. "Expository Preaching Revitalized." *Pulpit Digest* 45 (1965) 9–14.

Kirkpatrick, A. J. *The Book of Psalms.* Grand Rapids: Baker, 1902.

————. *Reflections on the Psalms.* New York: Harcourt, Brace, and World, 1958.

Kleinig, John W. *The Lord's Song: The Basis, Function, and Significance of Choral Music in Chronicles.* Sheffield, UK: Sheffield Academic Press, 1993.

Knowles, Michael J. *We Preach Not Ourselves: Paul on Proclamation.* Grand Rapids: Brazos, 2008.

Knust, Jenifer, and Tommy Wasserman. "The Biblical Odes and the Text of the Christian Bible: A Reconsideration of the Impact of Liturgical Singing on the Transmission of the Gospel of Luke." *Journal of Biblical Literature* 133 (2014) 341–65.

Koester, Craig R. "The Distant Triumph Song: Music and the Book of Revelation." *Word and World* 12 (1992) 243–62.

Kooy, V. H. "The Apocalypse and Worship: Some Preliminary Observations." *Reformed Review* 30 (1977) 198–209.

Kossler, John. *Folly, Grace, and Power: The Mysterious Act of Preaching.* Grand Rapids: Zondervan, 2011.

Kossler, John, ed. *The Moody Handbook of Preaching.* Chicago: Moody, 2008.

Krapohl, Robert H., and Charles H. Lippy. *The Evangelicals: A Historical, Theological, and Biographical Guide.* Westport, CT: Greenwood, 1999.

Kurtaneck, Nicholas. "Are Seminaries Preparing Prospective Pastors to Preach the Word of God?" *Grace Theological Journal* 6 (1985) 361–71.

Labberton, Mark. *The Dangerous Act of Worship: Living God's Call to Justice.* Downers Grove, IL: IVP, 2007.

Lacarni, Dan. *Why I Left the Contemporary Christian Music Movement: Confessions of a Former Worship Leader.* Darlington, UK: EP, 2002.

Lamb, Robin A. "Bach and Pietism." *Concordia Theological Journal* 55 (1991) 5–22.

Lang, Bernhard. *Sacred Games: A History of Christian Worship.* New Haven, CT: Yale University Press, 1997.

Larson, Craig Brian. *Prophetic Preaching.* Peabody, MA: Hendrickson, 2012.

LaRue, Cleophas J. *I Believe I'll Testify: The Art of African-American Preaching.* Louisville: Westminister John Knox, 2011.

———. *More Power in the Pulpit: How America's Most Effective Black Preachers Prepare Their Sermons.* Louisville: Westminster John Knox, 2009.

———. *Power in the Pulpit: How America's Most Effective Black Preachers Prepare Their Sermons.* Louisville: Westminster John Knox, 2002.

Lasor, William Sanford, et al. *Old Testament Survey: The Message, Form, and Background of the Old Testament.* 2nd ed. Grand Rapids: Eerdmans, 1996.

Lawrence, Michael. *Biblical Theology and the Church.* Wheaton, IL: Crossway, 2010.

Lawson, Steven J. *The Expository Genius of John Calvin.* Lake Mary, FL: Reformation Trust, 2007.

———. *Famine in the Land: A Passionate Plea for Expository Preaching.* Chicago: Moody, 2003.

———. "Sola Scriptura: The Sufficiency of Scripture in Expository Preaching." http://www.preaching.com/resources/articles/11565863/.

Leaver, Robin A. "The Hymn Explosion." *Christian History* 10 (1991) 14–17.

———. *J. S. Bach as Preacher: His Passions and Music in Worship.* St. Louis: Concordia, 1984.

———. *The Whole Church Sings: Congregational Singing in Luther's Wittenberg.* Grand Rapids: Eerdman, 2017.

Leech, Bryan J. "Truth, Taste and Tolerance." *Theology News & Notes* 29 (1982) 15–17.

Leiser, Burton M. "The Trisagion of Isaiah's Vision." *New Testament Studies* 6 (1960) 261–63.

Leith, John H. "Calvin's Doctrine of the Proclamation of the Word and its Significance for Today." In *John Calvin & The Church: A Prism of Reform,* edited by Timothy George, 206–29. Louisville: Westminster John Knox, 1990.

Lemke, Werner E. "Circumcision of the Heart: The Journey of a Biblical Metaphor." In *A God so Near: Essays on Old Testament Theology in Honor of Patrick D. Miller*, edited by Brent A. Strawn and Nancy R. Bowen, 299–320. Winona Lake, IN: Eisenbrauns, 2003.

L'Engle, Madeleine. *Walking on Water: Reflections on Faith & Art*. Wheaton, IL: Harold Shaw, 1980.

Leslie, Robert H. "Music and the Arts in Calvin's Geneva." PhD diss., McGill University, 1969.

Levi, Anthony. *Renaissance and Reformation: The Intellectual Genesis*. New Haven, CT: Yale University Press, 2002.

Lew, Timothy T'ingfang. "O Christ, the Great Foundation." In *Hymns of Universal Praise*, translated by Mildred A. Wiant, 273. Hong Kong: Chinese Christian Literature Council, 1977.

Lewis, C. S. *George MacDonald: An Anthology*. New York: Simon & Schuster, 1996.

———. *The Lion, the Witch, and the Wardrobe*. In *The Complete Chronicles of Narnia*, by C. S. Lewis, 76–134. New York: HarperCollins, 1998.

———. *Mere Christianity*. London: Macmillan, 1952.

———. *Miracles: A Preliminary Study*. New York: HarperCollins, 2001.

———. "On Church Music." In *C. S. Lewis: Christian Reflections*, edited by Walter Hooper, 94–99. Grand Rapids: Eerdmans, 1967.

———. *The Screwtape Letters*. New York: HarperCollins, 2001.

Liesch, Barry. *The New Worship: Straight Talk on Music and the Church*. Rev. ed. Grand Rapids: Baker, 2001.

———. *People in the Presence of God: Models and Directions for Worship*. Grand Rapids: Zondervan, 1988.

Lieth, John H. *Introduction to the Reformed Tradition*. Rev. ed. Atlanta: John Knox, 1981.

Lincoln, L. H. "The Message and Ministry of Howard G. Hendricks in Christian Higher Education." EdD diss., University of North Texas, 2001.

Lindbeck, George. *The Nature of Doctrine*. Philadelphia: Westminster, 1984.

Lindslay, Art. "Profiles in Faith: John Calvin." *Knowing and Doing* (2002) 1–21.

Linscott, Robert A., ed. *Complete Poems and Selected Letters of Michelangelo*. Translated by Creighton Gilbert. Princeton, NJ: Princeton University Press, 1980.

Lischer, Richard, ed. *The Company of Preachers: Wisdom on Preaching, Augustine to the Present*. Grand Rapids: Eerdmans, 2002.

Litfin, A. Duane. "The Perils of Persuasive Preaching." *Christianity Today* 21 (1977) 14–17.

Lloyd-Jones, D. Martyn. *Preaching and Preachers*. Grand Rapids: Zondervan, 1971.

Lockerbie, D. Bruce. *The Liberating Word: Art and the Ministry of the Gospel*. Grand Rapids: Eerdmans, 1974.

Long, Thomas G. *Beyond the Worship Wars: Building Vital and Faithful Congregations*. Herndon, VA: Alban, 2001.

———. *Preaching from Memory to Hope*. Louisville: Westminster John Knox, 2009.

———. "Reclaiming the Unity of Word and Sacrament in Presbyterian and Reformed Worship." *Reformed Liturgy & Worship* 16 (1982) 12.

———. *The Witness of Preaching*. Louisville: Westminster John Knox, 1989.

Longfellow, Henry Wadsworth. *The Complete Poetical Works of Henry Wadsworth Longfellow*. Oxford: Benediction Classics, 2011.

Longfield, Bradley J. *The Presbyterian Controversy: Fundamentalists, Modernists, and Moderates*. New York: Oxford University Press, 1991.

Longman, Tremper, III. *Immanuel in Our Place: Seeing Christ in Israel's Worship.* Phillipsburg, NJ: P&R, 2001.

———. *Old Testament Commentary Survey.* 4th ed. Grand Rapids: Baker Academic, 2007.

Longyear, Rey M. *Nineteenth-Century Romanticism in Music.* Englewood Cliffs, NJ: Prentice-Hall, 1973.

Loosemore, Henry. "O Lord, Increase Our Faith." In *The New Church Anthem Book,* edited by Lionel Dakers, 284–87. New York: Oxford University Press, 1992.

Love, Anthony N. S. *John Calvin: Student of the Church Fathers.* Grand Rapids: Baker, 1999.

Lovelace, Austin C. *The Anatomy of Hymnody.* Chicago: GIA, 1965.

Lovelace, Austin C., and William C. Rice. *Music and Worship in the Church.* Rev. ed. Nashville: Abingdon, 1960.

Lowery, Eugene L. *The Homiletical Plot: The Sermon as Narrative Form.* Rev. ed. Philadelphia: Westminster John Knox, 2001.

Lugo, Luis, et al. *"Nones" on the Rise: One-in-Five Adults Has No Religious Affiliation.* Washington, DC: Pew Research Center Forum on Religion & Public Life, 2012.

Lukianoff, Greg and Jonathan Haidt. "The Coddling of the American Mind." http://www.theatlantic.com/magazine/archive/2015/09/the-coddling-of-the-american-mind/399356/.

Lutkin, Peter C. *Music in the Church.* New York: American Musicological Society, 1970.

MacArthur, John, Jr., ed. *Rediscovering Expository Preaching: Balancing the Science and Art of Biblical Exposition.* Dallas: Word, 1992.

———. "A Reminder to Shepherds." In *Feed My Sheep: A Passionate Plea for Preaching,* edited by Don Kistler, 269–85. Morgan, PA: Soli Deo Gloria, 2002.

———. *Worship: The Ultimate Priority.* Chicago: Moody, 1983.

MacDonald, George. *Unspoken Sermons: Second Series.* Grand Rapids: Christian Classics Ethereal Library, n.d. https://www.ccel.org/ccel/macdonald/unspoken2.pdf.

———. *Unspoken Sermons: Series One.* Grand Rapids: Christian Classics Ethereal Library, n.d. https://www.ccel.org/ccel/macdonald/unspoken1.pdf.

———. *Unspoken Sermons: Third Series.* Grand Rapids: Christian Classics Ethereal Library, n.d. https://www.ccel.org/ccel/macdonald/unspoken3.pdf.

MacLeod, Donald. *Christ Crucified: Understanding the Atonement.* Downers Grove, IL: IVP Academic, 2014.

Macmillan, John B. "The Calvinist Psalmody of Claude LeJeune." PhD diss., New York University, 1966.

Magruder, Jeff C. "Why Pentecostals Don't Preach Expository Sermons." http://www.preaching.com/resources/articles/11547311/.

Mahler, Gustav. "Tradition is not the worship of ashes." http://www.goodreads.com/author/quotes/94724/gustav_mahler, lines 1–4.

———. "Tradition ist nicht die Anbetung der Asche." http://www.ruter.de/?p=2402.

Maleyft, Norma deWaal, and Howard Vanderwell. *Designing Worship Together: Models and Strategies for Worship Planning.* Herndon, VA: Alban, 2005.

Malligan, Mary Alice, and Ronald J. Allen. *Make the Word Come Alive: Lessons from the Laity.* St. Louis: Chalice, 2005.

Man, Ron. *Proclamation and Praise: Hebrews 2:12 and the Christology of Worship.* Eugene, OR: Wipf & Stock, 2007.

Manning, Bernard. *The Hymns of Watts and Wesley.* London: Epworth, 1942.

Manschreck, Clyde L., ed. *A History of Christianity: Readings in the History of the Church.* Vol. 2, *The Church from the Reformation to the Present.* Grand Rapids: Baker, 1964.

Mapson, J. Wendell, Jr. *The Ministry of Music in the Black Church.* Valley Forge, PA: Judson, 1984.

Marshall, I. Howard. *Last Supper and Lord's Supper.* Grand Rapids: Eerdmans, 1981.

———. *New Testament Theology: Many Witnesses, One Gospel.* Downers Grove, IL: IVP Academic, 2004.

———. "Preaching from the New Testament." *Scottish Bulletin of Evangelical Theology* 9 (1991) 104–17.

Marshall, I. Howard, ed. *New Testament Interpretation: Essays on Principles and Methods.* Grand Rapids: Eerdmans, 1977.

Marshall, Madeleine Forell. "A New Species of Christian Song: Where did the English Hymn Come from?" *Christian History X* 31 (1991) 32–34.

Martin, Ralph P. *The Spirit and the Congregation: Studies in 1 Corinthians 12–15.* Grand Rapids: Eerdmans, 1984.

———. *Worship in the Early Church.* Grand Rapids: Eerdmans, 1964.

———. *The Worship of God: Some Theological, Pastoral, and Practical Implications.* Grand Rapids: Eerdmans, 1982.

Marty, Martin E. *A Short History of Christianity.* Philadelphia: Fortress, 1959.

Massey, James Earl. *The Burdensome Joy of Preaching.* Nashville: Abingdon, 1996.

———. *Stewards of the Story: The Task of Preaching.* Louisville: Westminster John Knox, 2006.

Mathewson, Steven. *The Art of Preaching Old Testament Narrative.* Grand Rapids: Baker Academic, 2002.

Mauldin, David C. "Nurturing a Reformed Sacramental Piety of the Lord's Supper at Westminster Presbyterian Church, Mobile, Alabama." DMin diss., Samford University, 2012.

Maxwell, William D. *A History of Christian Worship: An Outline of its Development and Forms.* Grand Rapids: Baker, 1982.

———. *A History of Worship in the Church of Scotland.* London: Oxford University Press, 1955.

———. *An Outline of Christian Worship: Its Developments and Forms.* London: Oxford University Press, 1936.

Maynard-Reid, Pedrito D. *Diverse Worship: African-American, Caribbean, & Hispanic Perspectives.* Downers Grove, IL: InterVarsity, 2000.

Mayne-Treathick, Jessica-Robyn. "The Effectiveness of the Arts in Preaching and Worship." Lecture at the meetings of the Evangelical Homiletics Society, Deerfield, IL, October 14–16, 2010.

Mays, James L. "Calvin's Commentary on the Psalms: The Preface as Introduction." In *John Calvin & the Church: Prism of Reform,* edited by Timothy George, 195–204. Louisville: Westminster John Knox, 1990.

———. *Preaching and Teaching the Psalms.* Louisville: Westminster John Knox, 2006.

McAlpine, William R. "Mystery in Preaching and Worship." Lecture at annual meeting of the Evangelical Homiletics Society, Deerfield, IL, October 14–16, 2010.

McClaren, Brian. *A Generous Orthodoxy.* Grand Rapids: Zondervan, 2004.

McCracken, Brett. *Hipster Christianity: When Church and Cool Collide.* Grand Rapids: Baker, 2010.

McCullough, David. "The American Adventure of Louis Agassiz." In *Brave Companions: Portraits in History*, by David McCullough, 20–36. New York: Simon & Schuster, 1992.

McDill, Wayne. "Giving Voice to the Bible: Expository Scripture Reading." *Preaching* 24 (2008) 36–39.

———. *12 Essential Skills for Great Preaching*. Nashville: B&H, 2006.

McGowan, Andrew B. *Ancient Christian Worship: Early Church Practices in Social, Historical, and Theological Perspective*. Grand Rapids: Baker Academic, 2014.

McGrath, Alister E. *C. S. Lewis—A Life: Eccentric Genius, Reluctant Prophet*. Carol Stream, IL: Tyndale House, 2013.

———. *Evangelicalism and the Future of Christianity*. Downers Grove, IL: InterVarsity, 1995.

———. *Historical Theology: An Introduction to the History of Christian Thought*. Oxford: Blackwell, 1998.

———. *A Life of John Calvin: A Study in the Shaping of Western Culture*. Oxford: Blackwell, 1990.

———. *Luther's Theology of the Cross: Martin Luther's Theological Breakthrough*. Oxford: Blackwell, 1985.

———. *Reformation Thought: An Introduction*. 3rd ed. Oxford: Blackwell, 2001.

McGrath, Alister E., ed. *The Christian Theology Reader*. 2nd ed. Oxford: Blackwell, 2001.

McKee, Elsie Anne. *The Cambridge Companion to John Calvin*. Cambridge: Cambridge University Press, 2004.

———. "Context, Contours, Contents: Towards a Description of the Classical Reformed Teaching on Worship." *Princeton Seminary Bulletin* 16 (1995) 172–201.

———. *The Pastoral Ministry and Worship in Calvin's Geneva*. Geneva: Librairie Droz, 2016.

———. "Reformed Worship in the Sixteenth Century." In *Christian Worship in Reformed Churches Past and Present*, edited by Lukas Vischer, 3–34. Grand Rapids: Eerdmans, 2003.

McKee, Elsie Anne, ed. *John Calvin: Writings on Personal Piety*. New York: Paulist, 2001.

McKee, Elsie Anne, and Brian G. Armstrong, eds., *Probing the Reformed Tradition: Historical Studies in Honor of Edward A. Dowey, Jr*. Louisville: Westminster John Knox, 1989.

McKim, Donald K., ed. *Historical Handbook of Major Biblical Interpreters*. Downers Grove, IL: InterVarsity, 1998.

McKim, LindJo H. "Hymnody." In *The Westminster Handbook to Reformed Theology*, edited by Donald McKim, 116–18. Louisville: Westminster John Knox, 1995.

McKim, LindJo H., ed. *The Presbyterian Hymnal: Hymns, Songs, and Spiritual Songs*. Louisville: Westminster John Knox, 1990.

———. *The Presbyterian Hymnal Companion*. Louisville: Westminster John Knox, 1993.

McLean, Terri Bockland. *New Harmonies: Choosing Contemporary Music for Worship*. Herndon, VA: Alban, 1998.

McLaughlin, R. Emmet. "The Word Eclipsed: Preaching in the Early Middle Ages." *Traditio* 46 (1991) 77–122.

McLeod, Donald. *Presbyterian Worship: Its Meaning and Method*. Richmond, VA: John Knox, 1966.

———. *Word and Sacrament: A Preface to Preaching and Worship*. Englewood Cliffs, NJ: Prentice-Hall, 1960.

McNeill. John T. *The History and Character of Calvinism*. London: Oxford University Press, 1954.

Melton, James. *Presbyterian Worship in America: Changing Patterns Since 1787*. Richmond, VA: John Knox, 1967.

Merida, Tony. *Declaring Scripture with Responsibility, Passion, and Authenticity*. Nashville: B&H, 2009.

Merrill, Eugene H. *Everlasting Dominion: A Theology of the Old Testament*. Nashville: B&H, 2006.

———. *Kingdom of Priests: A History of Old Testament Israel*. Grand Rapids: Baker, 1987.

———. "Old Testament Scholarship and the Man in the Street: Whence and Whither?" *Journal of the Evangelical Theological Society* 54 (2011) 5–17.

Metaxas, Eric. "Are Atheists Afraid of God?" http://www.wsj.com/articles/are-atheists-afraid-of-god-1464907324.

———. *Dietrich Bonhoeffer: Pastor, Martyr, Prophet, Spy*. Nashville: Thomas Nelson, 2011.

Metzger, Bruce M. *The Text of the New Testament: Its Transmission, Corruption, and Restoration*. New York: Oxford University Press, 1968.

Meye, Robert P. "Christian Song and Music—Some Reflections." *Theology News & Notes* 29 (1982) 6–9.

Meyer, Leonard B. *Emotion and Meaning in Music*. Chicago: University of Chicago Press, 1956.

Millbank, John. *Theology and Social Theory*. Oxford: Blackwell, 1990.

Miller, Calvin. *Preaching: The Art of Narrative Exposition*. Grand Rapids: Baker, 2006.

———. *Spirit, Word, and Story: A Philosophy of Preaching*. Dallas: Word, 1989.

Miller, Charles E. *Ordained to Preach: A Theology and Practice of Preaching*. Eugene, OR: Wipf & Stock, 2003.

Miller, Donald G. *Fire in My Mouth*. Nashville: Abingdon, 1954.

———. *The Way to Biblical Preaching*. Nashville: Abingdon, 1957.

Miller, Patrick D., Jr. "Current Issues in Psalms Studies." *Word & World* 5 (1985) 132–43.

———. *Interpreting the Psalms*. Philadelphia: Fortress, 1986.

———. *The Lord of the Psalms*. Louisville: Westminster John Knox, 2014.

———. *They Cried to the Lord: The Form and Theology of Biblical Prayer*. Minneapolis: Fortress, 1994.

Miller, Paul M. "Worship Among the Early Anabaptists." *Mennonite Quarterly Review* 30 (1956) 235–46.

Miller, Steve. *The Contemporary Christian Music Debate*. Wheaton, IL: Tyndale House, 1993.

Minear, Paul S. *Death Set to Music: Masterworks by Bach, Brahms, Penderecki, Bernstein*. Atlanta: John Knox, 1987.

———. *Images of the Church in the New Testament*. Philadelphia: Westminster, 1970.

Mitchell, Robert H. *Ministry and Music*. Philadelphia: Westminster, 1978.

Mitman, F. Russell. *Worship in the Shape of Scripture*. Cleveland: Pilgrim, 2001.

Mohler, R. Albert Jr. "Creating the Bridge: An Interview with John R. W. Stott." http://www.preaching.com/resources/articles/11567090/.

———. "Expository Preaching and the Recovery of Christian Worship: Part One. http://www.albertmohler.com/2005/08/09/expository-preaching-and-the-recovery-of-christian-worship-part-one/.

———. "Expository Preaching and the Recovery of Christian Worship: Part Three. http://www.albertmohler.com/2005/08/11/expository-preaching-and-the-recovery-of-christian-worship-part-three/.

———. "Expository Preaching and the Recovery of Christian Worship: Part Two. http://www.albertmohler.com/2005/08/10/expository-preaching-and-the-recovery-of-christian-worship-part-two/.

———. *Feed My Sheep: A Passionate Plea for Preaching*. Lake Mary, FL: Reformation Trust, 2008.

———. *He is Not Silent: Preaching in a Post-Modern World*. Chicago: Moody, 2008.

Morgan, Robert P. *Twentieth-Century Music*. New York: Norton, 1991.

Morgenthaler, Sarah. *Worship Evangelism: Inviting Unbelievers into the Presence of God*. Rev. ed. Grand Rapids: Zondervan, 1999.

Moriah, Lionel M. "Imagination: Matchmaker for Preaching and Worship." Lecture at the annual meeting of the Evangelical Homiletics Society, Deerfield, Il, October 14–16, 2010.

Morris, Leon. "The Gospel According to John." In *The New International Commentary on the New Testament*, edited by F. F. Bruce, 251–75. Grand Rapids: Eerdmans,1971.

———. "The Saints & the Synagogue." In *Worship, Theology & Ministry in the Early Church: Essays in Honor of Ralph P. Martin*, edited by Michael J. Wilkins and Terrence Paige, 39–52. Sheffield, UK: Manchester University Press, 1992.

Morrow, Jonathan. *Think Christianly: Looking at the Intersection of Faith and Culture*. Grand Rapids: Zondervan, 2011.

Mortimer, Anthony, ed. *Selected Poems from Michelangelo Buonarroti: With Translations from Various Sources*. 1885. Reprint, London: Penguin, 2013.

Moses, Steven R. "Meeting the Challenge of Postmodernism: An Integrative Approach to Expository Preaching." MDiv thesis, Trinity Evangelical Divinity School, 2003.

Moule, C. F. D. "The Epistles to the Colossians and Philemon." In *The Cambridge Greek New Testament Commentary*, edited by C. F. D. Moule, 125. Cambridge: Cambridge University Press, 1957.

———. *Worship in the New Testament*. Richmond, VA: John Knox, 1961.

Mounce, William D. *Interlinear for the Rest of Us: The Reverse Interlinear for New Testament Word Studies*. Grand Rapids: Zondervan, 2006.

Mouw, Richard J. *The Smell of Sawdust: What Evangelicals Can Learn from Their Fundamentalist Heritage*. Grand Rapids: Zondervan, 2000.

Mouw, Richard J., and Mark A. Noll, eds. *Wonderful Words of Life: Hymns in American Protestant History and Theology*. Grand Rapids: Eerdmans, 2004.

Mowinckel, Sigmund. *The Psalms and Israel's Worship*. Nashville: Abingdon, 1960.

Mueller, Richard A. *After Calvin: Studies in the Development of a Theological Tradition*. New York: Oxford University Press, 2003.

———. *Post-Reformation Reformed Dogmatics: The Rise and Development of Reformed Orthodoxy, c. 1520 to c. 1725*. 4 vols. Grand Rapids: Baker Academic, 2003.

———. *The Unaccommodated Calvin: Studies in the Foundation of a Theological Tradition*. Oxford: Oxford University Press, 2000.

Mueller, Richard A., and Rowland S. Ward. *Scripture and Worship: Biblical Interpretation and the Directory for Public Worship*. Phillipsburg, NJ: P&R, 2007.

Murray, Iain H. *David Martyn Lloyd Jones*. Edinburgh: Banner of Truth, 1990.

Murray, Peter and Linda Murray. *The Oxford Companion to Christian Art and Architecture*. New York: Oxford University Press, 1996.

Music, David. W. *Christian Hymnody in Twentieth-Century Britain and America: An Annotated Bibliography*. Westport, CT: Greenwood, 2001.

―――. *Hymnology: A Collection of Source Readings*. London: Scarecrow, 1996.

Music, David W., and Paul Westermeyer. *Church Music in the United States 1760–1901*. Fenton, MO: Morningstar, 2014.

Naegeli, Mary Holder, ed. *What is Christian Worship?* Louisville: Presbyterians for Renewal, 2000.

Nauert, Charles G. "The Clash of Humanists and Scholastics: An Approach to Pre-Reformation Controversies." *Sixteenth Century Journal* 4 (1979) 1–18.

Navarro, Kevin. *The Complete Worship Service: Creating a Taste of Heaven on Earth*. Grand Rapids: Baker, 2005.

Nelson, David P. "Voicing God's Praise: The Use of Music in Worship." In *Authentic Worship*, edited by Herbert Bateman IV, 145–69. Grand Rapids: Kregel, 2002.

Nelson, Timothy J. "At Ease with Our Own Kind: Worship Practices and Class Segregation in American Religion." In *Religion and Class in America: Culture, History, and Politics*, edited by Sean McCloud and William A. Mirola, 45–68. Leiden, the Netherlands: Brill, 2009.

Nettle, Paul. *Luther and Music*. New York: Russell & Russell, 1967.

Newbigin, Leslie. *Foolishness to the Greeks: The Gospel and Western Culture*. Grand Rapids: Eerdmans, 1986.

Newton, Tim. "Our Changing Music: New Sounds in the Middle Ages." *Decision* 37 (1996) 16–18.

Nicholson, Sir Sydney, et al., eds. *Hymns Ancient & Modern*. Rev. ed. Norwich: Canterbury, 1950.

Nieman, James R., and Thomas G. Rogers. *Preaching to Every Pew: Cross-Cultural Strategies*. Minneapolis: Fortress, 2001.

Nixon, LeRoy. *John Calvin, Expository Preacher*. Grand Rapids: Eerdmans, 1950

Noll, Mark A. *America's God: From Jonathan Edwards to Abraham Lincoln*. Oxford: Oxford University Press, 2002.

―――. *The Scandal of the Evangelical Mind*. Grand Rapids: Eerdmans, 1994.

Noll, Mark A., and Carolyn Nystrom. *Is the Reformation Over? An Evangelical Assessment of Contemporary Roman Catholicism*. Grand Rapids: Baker Academic, 2005.

Northcutt, Cecil. *Hymns in Christian Worship*. *Eccumenical Studies in Worship* 3. Atlanta: John Knox, 1964.

Oesterly, W. O. E. *The Jewish Background of Christian Liturgy*. Gloucester, UK: Peter Smith, 1965.

―――. *Sacrifices in Ancient Israel: Their Origin, Purposes, and Development*. London: Hodder and Stoughton, 1937.

Office of the General Assembly of the Presbyterian Church U.S.A. *The Constitution of the Presbyterian Church U.S.A., 2011–2013*. Louisville: The Office of the General Assembly of the Presbyterian Church, 2011.

Office of Theology and Worship for the Presbyterian Church (U.S.A). *Book of Occasional Services: A Liturgical Resource Supplementing the Book of Common Worship, 1993*. Louisville: Geneva, 1999.

Okholm, Dennis L. "I Don't Think We're in Kansas Anymore, Toto!—Postmodernism in Our Everyday Lives." *Theology Matters* 5 (1999) 1–6.

Old, Hughes Oliphant. "Calvin's Theology of Worship." In *Give Praise to God: A Vision for Reforming Worship*, edited by Philip Ryken et al., 412–35. Phillipsburg, NJ: P&R, 2004.

———. *Holy Communion in the Piety of the Reformed Church*. Dallas, GA: Tolle Lege, 2014.

———. "John Calvin and the Prophetic Criticism of Worship." In *John Calvin & the Church: Prism of Reform*, edited by Timothy George, 230–46. Louisville: Westminster John Knox, 1990.

———. "A 'New Breed' of Presbyterians." In *The Reading and Preaching of the Scriptures in the Worship of The Christian Church*. Vol. 7, *Our Own Time*, edited by Hughes Oliphant Old, 87–169. Grand Rapids: Eerdmans, 2010.

———. *The Patristic Roots of Reformed Worship*. Zurich: Theologischer Verlag, 1975.

———. "Preaching as Worship in the Pulpit of John Calvin." In *Tributes to John Calvin: A Celebration of His Quincentenary*, edited by David W. Hall, 95–117. Phillipsburg, NJ: P&R, 2010.

———. *Themes and Variations for a Christian Doxology*. Grand Rapids: Eerdmans, 1992.

———. *Worship: Reformed According to Scripture*. Rev. ed. Louisville: Westminster John Knox, 2002.

Olford, Stephen F., and David L. Olford. *Anointed Expository Preaching*. Nashville: B&H, 1998.

Ortberg, John C. "My Holy of Holies: How All-too-human Preachers can Prepare Their Souls to Preach." http://www.christianitytoday.com/le/2007/spring/21.38.html.

Osbeck, Kenneth. *Beyond the Sunset: 25 Hymn Stories Celebrating the Hope of Heaven*. Grand Rapids: Kregel, 2001.

Osborne, Grant R. *The Hermeneutical Spiral: A Comprehensive Introduction to Biblical Interpretation*. Rev. ed. Downers Grove, IL: InterVarsity, 2006.

Otto, Rudolf. *The Idea of the Holy*. New York: Oxford University Press, 1950.

Overstreet, Mark M. "Preaching Rediscovered: Broadus' Lost Lectures and the Recovery of Exposition." http://www.preaching.com/resources/articles/11605341/.

Packer, J. I. "The Puritan Approach to Worship." In *A Quest for Godliness: The Puritan Vision of the Christian Life*. Wheaton, IL: Crossway, 1990.

———. "Worship." In *New Dictionary of Biblical Theology*, edited by T. Desmond Alexander et al., 855–63. Downers Grove, IL: InterVarsity, 2000.

Palisca, Claude V. *Baroque Music*. 2nd ed. Englewood Cliffs, NJ: Prentice-Hall, 1981.

Palmer, Earl F. *The Book that John Wrote*. Vancouver: Regent College Press, 2002.

———. "The Case for Expositional Preaching." *Theology News and Notes* 32 (1985) 8–13.

———. *The Enormous Exception: Meeting Christ in the Sermon on the Mount*. Vancouver: Regent College Press, 2001.

———. *Love has its Reasons: An Inquiry into New Testament Love*. Waco, TX: Word, 1977.

———. "The Love of Jesus Christ," (sermon). 1976. Audiocassette.

———. "The Making of a Sermon." *Theology News and Notes* 27 (1980) 20–23.

———. *Old Law—New Life: The Ten Commandments and New Testament Faith*. Nashville: Abingdon, 1984.

———. "Revelation." In *1, 2, 3 John & Revelation*, vol. 35 of *The Preacher's Commentary*, edited by Lloyd J. Ogilvie, 89–243. Nashville: Thomas Nelson, 1982.

———. *To Run the Race: St. Paul's Second Letter to Timothy*. Vancouver: Regent College Press, 2014.

Palmer, Earl F., et al. *Mastering Teaching*. Portland: Multnomah, 1991.

Panel on Worship in the Church of Scotland. "Prayers from the Book of Common Order." http://www.oremus.org/laborum/maincommonorder.htm.

Park, Hyun Shin. "Toward a Life-Changing Application Paradigm in Expository Preaching." PhD diss., Southern Baptist Theological Seminary, 2012.

Parker, Alice. *Melodious Accord: Good Singing in Church*. Chicago: Liturgy Training, 1991.

Parker, T. H. L. *Calvin's Preaching*. Louisville: Westminster John Knox, 1992.

———. *John Calvin: A Biography*. Philadelphia: Westminster, 1975.

Parry, Robin. *Worshiping Trinity*. Carlisle, UK: Paternoster, 2005.

Partee, Charles. *The Theology of John Calvin*. Louisville: Westminster John Knox, 2008.

Pascal, Blaise. "Theology & Philosophy." In *Pensées of Blaise Pascal*, translated by W. F. Trotter, 236. London: Dent, 1931.

Pasquarello, Michael, III. *Christian Preaching: A Trinitarian Theology of Proclamation*. Grand Rapids: Baker, 2006.

———. *Sacred Rhetoric: Preaching as a Theological and Pastoral Practice of the Church*. Grand Rapids: Eerdmans, 2005.

Paul, Gregory S. "Atheism on the Upswing in America." http://www.washingtonpost.com/blog/guest-voices/post/atheism-on-the-upswing-in-america.

Pauly, Reinhard G. *Music in the Classic Period*. 2nd ed. Englewood Cliffs, NJ: Prentice-Hall, 1973.

Payton, Leonard R. "Congregational Singing and the Ministry of the Word." *Revival and Reformation* 7 (1998) 119–66.

Pearcey, Nancy. *Total Truth: Liberating Christianity from its Cultural Captivity*. Wheaton, IL: Crossway, 2005.

Pelikan, Jaroslav. *Bach among the Theologians*. Philadelphia: Fortress, 1986.

Penny, Robert Lee. "An Examination of the Principles of Expository Preaching of David Martyn Lloyd-Jones." DMin diss., Asbury Theological Seminary, 1980.

Perry, Lloyd M. *Biblical Preaching for Today's World*. Chicago: Moody, 1973.

Peters, J. P. "The Religion of Moses." *Journal of Biblical Literature* 20 (1901) 101–28.

Peterson, David G. *Engaging God: A Biblical Theology of Worship*. Downers Grove, IL: InterVarsity, 1992.

Peterson, Eugene H. *Christ Plays in Ten Thousand Places: A Conversation in Spiritual Theology*. Grand Rapids: Eerdmans, 2005.

———. *Eat this Book: A Conversation in the Art of Spiritual Reading*. Grand Rapids: Eerdmans, 2006.

———. *The Jesus Way: A Conversation on the Ways that Jesus is the Way*. Grand Rapids: Eerdmans, 2007.

Petry, Ray C., ed. *A History of Christianity: Readings in the History of the Church*, vol. 1, *The Early and Medieval Church*. Grand Rapids: Baker, 1981.

Philip, James. "Preaching in History." *Evangelical Review of Theology* 8 (1984) 298–307.

Pinson, J. Matthew, ed. *Perspectives on Christian Worship: 5 Views*. Nashville: B&H Academic, 2009.

Piper, John. *Brothers, We Are Not Professionals: A Plea to Pastors for Radical Ministry*. Nashville: B&H, 2002.

———. "The Divine Majesty of the Word: John Calvin, the Man and His Preaching." *Southwestern Baptist Journal of Theology* (2009) 4–15.

———. *John Calvin and His Passion for the Majesty of God*. Wheaton, IL: Crossway, 2009.

———. "Preaching as Worship: Meditations on Expository Exultation." *Trinity Journal* 16 (1995) 29–45.

———. *The Supremacy of God in Preaching*. Grand Rapids: Baker, 1990.

———. "What Kind of Preaching Produces Holiness? The Link between Worship and Obedience." *Leadership* 20 (1999) 41–42.

Piper, John, and Justin Taylor. *The Power of Words and the Wonder of God*. Wheaton, IL: Crossway, 2009.

Piper, Otto. "The Apocalypse of John and the Liturgy of the Ancient Church." *Church History* 20 (1951) 10–22.

Pitt-Watson, Ian. *Preaching: A Kind of Folly*. Edinburgh: St. Andrews University Press, 1976.

———. "Preaching as His Story in Our Stories." *Theology News and Notes* 32 (1980) 5.

———. *A Primer for Preachers*. Grand Rapids: Baker, 1986.

Plank, Steven. *The Way to Heavens Doore: An Introduction to Liturgical Process and Musical Style*. Metuchen, NJ: Scarecrow, 1994.

Plantinga, Cornelius, and Sue A. Rozeboom. *Discerning the Spirits: A Guide to Thinking about Christian Worship Today*. Grand Rapids: Eerdmans, 2003.

Plantinga, Richard A. "The Union of Music and Theology in the Sacred Compositions of J. S. Bach." *Theology, News and Notes* 53 (2006) 12–15.

Postman, Neil. *Amusing Ourselves to Death: Public Discourse in the Age of Show Business*. Rev. ed. New York: Penguin, 2005.

Poultney, David. *Dictionary of Western Church Music*. Chicago: American Library, 1991.

Powell, Mark Allen. *Encyclopedia of Contemporary Christian Music*. Peabody, MA: Hendrickson, 2002.

Prince, David E. "The Necessity of a Christocentric, Kingdom-Focused Model of Expository Preaching." PhD diss., The Southern Baptist Theological Seminary, 2011.

Prothero, Stephen. *Religious Literacy: What Every American Needs to Know—And Doesn't*. New York: HarperCollins, 2008.

Proulx, Richard. *O God, Beyond All Praising*. Chicago: GIA, 1982.

Pruitt, Todd. "Is Your Church Worship More Pagan than Christian?" http://www.christianity.com/church/worship-and-hymns/is-your-church-worship-more-pagan-than-christian.html.

———. "Is Your Worship Christian or Pagan? (7 tests)." http://www.christianity.com/church/worship-and-hymns/is-your-worship-christian-or-pagan-7-tests.html.

Putnam, Robert D. *Bowling Alone: The Collapse and Revival of American Community*. New York: Simon & Schuster, 2000.

Putnam, Robert D., and David E. Campbell. *American Grace: How Religion Divides and Unites Us*. New York: Simon & Schuster, 2012.

———. "Preaching and Trinitarian Worship." http://www.preaching.com/resources/articles/11562921/.

Quickie, Michael J. *Preaching as Worship: An Integrative Approach to Formation in Your Church*. Grand Rapids: Baker, 2011.

———. *360-Degree Preaching: Hearing, Speaking, and Living the Word*. Grand Rapids: Baker, 2003.

Rainer, Thom S. *Who Moved My Pulpit? Leading Change in the Church*. Nashville: B&H, 2016.

Ralston, Timothy J. "Showing the Relevance: Application, Ethics, and Preaching." In *Interpreting the New Testament Text: Introduction to the Art and Science of Biblical Exegesis*, edited by Darrell L. Bock and Buist M. Fanning, 293–311. Wheaton, IL: Crossway, 2006.

Ramshaw, Gail. *Christian Worship: 100,000 Sundays of Symbols and Rituals*. Minneapolis: Fortress, 2009.

———. "Words Worth Signing." In *The Hymn* 46 (April 1995) 17–19.

Rattenbury, J. Ernest. *The Evangelical Doctrines of Charles Wesley's Hymns*. London: Epworth, 1941.

Ratzinger, Joseph Cardinal, et al. *Catechism of the Catholic Church*. 2nd ed. Rome: Liberia Editrice Vaticana, 2000.

Rayburn, Robert G. *O Come, Let Us Worship*. Grand Rapids: Baker, 1980.

———. "Worship in the Church." In *Evangelical Dictionary of Theology*, edited by Walter A. Elwell, 1193–96. Grand Rapids: Baker, 1984.

Reid, Robert S. *The Four Voices of Preaching: Connecting Purpose and Identity Behind the Pulpit*. Grand Rapids: Brazos, 2006.

Reid, W. Stanford. "The Battle Hymn of the Lord: Calvinist Psalmody of the Sixteenth Century." In *Sixteenth Century Essays and Studies*, vol. 2, edited by Carl S. Meyer. St. Louis: Foundation for Reformation Studies, 1971.

Renwick, David A. *Paul, the Temple, and the Presence of God*. Atlanta: Scholars, 1991.

Reynolds, William J. *Songs of Glory: Great Hymns and Gospel Songs*. Grand Rapids: Zondervan, 1990.

———. "Three Hymnals that Shaped Today's Worship." *Christian History* 10 (1991) 36–37.

Reynolds, William J., and Milburn Price. *A Survey of Christian Hymnody*. 4th ed. Carol Stream, IL: Hope, 1999.

Rice, Howard L., and James C. Huffstutler. *Reformed Worship*. Louisville: Geneva, 2001.

Richard, Ramesh P. "Levels of Biblical Meaning." *Bibliotheca Sacra* 143 (1986) 123–33.

———. *Preparing Expository Sermons: A Seven-Step Method for Biblical Preaching*. Grand Rapids: Baker, 2001.

———. *Scripture Sculpture*. Grand Rapids: Baker, 1995.

Richard, William A. "Preaching the Dark Side of the Gospel." *Worship* 61 (1987) 141–51.

Riedel, Johannes. *The Lutheran Chorale: Its Basic Traditions*. Minneapolis: Augsburg/ Fortress, 1967.

Ringern, Helmer. *Sacrifice in the Bible*. New York: Association, 1962.

Ritchie, James H., Jr. *Always in Rehearsal: The Practice of Worship and the Presence of Children*. Nashville: Upper Room, 2005.

Robinson, Haddon W. *Biblical Preaching: The Development and Delivery of Expository Messages*. 3rd ed. Grand Rapids: Baker Academic, 2014.

———. *Biblical Sermons: How Twelve Great Preachers Apply the Principles of Biblical Preaching*. Grand Rapids: Baker, 1981.

———. "The Heresy of Application." *Leadership* 18 (1997) 21–27.

———. "What is Expository Preaching?" *Bibliotheca Sacra* 131 (1974) 55–60.

Robinson, Haddon W., and Craig Brian Larson. *The Art and Craft of Biblical Preaching*. Grand Rapids: Zondervan, 2005.

Robinson, Haddon W., and Torrey W. Robinson. *It's All in How You Tell It: Preaching First-Person Expository Messages*. Grand Rapids: Baker, 2003.

Rookmaaker, H. R. *The Creative Gift: Essays on Art and the Christian Life*. Wheaton, IL: Crossway, 1981.

Rosen, Charles. *The Classical Style: Haydn, Mozart, Beethoven*. Rev. ed. New York: Norton, 1997.

———. *Sonata Form*. Rev. ed. New York: Norton, 1988.

Rosentiel, Léonie, ed. *Schirmer History of Music*. New York: G. Schirmer, 1982.

Ross, Allen P. *A Commentary on the Psalms*, vol. 1, *1–41*. *Kregel Exegetical Library*. Grand Rapids: Kregel Academic, 2012.

———. *A Commentary on the Psalms*, vol. 2, *42–89*. *Kregel Exegetical Library*. Grand Rapids: Kregel Academic, 2013.

———. *A Commentary on the Psalms*, vol. 3, *90–150*. *Kregel Exegetical Library*. Grand Rapids: Kregel Academic, 2015.

———. *Creation and Blessing: A Guide to the Study and Exposition of the Book of Genesis*. Grand Rapids: Baker, 1988.

———. *Holiness to the Lord: A Guide to the Study of Leviticus*. Grand Rapids: Baker Academic, 2002.

———. "Psalms." In *The Bible Knowledge Commentary*, edited by John F. Walvoord and Roy B. Zuck, 779–899. Wheaton, IL: Victor, 1985.

———. *Recalling the Hope of Glory: Biblical Worship from the Garden to the New Creation*. Grand Rapids: Kregel Academic, 2006.

———. "Worship with Proclamation: The Development of True Worship in a Religious World." In *Recalling the Hope of Glory: Biblical Worship from the Garden to the New Creation*, 121–51. Grand Rapids: Kregel Academic, 2006.

Routley, Erik. *Christian Hymns Observed: When in Our Music God Is Glorified*. Princeton, NJ: Prestige, 1982.

———. *Church Music and the Christian Faith*. Carol Stream, IL: Agape, 1978.

———. *Hymns Today and Tomorrow*. New York: Abingdon, 1964.

———. *I'll Praise My Maker: A Study of the Hymns of Certain Authors Who Stand in or Near the Tradition of English Calvinism, 1700–1850*. London: Independent, 1951.

———. *The Music of Christian Hymns*. Chicago: GIA, 1981.

Routley, Erik. *A Panorama of Christian Hymnody*. Edited by Paul A. Richardson. Chicago: GIA, 2005.

Rowley, H. H. *Worship in Ancient Israel: Its Forms and Meanings*. Philadelphia: Fortress, 1967.

Rummage, Stephen Nelson. *Planning Your Preaching: A Step-by-Step Guide for Developing a One-Year Preaching Calendar*. Grand Rapids: Kregel, 2002.

Runia, Klaas. "What Is Preaching According to the New Testament?" *Tyndale Bulletin* 29 (1978) 3–48.

Rushton, Julian. *Classical Music: A Concise History from Gluck to Beethoven*. London: Thames and Hudson, 1986.

Ruth, Lester. "How Great Is Our God: The Trinity in Contemporary Worship Music." In *The Message in the Music: Studying Contemporary Praise and Worship*, edited by Robert Woods and Brian Walrath, 29–42. Nashville: Abingdon, 2007.

Rutledge, Fleming. *And God Spoke to Abraham: Preaching from the Old Testament*. Grand Rapids: Erdmans, 2011.

Rutter, John. *Open Thou Mine Eyes*. Chapel Hill, NC: Hinshaw, 1980.

Ryken, Leland. *Culture in Christian Perspective: A Door to Understanding & Enjoying the Arts*. Portland: Multnomah, 1986.

———. *The Liberated Imagination: Thinking Christianly about the Arts*. Wheaton, IL: Harold Shaw, 1989.

———. *Words of Delight: A Literary Introduction to the Bible*. Grand Rapids: Baker, 1987.

Ryken, Leland, ed. *The Christian Imagination: Essays on Literature and the Arts*. Grand Rapids: Baker, 1981.

Ryken, Leland, and Todd A. Wilson, eds. *Preach the Word: Essays on Expositional Preaching in Honor of R. Kent Hughes.* Wheaton, IL: Crossway, 2007.

Ryken, Philip G., et al., eds. *Give Praise to God: A Vision for Reforming Worship.* Phillipsburg, NJ: P&R, 2011.

Saad, Lydia. "Sermon Content is What Appeals to Churchgoers." https://www.gallup.com/poll/208529/sermon-content-appeals-churchgoers-aspx.

Sadie, Stanley, ed. *The New Grove Dictionary of Music and Musicians.* London: Macmillan, 1980.

Sakenfeld, Katharine Doob. *The Meaning of Hesed in the Hebrew Bible.* Eugene, OR: Wipf & Stock, 2002.

Saliers, Don E. *Music and Theology.* Nashville: Abingdon, 2007.

———. *Worship and Spirituality.* Philadelphia: Westminster, 1984.

———. *Worship as Theology: Foretaste of Divine Glory.* Nashville: Abingdon, 1994.

———. *Worship Come to Its Senses.* Nashville: Abingdon, 1996.

Salzman, Eric. *Twentieth-Century Music.* 3rd ed. Englewood Cliffs, NJ: Prentice-Hall, 1988.

Sandmel, Samuel. *Judaism and Christian Beginnings.* New York: Oxford University Press, 1978.

Sargent, Tony. *The Sacred Anointing: The Preaching of Dr. Martyn Lloyd-Jones.* Wheaton, IL: Crossway, 1994.

Saylor, L. Jonathan. "Our Changing Music: Dramatic New Styles." *Decision* 37 (1996) 16–18.

Schaeffer, Franky. *Addicted to Mediocrity: 20th Century Christians and the Arts.* Wheaton, IL: Crossway, 1981.

Schalk, Carl, ed. *Key Words in Church Music.* St. Louis: Concordia, 1978.

Schaper, Robert, et al. "Music in Worship: A Dialogue with Ministers of Music." *Theology News & Notes* 29 (1982) 10–14.

Schilling, Paul. *The Faith We Sing: How the Message of Hymns Can Enhance Christian Belief.* Philadelphia: Westminster: 1983.

Schmit, Clayton J. "Art for Faith's Sake." *Theology, News and Notes* 48 (Fall 2001) 3–5.

———. "Feeling and Form in Worship." PhD diss., Graduate Theological Union, 1997.

———. *Public Reading of Scripture: A Handbook.* Nashville: Abingdon, 2002.

Schreiner, Thomas R. *The King in His Beauty: A Biblical Theology of the Old and New Testaments.* Grand Rapids: Baker Academic, 2013.

Schultze, Quentin J. *High-Tech Worship? Using Presentational Technologies Wisely.* Grand Rapids: Baker, 2004.

———. *Televangelism and American Culture: The Business of Popular Religion.* Grand Rapids: Baker, 1991.

Schulz, Samuel J. *The Gospel of Moses.* New York: Harper & Row, 1974.

Scudder, Samuel H. "In the Laboratory with Agassiz." *Every Saturday* 16 (1974) 369–70.

Seay, Albert. *Music in the Medieval World.* 2nd ed. Englewood Cliffs, NJ: Prentice-Hall, 1975.

Segler, Franklin M., and Randall Bradley. *Christian Worship: Its Theology and Practice.* 3rd ed. Nashville: B&H, 2006.

Selderhuis, Herman J. *Calvin's Theology of the Psalms.* Grand Rapids: Baker Academic, 2007.

Sellers, Ovid R. "Musical Instruments of Israel." In *Biblical Archeologist Reader*, edited by George Ernest Wright and David Noel Friedman, 81–94. New York: Doubleday, 1961.

Senn, Frank. *Christian Liturgy*. Minneapolis: Augsburg, 1997.

Sexton, Ronald Thomas. "A Critical Examination of the Preaching of Donald Grey Barnhouse." PhD diss., New Orleans Baptist Theological Seminary, 1984.

Shaddix, Jim. *The Passion-Driven Sermon*. Nashville: B&H, 2003.

Shannon, Martin. "Soli Deo Gloria." In *The Sacred Choral Music of J. S. Bach: A Handbook*, edited by John Butt, 40–47. Brewster, MA: Paraclete, 1997.

Sharp, Avery T., and Michael James Floyd. *Church and Worship Music: An Annotated Bibliography of Contemporary Scholarship, A Research and Information Guide*. New York: Routledge, 2005.

Sheff, Donald. "Izzy, Did You Ask a Good Question Today." http://www.nytimes.com/1988/01/19/opinion/l-izzy-did-you-ask-a-good-question-today-712388.html.

Shelley, Bruce L. *Church History in Plain Language*. Dallas: Word, 1982.

Shepherd, Jerry Eugene. "The Book of Psalms as the Book of Christ: A Christo-Canonical Approach to Expository Preaching." PhD diss., Westminster Theological Seminary, 1995.

Shorney, George, et al., eds. *Worship and Rejoice*. Carol Stream, IL: Hope, 530.

Sizer, Sandra S. *Gospel Hymns and Social Religion: The Rhetoric of Nineteenth-Century Revivalism*. Philadelphia: Temple University Press, 1978.

Sloyan, Gerard S. *Worshipful Preaching*. Philadelphia: Fortress, 1984.

Small, Joseph D., ed. *Proclaiming the Great Ends of the Church: Mission and Ministry for Presbyterians*. Louisville: Geneva, 2010.

Smart, James D. *The Strange Silence of the Bible in the Church: A Study in Hermeneutics*. Philadelphia: Westminster, 1972.

Smick, Elmer B. *Job*. The Expositor's Bible Commentary Series, vol. 4. Grand Rapids: Zondervan, 1988.

Smith, Christian, and Patricia Snell. *Souls in Transition: The Religious and Spiritual Lives of Emerging Adults*. New York: Oxford University Press, 2009.

Smith, J. A. "The Ancient Synagogue, the Early Church, and Singing." *Music and Letters* 65 (1984) 1–16.

———. "First Century Singing and its Relationship to Contemporary Jewish Religious Song." *Music and Letters* 75 (1994) 1–15.

Smith, James D., III. "Where Did We Get the Doxology?" *Christian History* 10 (1991) 18.

Smith, James K. A. *Desiring the Kingdom: Worship, Worldview, and Cultural Formation*. Grand Rapids: Baker Academic, 2009.

———. *Imagining the Kingdom: How Worship Works*. Grand Rapids: Baker Academic, 2013.

Smith, Robert, Jr. *Doctrine that Dances*. Nashville: B&H, 2008.

———. "The Importance of Dramatic Narration and Storytelling in Preaching." *The African American Pulpit* 11 (2008) 8–10.

———. "Is there a Word from the Lord?" *Preaching* 23 (2008) 16–19.

Smith, Steven W. *Dying to Preach: Embracing the Cross in the Pulpit*. Grand Rapids: Kregel, 2009.

Snyder, James L., ed. *Tozer on Worship and Entertainment: Selected Excerpts*. Camp Hill, PA: Wingspread, 1997.

Sollod, Robert N. "The Hollow Curriculum: The Place of Religion and Spirituality in Society Is Too Often Missing." *The Chronicle of Higher Education* 38.28 (March 18, 1992) 60.

Spinks, Bryan D. *The Worship Mall: Contemporary Responses to Contemporary Culture.* New York: Church, 2010.

Spinks, Brian, and Iain Torrance, eds. *To Glorify God: Essays on Modern Reformed Liturgy.* Edinburgh: T. & T. Clark, 1999.

Spitz, Lewis W. "Humanism and the Protestant Reformation." In *Renaissance Humanism: Foundations, Forms, and Legacy*, vol. 3, edited by Albert Rabil, Jr., 380–411. Philadelphia: University of Pennsylvania Press, 1988.

Sproul, R. C. *The Consequences of Ideas: Understanding the Concepts that Shaped Our World.* Wheaton, IL: Crossway, 2000.

———. "The Recovery of Worship." *Reformation and Revival* 2 (1993) 23–42.

Sri, Edward. *A Biblical Walk through the Mass: Understanding What We Say and Do in the Liturgy.* Westchester, NY: Ascension, 2011.

Stacey, John. "John Wycliffe and the Ministry of the Word." *The London Quarterly and Holborn Review* 190 (1965) 50–54.

Stacker, Joe R., and Wesley Forbis. *Authentic Worship: Exalting God and Reaching People.* Nashville: Convention, 1990.

Stackhouse, John G., Jr. "The True, the Good, the Beautiful Christian." *Christianity Today* 46 (2002) 58–61.

Stanley, Andy, and Ronald Lane Jones. *Communicating for a Change.* Portland, OR: Multnomah, 2006.

Stapert, Calvin R. *A New Song in an Old World: Musical Thought in the Early Church.* Grand Rapids: Eerdmans, 2007.

Stark, Rodney, et al. *What Americans Really Believe: New Findings from the Baylor Surveys of Religion.* Waco, TX: Baylor University Press, 2008.

Statom, Gabriel. *Practice for Heaven: Music for Worship that Looks Higher.* Eugene, OR: Wipf & Stock, 2015.

Steckel, Clyde J. "How Can Music have Theological Significance?" In *Theomusicology*, edited by John Michael Spencer, 13–35. Durham, NC: Duke University Press, 1994.

Stedman, Raymond C. "Whatever Happened to Preaching," *Theology News and Notes* 27 (1980) 6–24.

Steer, Roger. *Guarding the Holy Fire: The Evangelicalism of John R. W. Stott, J. I. Packer, and Alister McGrath.* Grand Rapids: Baker, 1999.

Stein, Gertrude. *Everybody's Autobiography.* New York: Cooper Square, 1971.

Stewart, James S. "Our Duty of Praise." In *Classic Sermons on Worship*, edited by Warren K. Wiersbe, 84–93. Grand Rapids: Kregel, 1988.

Stitzinger, James F. "The History of Expository Preaching." *The Master's Seminary Journal* 31 (1992) 5–32.

Stolba, K. Marie. *The Development of Western Music: A History.* 2nd ed. Madison, WI: Brown & Benchmark, 1990.

Stott, John R. W. *Between Two Worlds: The Art of Preaching in the Twentieth Century.* Grand Rapids: Eerdmans, 1982.

———. *The Living Church: Convictions of a Lifelong Pastor.* Downers Grove, IL: InterVarsity, 2007.

———. *The Preacher's Portrait: Some New Testament Word Studies.* Grand Rapids: Eerdmans, 1961.

———. *The Radical Disciple: Some Neglected Aspects of Our Calling*. Downers Grove, IL: InterVarsity, 2010.

Strimple, Nick. *Choral Music in the Twentieth Century*. Portland: Amadeus, 2002.

Stringer, Martin D. *A Sociological History of Christian Worship*. Cambridge: Cambridge University Press, 2006.

Strunk, Oliver, ed. "The Early Christian View of Music." In *Source Readings in Music History: Antiquity and the Middle Ages*, 59–75. New York: Norton, 1965.

———. "Reformation and Counter-Reformation." In *Source Readings in Music History: The Renaissance*, 151–69. New York: Norton, 1965.

Sunukjian, Donald R. *Invitation to Biblical Preaching: Proclaiming Truth with Clarity and Relevance*. Grand Rapids: Kregel, 2007.

Sweet, Leonard, ed. *The Church in Emerging Culture: Five Perspectives*. El Cajon, CA: emergentYS, 2003.

Swindoll, Charles R. *Saying it Well: Touching Others with Your Words*. New York: Faithwords, 2012.

Talley, Thomas J. *Origins of the Liturgical Year*. New York: Pueblo, 1986.

Taylor, Barbara Brown. *The Preaching Life*. Cambridge: Cowley, 1993.

Taylor, Gardner. "Shaping Sermons by the Shape of the Text and Preacher." In *Preaching Biblically: Creating Sermons in the Shape of Scripture*, edited by Don M. Wardlaw, 137–52. Philadelphia: Westminster, 1983.

Taylor, W. David O. *For the Beauty of the Church: Casting a Vision for the Arts*. Grand Rapids: Baker, 2010.

Tell, Martin. "Truthfulness in Church Music." *The Princeton Seminary Bulletin* 19 (1998) 26–39.

Tell, Martin, et al. *Psalms for All Seasons: A Complete Psalter for Worship*. Grand Rapids: Faith Alive, 2012.

Temperley, Nicholas. *The Music of the English Parish Church*. Vol. 1. Cambridge: Cambridge University Press, 1972.

Temperley, Nicholas, and Stephen O. Banfield, eds. *Music and the Wesleys*. Urbana, IL: University of Illinois Press, 2010.

Temple, William. *Readings in St. John's Gospel, First and Second Series*. London: Macmillan, 1952.

ten Boom, Corrie. *The Hiding Place*. 35th Anniversary Edition. Grand Rapids: Chosen, 2006.

Tenney, Merrill C. *New Testament Times*. Grand Rapids: Eerdmans, 1965.

Theology and Ministry Unit for The Presbyterian Church (U.S.A), and The Cumberland Presbyterian Church. *Book of Common Worship*. Louisville: Westminster John Knox, 1993.

Thielicke, Helmut. *The Evangelical Faith*, vol. 2, *The Doctrine of God and of Christ*. Grand Rapids: Eerdmans, 1977.

———. *Our Heavenly Father: Sermons on the Lord's Prayer*. Grand Rapids: Baker, 1960.

Thielman, Frank. *A Theology of the New Testament: A Canonical and Synthetic Approach*. Grand Rapids: Zondervan, 2005.

Thiessen, Gesa Elsbeth, ed. *Theological Aesthetics: A Reader*. Grand Rapids: Eerdmans, 2005.

Thomas, André J. *Way Over in Beulah Land: Understanding and Performing Negro Spirituals*. Dayton, OH: Heritage, 2007.

Thomas, Derek W. H. "Expository Preaching." In *Feed My Sheep: A Passionate Plea for Preaching*, 35–52. Lake Mary, FL: Reformation Trust, 2008.

Thompson, Bard. *Liturgies of the Western Church*. Minneapolis: Fortress, 1980.

Tisdale, Lenora Tubbs. *Prophetic Preaching: A Pastoral Approach*. Louisville: Westminster John Knox, 2010.

Toone, Mark. "Reforming Reformed Worship." In *What Is Christian Worship?*, edited by Mary Holder Naegeli, 47–51. Louisville: Presbyterians for Renewal, 2000.

Torrance, James B. *Worship, Community, and the Triune God of Grace*. Downers Grove, IL: InterVarsity, 1996.

———. "Worship—Unitarian or Trinitarian?: Participating by the Holy Spirit in the Son's Communion with the Father." In *What is Christian Worship?* edited by Mary Holder Naegeli, 9–16. Louisville: Presbyterians for Renewal, 2000.

Tozer, A. W. *Whatever Happened to Worship?* Camp Hill, PA: Christian, 1985.

Traina, Robert A. *Methodical Bible Study*. Grand Rapids: Zondervan, 2002.

Tredinnick, Noël. "Our Changing Music: New Expressions of Faith." *Decision* 37 (1996) 16–18.

Troeger, Thomas H. *Creating Fresh Images for Preaching: New Rungs for Jacob's Ladder*. Valley Forge, PA: Judson, 1982.

———. "For God Risk Everything: Reconstructing a Theology of Church Music." *Reformed Liturgy and Music* 33 (1999) 3–7.

———. *Imagining a Sermon*. Nashville: Abingdon, 1990.

———. *Music as Prayer: The Theology and Practice of Church Music*. Oxford: Oxford University Press, 2013.

———. *Preaching and Worship*. St. Louis: Chalice, 2003.

———. *Wonder Reborn: Creating Sermons on Hymns, Music, and Poetry*. New York: Oxford University Press, 2010.

Ulrich, Homer. *A Survey of Choral Music*. New York: Harcourt Brace Janovich, 1973.

Underhill, Evelyn. *Worship*. New York: Crossroad, 1984.

Unger, Merrill F. *Principles of Expository Preaching*. Grand Rapids: Zondervan, 1955.

Van Dyk, Leanne. *A More Profound Alleluia: Theology and Worship in Harmony*. Grand Rapids: Eerdmans, 2005.

Vangemeren, Willem A., ed. *New International Dictionary of Old Testament Theology and Exegesis*, vol. 1. Grand Rapids: Zondervan, 1997.

Van Harn, Roger E. *Preacher, Can You Hear Us Listening?* Grand Rapids: Eerdmans, 2005.

Van Harn, Roger E., and Brent A. Strawn. *Psalms for Preaching and Worship: A Lectionary Commentary*. Grand Rapids: Eerdmans, 2009.

Vanhoozer, Kevin J. *The Drama of Doctrine: A Canonical-Linguistic Approach to Christian Theology*. Louisville: Westminster John Knox, 2005.

———. *Faith Speaking Understanding: Performing the Drama of Doctrine*. Louisville: Westminster John Knox, 2014.

Vaughan, Curtis. "Colossians." In *The Expositors Bible Commentary*, edited by Frank E. Gaebelein, 216. Grand Rapids: Zondervan,1978.

Vibert, Simon. *Excellence in Preaching: Studying the Craft of Leading Preachers*. Downers Grove, IL: InterVarsity, 2011.

Vines, Jerry, and David Allen. "Hermeneutics, Exegesis, and Proclamation." *Criswell Theological Review* 1 (1987) 333–34.

Vines, Jerry, and Jim Shaddix. *Power in the Pulpit: How to Prepare and Deliver Expository Sermons*. Chicago: Moody, 1999.

Vischer, Lukas, ed. *Christian Worship in Reformed Churches Past and Present.* Grand Rapids: Eerdmans, 2003.

———. "Worship as Christian Witness to Society." In *Christian Worship in Reformed Churches Past and Present,* edited by Lukas Vischer, 414–15. Grand Rapids: Eerdmans, 2003.

von Rad, Gerhard. *Old Testament Theology,* vol. 1. New York: Harper & Row, 1962.

———. *Old Testament Theology,* vol. 2. New York: Harper & Row, 1965.

Waddington, Samuel, ed. *The Sonnets of Europe: A Volume of Translations.* London: Walter Scott, 1888.

Wagner, E. Glenn. "Celebrating God in Authentic Worship." http://www.preaching.com/resources/articles/11565851/.

Wainwright, Geoffrey. *Doxology: The Praise of God in Worship, Doctrine, and Life.* New York: Oxford University Press, 1980.

———. "In Praise of God." *Worship* 53 (1979) 496–511.

Wainwright, Geoffrey, and Karen B. Westerfield Tucker, eds. *The Oxford Dictionary of Christian Worship.* New York: Oxford University Press, 2006.

Waite, Daniel J. "Toward a Holistic Preaching Model for Postmodern America: Integrating the Philosophy and Methodology of Haddon Robinson, David Buttrick, and Rick Warren." Lecture at annual meeting of the Evangelical Homiletics Society, Wenham, MA, October 12–14, 2006.

Wakefield, Gordon S. *An Outline of Christian Worship.* Edinburgh: T. & T. Clark, 1998.

Wallace, Robert Knowles. *Worshiping in the Small Church.* Nashville: Abingdon, 2008.

Wallis, Charles L. *Treasury of Poems for Worship and Devotion.* New York: Harper & Brothers, 1959.

Walters, Michael. *Can't Wait for Sunday: Leading Your Congregation in Authentic Worship.* Indianapolis: Wesleyan, 2006.

Waltke, Bruce K., and James M. Houston. *The Psalms as Christian Worship: An Historical Commentary.* Grand Rapids: Eerdmans, 2010.

Walton, John H. *Ancient Israelite Literature in its Cultural Context.* Grand Rapids: Zondervan, 1994.

———. "The Psalms: A Cantata about the Davidic Covenant." *Journal of the Evangelical Theological Society* 34 (1991) 21–31.

Ward, Keith. *The Big Questions in Science and Religion.* West Coshohocken, PA: Templeton, 2008.

———. *Is Religion Dangerous?* Grand Rapids: Eerdmans, 2007.

———. *Why There Almost Certainly Is a God: Doubting Dawkins.* Oxford: Lion and Hudson, 2008.

Warfield, Benjamin Breckenridge. *Calvin and Augustine.* Philadelphia: P&R, 1980.

———. *Calvin and Calvinism.* New York: Oxford University Press, 1931.

———. *The Lord of Glory: A Study of the Designations of Our Lord in the New Testament with Especial Reference to His Deity.* 1907. Reprint. Grand Rapids: Baker, 1974.

Warren, Rick. *The Purpose Driven Life: What on Earth Am I here for?* Grand Rapids: Zondervan, 2002.

Warren, Timothy S. "A Paradigm for Preaching." *Bibliotheca Sacra* 148 (1991) 464–87.

———. "The Theological Process in Sermon Preparation." *Bibliotheca Sacra* 156 (1999) 336–56.

Warrington, James. *Short Titles of Books Relating to or Illustrating the History and Practice of Psalmody in the United States, 1620–1820*. 1890. Reprint, New York: Burt Franklin, 1971.

Waschevski, Michael, and John G. Steven. *Rhythms of Worship: The Planning and Purpose of Liturgy*. Louisville: Westminster John Knox, 2014.

Watson, Richard J. *The English Hymn: A Critical and Historical Study*. New York: Oxford University Press, 1997.

Watts, Isaac. *The Psalms and Hymns of Isaac Watts*. Morgan, PA: Soli Deo Gloria, 1997.

———. *The Psalms of David Imitated in the Language of the New Testament, and Applied to the Christian State and Worship*. 1801. Reprint. London: Forgotten, 2017.

Webb, Stephen H. *The Divine Voice: Christian Proclamation and the Theology of Sound*. Grand Rapids: Brazos, 2004.

Webber, Robert E. *Ancient-Future Time: Forming Spirituality through the Christian Year*. Grand Rapids: Baker, 2004.

———. *Ancient-Future Worship: Proclaiming and Enacting God's Narrative*. Grand Rapids: Baker, 2008.

———. "Authentic Worship in a Changing World: What's Next?" *Theology Matters* 6 (2000) 1–5.

———. *Blended Worship: Achieving Substance and Relevance in Worship*. Peabody, MA: Hendrickson, 1994.

———. *Celebrating Our Faith: Evangelism through Worship*. San Francisco: Harper & Row, 1986.

———. *Enter His Courts with Praise: A Study of the Role of Music and the Arts in Worship*. Peabody, MA: Hendrickson, 1997.

———. *Liturgical Evangelism*. New York: Morehouse, 1992.

———. *Planning Blended Worship*. Nashville: Abingdon, 1998.

———. *Who Gets to Narrate the World? Contending for the Christian Story in an Age of Rivals*. Downers Grove, IL: InterVarsity, 2008.

———. *Worship Is a Verb: Celebrating God's Mighty Deeds of Salvation*. Peabody, MA: Hendrickson, 2004.

———. *Worship Old and New: A Biblical, Historical, and Practical Introduction*. Grand Rapids: Zondervan, 1994.

———. *The Younger Evangelicals: Facing the Challenges of the New World*. Grand Rapids: Baker, 2002.

Webber, Robert E., ed. *The Complete Library of Christian Worship*. Peabody, MA: Hendrickson, 1994.

Webster, Douglas D. *Follow the Lamb: A Pastoral Approach to The Revelation*. Eugene, OR: Cascade, 2014.

———. *Living in Tension: A Theology of Ministry*, vol. 1, *The Nature of Ministry: Faithfulness from the Beginning*. Eugene, OR: Cascade, 2012.

———. *Living in Tension: A Theology of Ministry*, vol. 2, *The Practice of Ministry: Faithfulness to the End*. Eugene, OR: Cascade, 2012.

———. *Selling Jesus: What's Wrong with Marketing the Church*. Eugene, OR: Wipf & Stock, 2009.

———. "Stay in the Story." In *Living in Tension: A Theology of Ministry*, vol. 2, *The Practice of Ministry: Faithfulness to the End*, by Douglas D. Webster, 45–58. Eugene, OR: Cascade, 2012.

———. *Text Messaging: A Conversation on Preaching*. Toronto: Clements, 2010.

Wells, David F. *The Courage to Be Protestant: Truth-lovers, Marketers, and Emergents in the Postmodern World*. Grand Rapids: Eerdmans, 2008.

Wells, Samuel. *Speaking Truth in a Pluralistic Culture*. Nashville: Abingdon, 2008.

Wenham, Gordon J. *Psalms as Torah: Reading Biblical Psalms Ethically*. Grand Rapids: Baker Academic, 2012.

———. "The Religion of the Patriarchs." In *Essays in the Patriarchal Narratives*, edited by A. R. Millard and D. J. Wiseman, 157–88. Leicester, UK: InterVarsity, 1980.

Wesley, Charles. "Jesus Comes with Clouds Descending." In *The Presbyterian Hymnal*, edited by LindJo McKim, 6. Louisville: Westminster John Knox, 1990.

———. "Love Divine, All Loves Excelling." In *The Presbyterian Hymnal*, edited by LindaJo McKim, 376. Louisville: Westminster John Knox, 1990.

Wesselschmidt, Quentin F., ed. "Psalms 51–150." In *Ancient Christian Commentary on Scripture*, vol. 8, edited by Thomas C. Oden, 164–69. Downers Grove, IL: IVP Academic, 2007.

Westermann, Claus. *Blessing in the Bible and the Life of the Church*. Translated by Keith R. Crim. Philadelphia: Fortress, 1978.

———. *Praise and Lament in the Psalms*. Atlanta: John Knox, 1981.

———. *The Praise of God in the Psalms*. 2nd ed. Translated by Keith R. Crim. Richmond, VA: John Knox, 1961.

Westermeyer, Paul. *Te Deum: The Church and Music*. Minneapolis: Fortress, 1998.

Whaley, Vernon M. *Called to Worship: The Biblical Foundations of Our Response to God's Call*. Nashville: Thomas Nelson, 2009.

———. *The Dynamics of Corporate Worship*. Grand Rapids: Baker, 2001.

Whaling, Frank, ed. *John and Charles Wesley: Selected Prayers, Hymns, Journal Notes, Sermons, Letters and Treatises*. Mahwah, NJ: Paulist, 1981.

Whalum, Wendell P. "Church Music: A Position Paper (with Special Consideration of Music in the Black Church)." In *Readings in African American Church Music and Worship*, edited by James Abbington, 499–518. Chicago: GIA, 2001.

White, James F. *A Brief History of Christian Worship*. Nashville: Abingdon, 1993.

———. *Documents of Christian Worship: Descriptive and Interpretive Resources*. Louisville: Westminster John Knox, 1992.

———. *Introduction to Christian Worship*. Rev. ed. Nashville: Abingdon, 1990.

———. *Protestant Worship and Church Architecture: Theological and Historical Considerations*. New York: Oxford University Press, 1964.

———. *Protestant Worship: Traditions in Transition*. Louisville: Westminster John Knox, 1989.

White, Susan J. *Foundations of Christian Worship*. Louisville: Westminster John Knox, 2006.

Whitesell, Faris D. *Power in Expository Preaching*. Old Tappan, NJ: Revell, 1963.

Wienandt, Elwyn A., ed. *Opinions on Church Music: Comments and Reports from Four-and-a-Half Centuries*. Waco, TX: Baylor University Press, 1974.

Wiersbe, Warren W. *Dynamics of Preaching*. Grand Rapids: Baker, 1999.

———. *Preaching and Teaching with Imagination: The Quest for Biblical Ministry*. Grand Rapids: Baker, 1994.

———. *Real Worship: It Will Transform Your Life*. Nashville: Nelson, 1986.

———. *Real Worship: Playground, Battleground, or Holy Ground?* Grand Rapids: Baker, 2000.

Wilhite, Keith. "Audience Relevance and Rhetorical Argumentation in Expository Preaching: A Historical-Critical Comparative Analysis of Selected Sermons of John F. MacArthur, Jr., and Charles R. Swindoll, 1970–1990." PhD diss., Purdue University, 1990.

———. *Preaching with Relevance without Dumbing Down*. Grand Rapids: Kregel, 2001.

Wilhite, Keith, and Scott M. Gibson, eds. *The Big Idea of Biblical Preaching*. Grand Rapids: Baker, 1998.

Williams, Edgar. *Reasons of the Heart: Recovering Christian Persuasion*. Phillipsburg, NJ: P&R, 2003.

Willimon, William H. *The Bible: A Sustaining Presence in Worship*. Valley Forge, PA: Judson, 1981.

———. *The Gospel for the Person Who Has Everything*. Valley Forge, PA: Judson, 1978.

———. *A Guide to Preaching and Leading Worship*. Philadelphia: Westminster John Knox, 2008.

———. *The Intrusive Word: Preaching to the Unbaptized*. Grand Rapids: Eerdmans, 1994.

———. *Preaching to the Baptized*. Grand Rapids: Eerdmans, 1992.

———. *Proclamation and Theology*. Nashville: Abingdon, 2005.

———. *The Service of God: Christian Work and Worship*. Nashville: Abingdon, 1983.

———. *Worship as Pastoral Care*. Nashville: Abingdon, 1979.

Willimon, William H., and Richard Lischer, eds. *Concise Encyclopedia of Preaching*. Louisville: Westminster John Knox, 1995.

Willmington, Edwin M. "Convergence: Coming to a Worship Service Near You." *Theology News and Notes* 53 (2006) 9–11.

Wilson, Jonathan. *Why Church Matters: Worship, Ministry, and Missions in Practice*. Grand Rapids: Brazos, 2006.

Wilson, Len, and Jason Moore. *Taking Flight with Creativity: Worship Design Teams that Work*. Nashville: Abingdon, 2009.

Wilson, Marvin R. *Our Father Abraham: Jewish Roots of the Christian Faith*. Grand Rapids: Eerdmans, 1991.

Wilson, Paul Scott, et al., eds. *The New Interpreter's Handbook of Preaching*. Nashville: Abingdon, 2008.

Wilson-Dixon, Andrew. *A Brief History of Christian Music: From Biblical Times to the Present*. Oxford: Lion, 1992.

Witham, Larry. *A City Upon a Hill: How Sermons Changed the Course of American History*. New York: HarperOne, 2007.

Witvliet, John D. *The Biblical Psalms in Christian Worship: A Brief Introduction and Guide to Resources*. Grand Rapids: Eerdmans, 2007.

———. "Images and Themes in Calvin's Theology of Liturgy: One Dimension of Calvin's Liturgical Legacy." In *The Legacy of John Calvin*, edited by David Foxgrover, 130–52. Grand Rapids: CRC, 2000.

———. "The Spirituality of the Psalter: Metrical Psalms in Liturgy and Life in Calvin's Geneva." *Calvin Theological Journal* 32 (1997) 273–97.

———. *Worship Seeking Understanding: Windows into Christian Practice*. Grand Rapids: Baker Academic, 2003.

Witvliet, John, and Emily R. Brink. "Contemporary Developments in Music in Reformed Churches Worldwide." In *Christian Worship in Reformed Churches Past and Present*, edited by Lukas Vischer, 324–47. Grand Rapids: Eerdmans, 2003.

———. *The Worship Sourcebook*. Grand Rapids: Calvin Institute, Faith Alive, 2004.

Wolfe, Alan. "The Opening of the Evangelical Mind." *The Atlantic Monthly* 286 (2000) 55–76.

———. *The Transformation of American Religion*. New York: Free Press, 2003.

Wolterstorff, Nicholas P. *Art in Action: Toward a Christian Aesthetic*. Grand Rapids: Eerdmans, 1980.

———. "Thinking about Church Music." In *Music in Christian Worship: At the Service of Liturgy*, edited by Charlotte V. Kroeker, 3–16. Collegeville, MN: St. Benedict, 2005.

Wood, A. Skevington. "The Apostolic Church." In *The Expositor's Bible Commentary*, edited by Frank E. Gaebelein, 577–89. Grand Rapids: Zondervan, 1979.

Wood, Leon J. *The Prophets of Israel*. Grand Rapids: Baker, 1979.

Wordsworth, William. *The Collected Poems of William Wordsworth*. Ware, UK: Wordsworth Editions, 1998.

Wren, Brian. *Praying Twice: The Music and Words of Congregational Singing*. Louisville: Westminster John Knox, 2000.

Wright, N. T. *For All God's Worth: True Worship and the Calling of the Church*. Grand Rapids: Eerdmans, 1997.

———. "Preaching in a Changing Culture." http://www.preaching.com/resources/articles/11547621/.

———. *Scripture and the Authority of God: How to Read the Bible Today*. New York: HarperOne, 2011.

———. *Simply Jesus: A New Vision of Who He was, What He Did, and Why it Matters*. New York: HarperCollins, 2011.

Wright, Timothy. *A Commitment of Joy: How to Create Contemporary Worship*. Nashville: Abingdon, 1994.

Wuthnow, Robert. *After the Baby Boomers: How Twenty and Thirty-Somethings are Shaping the Future of American Religion*. Princeton, NJ: Princeton University Press, 2010.

———. *All in Sync: How Music and Art Are Revitalizing American Religion*. Berkeley: University of California Press, 2006.

———. *Red State Religion: Faith and Politics in America's Heartland*. Princeton, NJ: Princeton University Press, 2014.

———. *The Struggle for America's Soul: Evangelicals, Liberals, and Secularism*. Grand Rapids: Eerdmans, 1989.

Yee, Russell. "The Shared Meaning and Significance in Congregational Singing." *The Hymn* 48 (1997) 7–11.

York, Hershael W. "Text, Emotion, and Audience: Finding the Line between Planning and Manipulation in Worship and Preaching." Lecture at the annual meeting of Evangelical Homiletics Society, Deerfield, IL, October 14–16, 2010.

York, Hershael W., and Bert Decker. *Preaching with Bold Assurance: A Solid and Enduring Approach to Engaging Exposition*. Nashville: B&H, 2003.

York, Hershael W., and Scott A. Blue. "Is Application Necessary in the Expository Sermon?" *Southern Baptist Journal of Theology* 3 (1999) 70–84.

Young, Carlton R. *Music of the Heart: John and Charles Wesley on Music and Musicians*. Carol Stream, IL: Hope, 1995.

Zaninelli, Luigi. *Five Folk Songs*. Delaware Water Gap, PA: Shawnee, 1979.

Zuckerman, Phil. *Living the Secular Life: New Answers to Old Questions*. New York: Penguin, 2014.

Name Index

Adam, P. J. H., 4n8
Agassiz, Louis, 68
Alford, H., 86n12
Allen, Leslie C., 13n4
Andrewes, Lancelot, 93n20
Aniol, Scott, 106n15
Armstrong, Kevin R., 98n1
Asaph, 22, 23
Atchinson, Thomas, 105n12

Baker, H. W., 90n17
Balmer, Randall, 41n19
Barna, George, 105n12
Barnes, M. Craig, 45, 45n33
Barth, Karl, 92, 114, 116n4, 119
Bateman, Christian Henry, 1n2
Bateman, Herbert, IV, 106n15
Battles, Ford Lewis, 14n5
Bauer, Walter, 13n2, 14n8, 25n33, 26n34,
  26n35, 30n45, 31n46, 34n54,
  40n18, 55n7, 56n12, 62n25,
  63n26
Bayly, Albert F., 15n10
Begbie, Jeremy S., 106n15, 121n9
Benson, Luis F., 85n8
Best, Harold M., 106n15
Block, Daniel I., 5n12, 28n37, 57n13,
  106n15
Boice, James Montgomery, 1n1
Bonhoeffer, Dietrich, 46, 92, 95n23, 116
Borden, Paul, 68n3
Bradley, C. Randall, 106n15
Brooke, S., 88n13
Brooks, David, 40n14

Brown, Francis, 15n9, 19n20, 20n24,
  31n46, 32n49–33n50, 40n18,
  52n3, 55n7, 56n10
Brown, Raymond E., 49n44, 63n26
Bruce, F. F., 33n50, 41n18, 49n44, 60n21
Buck, P. C., 81n1
Bultmann, Rudolf, 118, 118n6
Burge, Gary, 10n22
Burns, J. Lanier, 30n44

Cain, Susan, 104, 104n10, 105, 105n13
Calvin, John, 2n4, 13, 14, 14n5, 36–37,
  36n2–37n2, 37, 67, 92, 93, 115
Carson, Donald A., 8n18, 106n15
Cassuto, Umberto, 18n15
Chapell, Bryan, 4n8, 106n15
Cherry, Constance M., 42n24
Chesterton, G. K., 46–47, 47n39
Childs, Brevard S., 18n15
Clancy, Robert A. D., 13n4
Coffin, William Sloane, 48, 49n43
Collins, Owen, 93n21
Conzelmann, Hans, 119n7
Copland, Aaron, 80, 82, 82n4
Counsell, Michael, 85n9
Courtney, Craig, 80, 81, 82n3, 84, 85,
  86n11, 87–88, 90n16
Cranfield, C. E. B., 12n1
Crosby, Fanny Jane, 59n17

Davis, Taylor, 94, 94n22
Dawkins, Richard, 42n22
Denham, Michael, 83n6, 84n7, 89n15,
  96n24

171

Subject Index

biblical worship
in contrast to ancient near eastern
(ANE) patterns and practices, 16
as not speculative, 13
qualities of, 13n3
blessing, as a key worship word, 52
blood sacrifice, 1, 33
Book of Occasional Services, 50n49
"Book of the Law," 24
"bowing down," 9n12, 24n32, 31n46, 52
Buddhist woman, coming to faith, 117
burden, of the prophet, 20n24
burning bush, 58
"By Gracious Powers So Wonderfully
Sheltered," 94–95
"By the Waters of Babylon," 80

"call of distress" (lament), 19n17
Calvin, John
on God's self-revelation in Scripture,
36–37
on the OT, 115
on the persuasiveness of holy
Scripture, 67
prayer of confession by, 93
preached through whole books of the
Bible, 36n2–37n2
Cathedral of St. Peter, in Geneva,
Switzerland, 2n4
celestial beings, 55
China, Three-Self Church, 116
choral introit, example, 93
choral material, example, 80, 84
choral meditation, example, 81
choral response, example, 81, 85
Christ. *See* Jesus Christ
"Christ is Made the Sure Foundation," 92
Christian faith, 46
Christian ministry. *See* ministry
Christian moral endeavor, as theocentric,
12n1
Christian spirituality, forming, 39
Christianity, 14, 107, 120
Christians
consecrated status of, 55
struggling daily, 106

treating each other with deference
and mutual concern, 63
Christlikeness, 46
Christ's church, persecution of, 106
churches
differences among, 103
unique personality of each, xii–xiii
circumcision, 37
"cloud of witnesses," 3
"Come Christians, Join to Sing" (hymn),
1
commandments, of God, 92
communication, through music, xi–xii,
8–9
confession of sin
example, 81, 85, 93
in personal and corporate worship,
27n36
congregational hymns, example, 83, 87
consecration, 55
consideration, careful, 121
covenant, invitation to, 18n15
creation
Bible a story of, 43
as a fundamental act of God, 14–15
our position in, 49
creatures and elders, falling down and
singing, 31
critical scholarship, contributing to
mistrust, 118
"crowns," implying position and
authority, 31
cultural contexts, of Scripture, 42, 42n22
culture, current, 104

Damascus Road vision, of Paul, 60
dangerous goodness of God, 59–60
Daniel 1:1-2, sample worship
components for, 80–83
David
deliverance from danger or judgment,
18n17–19n17
God's preservation of, 19n18
heart-felt repentance, 44
penitence of, 19
sin against Bathsheba and her
husband Uriah, 44

Scripture Index

Ancient Near Eastern Documents

Old Testament

New Testament